ANTHROPOLOGICAL PAPERS
MUSEUM OF ANTHROPOLOGY, UNIVERSITY OF MICHIGAN
NO. 20

THE ACCOKEEK CREEK SITE
A MIDDLE ATLANTIC SEABOARD CULTURE SEQUENCE

by

ROBERT L. STEPHENSON

and

ALICE L. L. FERGUSON

with sections by

HENRY G. FERGUSON

ANN ARBOR
THE UNIVERSITY OF MICHIGAN, 1963

ISBN (print): 978-1-949098-25-9
ISBN (ebook): 978-1-951519-47-6

Browse all of our books at
sites.lsa.umich.edu/archaeology-books.

Order our books from the University of Michigan
Press at www.press.umich.edu.

For permissions, questions, or manuscript queries,
contact Museum publications by email at umma-
pubs@umich.edu or visit the Museum website at
lsa.umich.edu/ummaa.

PREFACE

Henry G. Ferguson

Mrs. Ferguson purchased "Hard Bargain" farm in 1923. The farm, located in the southwestern corner of Prince George's County, Maryland, had been deserted and was largely overgrown with brush. Her first years on the ground were devoted to the reconditioning of the farm land and building the necessary houses and barns. In those early years it became more and more apparent that a large prehistoric Indian village had once occupied a part of the farm lying along the edge of the Potomac River, and she grew more and more interested in the meaning of the bits of pottery and arrowheads found there.

The excavation of the site of this Indian village on our farm began in a small way in 1935 and continued on a larger scale in the following years with the employment of a small and variable labor force, mostly high school boys, helped, when opportunity afforded, by the regular farm labor. Work at the site concluded to be that of the Indian village called "Moyaone" by Captain John Smith (Smith, 1910), together with a considerable amount of unproductive exploration, was completed in 1939. The Mockley Point area and the Susquehannock Fort were explored in 1939 and 1940. During the latter part of this period an ossuary at the site of the old Piscataway Fort, two miles east of the site of Moyaone, was also excavated. A description of this latter has been published (Ferguson, 1941).

During the war years the farm, as a farm, absorbed all of Mrs. Ferguson's energies and it was not until 1945 that she could give serious attention to the preparation of a report of her excavations at Moyaone. By then she was working under the handicap of increasing ill-health. A manuscript was completed in the spring of 1948 and submitted to Dr. Irving Rouse, Editor of *American Antiquity*, for publication as a Memoir of the Society for American Archaeology. It was returned with helpful suggestions for revision, particularly in those portions dealing with ceramics. By this time, her health was too poor to enable her to do the necessary work of revision.

To my regret, my own work with the United States Geological Survey took me west during the summers that excavation was in progress, so that, except for the beginnings and ends of the seasons, I had little share in the actual digging. I was able, though, to help somewhat as a critic and, more directly, in the study of the topography of the site and in speculation as to the possible topographic changes during and since the period of Indian occupation.

Mrs. Ferguson's own words in the preface to her original manuscript of 1948 provides an illuminating insight into the work. The following quotation constitutes her original preface almost in its entirety:

> The first thing we had to do, of course, was to become acquainted with our land and find out what our soil was like. We very soon discovered that the soil of one of the river fields was much darker than the other fields and that it was covered with a profusion of potsherds and arrowheads. We also found that a great many people knew of our abundant arrowheads and were accustomed to coming down to the farm to hunt for them. We were very obliging in those days and we even used to write to a local amateur archeologist, telling him when that field had been plowed so that he could come down after the next rain and add to his collection.
>
> There was a sharp boundary between the land with the potsherds and the other fields, which puzzled us. Very slowly it dawned on us that we had an archeological site and slowly and steadily the conviction grew that it was of some importance. We had always understood that sites were rare and that archeologists were eager to find them. There are a good many universities and museums within a day's journey and many of them send expeditions to the far corners of the earth. We wrote to every organization that seemed at all hopeful, offering them the site, but no one was interested enough to come down to look at it. I had been in New Mexico with Dr. Hewitt while he was excavating the Puÿe and had seen many of the excavations in South America and Spain but it never occurred to me that I could do any digging myself. One day a group of lads came down without permission, dug a trench across part of the field and went off with considerable loot. We decided that if digging was such a fascinating occupation we would like to try it ourselves. The first spade accidentally plunged into a big refuse pit and we and our friends dug in that one refuse pit all our spare time that spring. By the time my husband and most of our friends had gone west on their field trips, I was convinced that the site was much too important to be thrown away. Since no one wanted it, and there it was in my front yard, the development seemed up to me. At the least, I could record what was found and where it was found. With the help of Dr. Parker Trask and Dr. Thomas B. Nolan of the Geological Survey, a grid was laid out to

simplify the surveying and mapping, some workmen were employed and the excavation which was to take the better part of five years was begun.

In my abysmal ignorance questions were constantly cropping up and I was very grateful that the National Museum was so near. Dr. Henry B. Collins, Jr. was especially patient and helpful. It has always been a pleasure to remember that he was the first important visitor to the site. He was the first one to suggest that we had found the Moyaone of the Captain John Smith map. From the very beginning, and all through, Dr. A. Remington Kellogg always had time to cheerfully identify our little scraps of bone which soon piled up until they filled a large bin. Mr. Donald A. Cadzow was also one of our visitors that first season. He came in just as we were uncovering a burnt stockade line with the post molds full of charcoal. The second season we had several very helpful visitors like Dr. William A. Ritchie from New York, Dr. James B. Griffin from Ann Arbor and Dr. John Hack, then from Harvard University. The Heye Foundation sent down Mr. Charles O. Turbyfill for several days. We complained that so far no burials had been found. Mr. Turbyfill said that he was psychic about things like that and he felt that he was in the midst of burials. It afterward turned out that at the time he made the remark he was sitting on the third ossuary.

The first thing that happened in the third season of digging was the discovering of Ossuary No. 1. From then on, the burials poured in. Dr. Hrdlicka came down several times and Dr. T. D. Stewart was tremendously helpful to us as well as doing an immense amount of work for the National Museum on the material. We also had a great many tourists. Almost every Kiwanis Club and school in southern Maryland came to see what we were doing and Indian Head even sent up a top sergeant and a truck load of U. S. Marines.

The excavation of Moyaone was a magnificent adventure. The work was an education and it was especially so in the opportunity it gave to observe how scientists work. They were all absorbed in their own jobs but when they were asked questions there was no end to their patience and their generosity with both their time and knowledge. My thanks to them all is both deep and sincere.[1]

After Mrs. Ferguson's death in 1951, on the advice of Dr. Marshall T. Newman and Dr. Clifford Evans of the Smithsonion Institution, I asked assistance from Dr. James B. Griffin of the University of Michigan. Dr. Griffin arranged for the establishment of the Alice L. L. Ferguson Memorial Fellowship and assigned Robert L. Stephenson to a restudy of the ceramics and other artifacts. Mr. Stephenson was then on leave of absence from the Smithsonian Institution to complete his work toward a doctoral degree at The University of Michigan and the Moyaone project was accepted as the subject for his dissertation. He studied the enormous collection of specimens in the little log

[1]For an amusing account of the beginnings of the archaeological adventure see Alice L. L. Ferguson, "Adventures in Southern Maryland," 1941, pp. 157-66.

cabin museum at Hard Bargain during the summer of 1952 and later continued work on the material at The University of Michigan. Throughout the course of these studies he also gave me many valuable suggestions on the interpretation of the field archeology, particularly as related to the artifacts. The substance of this work was summarized in a popular paper in 1959 (Stephenson, 1959). The present monograph is a complete revision of the entire work.

Others who have contributed generously of their time and facilities, or discussed specific details of the work, include Margaret C. Blaker, of the Bureau of American Ethnology, Smithsonian Institution; Howard McCord, Gates Slattery, Carl Manson, and Hugh Stabler, all of Washington, D.C.; John Witthoft of the Pennsylvania Historical and Museum Commission; Carl F. Miller of the River Basin Surveys; William J. Mayer-Oakes then of the Carnegie Museum; Dorothy Cross of the New Jersey State Museum; Alfred K. Guthe of the Rochester Museum of Science; and Carlyle S. Smith of the University of Kansas. Sincere appreciation is expressed to all of these people. Laboratory assistance during the later study of the artifacts was generously provided by Dean E. Clark, Lawrence L. Tomsyck, and Lee G. Madison, of the River Basin Surveys. Herman L. Harpster, Evelyn B. Stewart, Wayne Nelson, and Jerry Livingston, also of the River Basin Surveys prepared the illustrations. Georgie E. Stephenson assisted in sorting and tabulating the artifacts and together with Ione Wilson of the River Basin Surveys, patiently typed the many drafts of the manuscript. This essential help is gratefully acknowledged. Finally, to Dr. Frank H. H. Roberts, Jr., Director of the River Basin Surveys, sincere thanks are expressed for allowing work already begun on a study of River Basin materials from Texas to be postponed while the Accokeek Creek site report was completed.

This publication is sponsored jointly by The University of Michigan and the Alice Ferguson Foundation, the latter an organization formed as a memorial to Mrs. Ferguson.

CONTENTS

ILLUSTRATIONS

Plates

(Plates I-XXVIII follow page 215)

CONTENTS

Figures

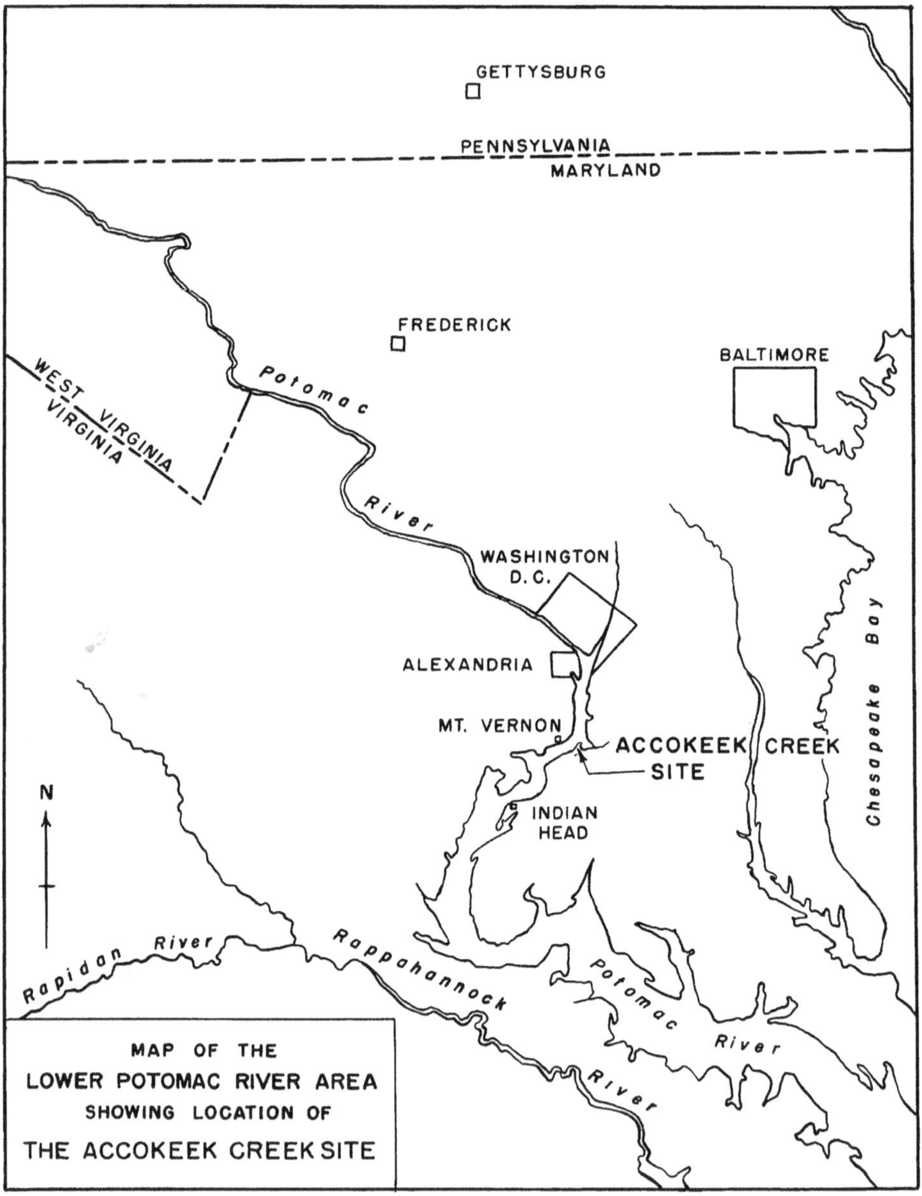
GETTYSBURG
PENNSYLVANIA
MARYLAND
FREDERICK
BALTIMORE
WEST VIRGINIA
VIRGINIA
Potomac
River
WASHINGTON
D. C.
ALEXANDRIA
MT. VERNON
ACCOKEEK CREEK
SITE
INDIAN
HEAD
Chesapeake Bay
N
Rapidan River
Rappahannock
River
Potomac
River
MAP OF THE
LOWER POTOMAC RIVER AREA
SHOWING LOCATION OF
THE ACCOKEEK CREEK SITE

Figure 1.

I

THE HISTORICAL SETTING

Alice L. L. Ferguson and Henry G. Ferguson[1]

INDIANS OF THE TIDEWATER REGION

At the beginning of the seventeenth century the tidewater region of Maryland and Virginia was occupied by Indians of Algonkin stock who had migrated from the north some three or more centuries earlier (Schmitt, 1952, p. 63). The Algonkins brought with them a culture superior to that of the earlier peoples, improved agriculture and pottery and at least the rudiments of political organization—stockaded villages grouped into loose confederacies, each with a single leader whose power varied according to his character. At the time of European contact, the Indians on the Virginia side formed the powerful confederacy governed by Powhatan. In Maryland there were several more loosely organized groups. The principal ones were the Nanticokes on the east and the Piscataways occupying the western peninsula.

Sometime before the beginning of Maryland settlement by

[1]The following section is a condensation of a booklet: Alice L. L. Ferguson and Henry G. Ferguson, *The Piscataway Indians of Southern Maryland*, Alice Ferguson Foundation, Accokeek, Maryland 1960—which in turn was based on a similar publication, Alice L. L. Ferguson, *Moyaone and the Piscataway Indians*, privately printed, Washington, 1937*a*.

The Nanticokes were most exposed to the Susquehannock invasion and during the first half of the seventeenth century were forced to migrate westward. At the time of the Maryland settlement in 1634 the Susquehannocks had already occupied the shores of Chesapeake Bay. A further complication was introduced by the raids of the Seneca tribe, a member of the powerful Iroquoian confederacy of the Five Nations. In their raids on Maryland, the Senecas were aided by the other allied tribes of the Five Nations, chiefly the Oneidas, but to what extent is uncertain. The Iroquoian Susquehannocks, not members of the Five Nations, were constantly at war with them.

The Piscataway Indians had probably lived in western Maryland since the fourteenth century, or before. Their principal town on the Potomac below the mouth of Piscataway Creek, called "Moyaone" by Captain John Smith, may have been in existence for about three hundred years before Smith's visit in 1608. This is indicated by the successive concentric lines of stockade post molds uncovered in the excavation of this village. Such a time span is also more or less supported by the Piscataway tradition, related to the Maryland authorities in 1674, of a succession of thirteen "Emperors" before that date.

Originally, as claimed by the Piscataways, the "Empire" may have been much larger, but by the beginning of Maryland settlement, pressure from the Susquehannocks had reduced its area to a belt bordering the Potomac south of the falls and extending up the principal tributaries. Roughly, the Empire covered the southern half of present Prince George's County and all, or nearly all, of Charles County. According to Smith's account in 1608 and the map credited to him, the principal towns of the Empire were Nacostan (Nacotchtank) on the site of modern Anacostia in the southern corner of what is now the District of Columbia; the village called Moyaone on the Smith map, the largest town; Pamunkey, on the Potomac about six miles further down stream; and Portobak, near the head of Port Tobacco River.

EARLY CONTACTS 1608 - 1634

Although the first known contacts with Europeans was Captain John Smith's visit in 1608, the Piscataways must have long known of their existence. The Spaniards had explored the lower

Potomac since the middle of the previous century. The story of the short-lived English Roanoke colony (1584-1589) must have been known to them, as also the massacre of the Jesuit mission (1571) in Virginia (near the site of Jamestown) and particularly the retribution by Mendenez, which left a legacy of hate and suspicion along the lower reaches of the river.

On Smith's voyage up the Potomac in 1608 he met a hostile reception on the Virginia side of the lower Potomac, but further upstream "at Moyaones, Nacotchtank (Nacostan) and Tauxenent (near the site of Mount Vernon) the people did their best to content us." The stockaded village, Moyaone, on the Maryland shore, was the chief town of the Piscataways and the seat of their principal chief or "emperor." The site, which can be certainly located on the map credited to Smith, is the same as that which we excavated, and covers a major part of the Accokeek Creek Site. Mrs. Ferguson's earlier paper has given the evidence for the location of the site of Moyaone (Ferguson, 1937*a*, pp. 4-11) and need not be repeated here.

There is some evidence, however, indicating that the name, Moyaone, was a mistake on Smith's part. Moyaone appears on maps derived from the Smith map, but is missing from maps based on Maryland sources beginning in 1635. The name appears only in Smith's account of his exploration and in Virginia official records up to 1623. In the latter there is the double reference to the Maryland Indians as "Moyancers and Pascaticons." The scrappy records of the fur traders do not mention Moyaone. Henry Fleet, describing his 1629 visit to what is almost certainly the same locality, calls the town Piscataway.

Interpreter service as early as 1608 must have been rudimentary, and a further complication was the difference in dialect between the Maryland and Virginia Indians, although all dialects were variants of the widespread Algonkin language. It is assumed, therefore, that the stockaded village was known as Piscataway.

Indians, however, sometimes referred to a town by the name of the ruling chief, and in one instance at least this custom was followed by the early Jesuit missionaries. It is not known whether there was an Indian *Tayac,* or king, of that name ruling the village at the time of Smith's visit, but it is a possible explanation of his mistake. Some twenty years later, presumably after the destruction of the village by the Senecas, the Indians moved to the site on Piscataway Creek, retaining the name Piscataway. For greater clarity we have kept the name Moyaone for the town visited by Smith, reserving Piscataway for the later Indian village and fort on Piscataway Creek.

Following Smith's exploration there is nothing known of the history of the Piscataways for several years, though other explorers and traders must have contributed data to the "Smith" map.

In Virginia the effective rule of Powhatan did not extend as far as the northern part of the Potomac. The towns of Potomac, Tauxenent, and neighboring villages were essentially independent, each governed by its own *Tayac*.

There was constant hostility between the Piscataways and the villages on the Virginia side. This consisted not of full-scale war, but rather of a succession of petty intertown wars, with generally inconclusive results. Commonly, they seem to have been reprisal raids. Both the Virginia Indians and the Piscataways, particularly those of the northern villages, suffered from the raids of the Senecas.

The massacre of the Virginia settlement in 1622, planned by Openanchancoko, the successor to Powhatan, took the lives of 340 settlers and, except for timely warning, would have wiped out the colony. Reprisal followed quickly. The orders from the London Company were to root out all the Indians except the young, who would be profitable as slaves, to starve them by burning their corn, and to destroy their canoes and everything they had. Apparently, this reprisal took place before the corn harvest of 1622 and by the next January the Virginia Council reported that they had "set upon the Indians in all places and by their own confession we have slain more than hath been slain before since the beginning of the colony."

This reprisal did not extend as far upriver as Potomac and Tauxenent, friendly to the Virginians, but the burning of the Indians' corn crop along the river created a food shortage in Jamestown which had to be supplied from the upper Potomac villages. Consequently, both fur traders and Virginia officials became involved in local politics and intervillage warfare.

Late in 1622 Captain Hamer came to Potomac, where Captain Crawshaw, the trader, was living, to get corn for Jamestown. He was told that Potomac was short, but Nacostan had plenty. Hamer and Crawshaw, with some other Englishmen and forty or fifty bowmen from Potomac, went to Nacostan and burned the town, which was soon rebuilt. They killed some of the people and drove the others into the woods. Moyaone, as ally of Nacostan, seems to have promptly revenged this by a raid on Potomac. In April, 1623, Henry Spelman, who had long lived among the Indians of the region, took the risk of a trading expedition into the disturbed country. At Nacostan he and nineteen of his men were murdered and a head, probably Spelman's, was seen to roll down the bank. One man, Henry Fleet, was held prisoner. Reprisal followed quickly, and Governor Wyatt reported in 1624 that he had "avenged the treason of the Pascaticons and their associates, the greatest people in these parts." It is inferred that the first burning of Moyaone, as revealed by the inner of the two lines of charcoal-filled post molds, took place at this time but the town was soon rebuilt.

Upon his release by Wyatt, Fleet resumed his trading on the Potomac. On his voyage in 1631 his main object was to open trade with the Susquehannocks above the falls. In this he was nearly successful but was finally frustrated by reports spread by his former captors, the Nacostans, who told the Susquehannocks that he was planning an attack on them. Nacostan jealously guarded its profitable position of exchange point between the traders and the northern Indians and from the time of Smith's visit did everything possible to prevent explorers and traders going beyond the falls of the Potomac.

Upon his return down river, Fleet visited the Emperor of Piscataway. The wording of his account strongly suggests that the Piscataway he mentions was the same as the town called Moyaone by Smith.

Fleet mentioned "the great change" that has come over the towns of Nacostan and Piscataway and in discussion of the opposition of his "neighbor Indians" to his plan of opening direct trade with the Susquehannocks said that "the Pascatowics having had a great slaughter by them to the number of one thousand persons in my time." From this fragmentary evidence it is inferred that this massacre and the second burning of Moyaone occurred before 1631 and after 1624, and that the Emperor and surviving inhabitants moved to the new site of Piscataway on Piscataway Creek shortly after the massacre and second burning of Moyaone. It is likely that the raiders were Senecas rather than Susquehannocks, whom Fleet found to be friendly. The fourth, and apparently latest, ossuary excavated at Moyaone contained 618 burials as compared with about 250 for each of the earlier three. This might indicate a major disaster, and if so, confirms Fleet's statement, allowing for reasonable exaggeration.

Fleet's account is the last description known to us of beaver trade along the Potomac. Apparently the trade fell off rather sharply after Maryland settlement, though it prospered for several years in the Chesapeake Bay and Eastern Shore regions, but by the year 1700 fur was no longer an important export from the Colony. In the Potomac area, the reckless killing of beaver and other large game, the increasing danger from the Senecas and intercolonial rivalry contributed to its decline—Maryland which by charter owned the entire river, required a license and a 10 per cent tax and attempted to restrict the Potomac trade to its citizens.

PISCATAWAYS AND THEIR NEIGHBORS (1634-1674)

The Jesuit Missions

The retreat of the Piscataways from the invading Susquehannocks was still in progress when the first Maryland colonists arrived. Hemmed in by their enemies, the Piscataways hopefully welcomed the Europeans as potential allies and protectors.

Henry Fleet was on another trading voyage on the Potomac, when, in March 1634, he met the *Ark* and the *Dove* carrying Governor Leonard Calvert and the first Maryland colonists and Jesuit missionaries. Fleet persuaded Calvert that it would be unwise to attempt settlement until permission of the Emperor at Piscataway had first been obtained. Consequently, Calvert, Fleet, Father White and some others sailed up to Piscataway in the *Dove*. The rumor (instigated by the fur traders, according to Father White) had spread that this was an attack by the Spaniards and the party found five hundred bowmen drawn up on the shore for defense. Good relations were soon established, but Wannis, the Emperor, was not too cordial and told Calvert he: "would not bid him go, neither would he bid him stay, but that he might use his own discretion." Accordingly, the first permanent settlement was made at St. Mary's on the site of a village which was being deserted from fear of the Susquehannocks.

Calvert did not permit the immediate establishment of missions to the Indians. The delay may have been due to doubts about the attitude of Wannis, whose reception of the colonists had not been overly cordial. The situation changed, however, when Kittamaquund, his younger brother, a friend of the English from the start, murdered and succeeded Wannis. As Governor Calvert wrote to his brother, Lord Baltimore in 1638: "He hath within this two yeares stept into the Empire of the Indians by killing his oldest brother, the old Emperor and enjoyeth (it) yet with peace through the good correspondence he keepeth with me."

When, in 1639, permission was granted, missionary work was confined to the tribes of the Piscataway Empire, including the Patuxents at the southeastern end of the peninsula. The headquarters and general supply depot of the mission, under charge of the Superior, Father Brock, was an extensive tract of land near Patuxent, granted by the local *Tayac*. In the Piscataway area Father White was in charge of the mission at Piscataway "having lived in the palace (!) with the Emperor himself of the place...from the month of June 1639." Shortly afterwards a mission was established at Port Tobacco, under Father Rigby.

Land granted directly by the Indian *Tayacs* to the missionaries soon became the source of a displute between Lord Baltimore and the Jesuits. Baltimore insisted that he alone had the power to grant lands within the colony, but was bitterly opposed by the Jesuits who claimed that the "immunity of the church has been violated." The controversy went so far that Baltimore appealed to the Congregation for Propogation of the Faith to recall the Jesuits and substitute secular priests. Eventually the Jesuits capitulated and agreed to hold their lands as tenants of the proprietor.

The Jesuits did not get along well with the fur traders, though they were obliged to use them as interpreters during the early stages of their work. This could not have been a very efficient way to inculcate Catholic doctrine. They accused the traders of impeding their efforts to give the Indians "proper clothing" by charging outrageous prices in beaver skins. "God forbid that we should ever do the like." On the other hand, the Jesuits, to support their mission, themselves engaged in the fur trade both by hiring Indian trappers and hunters and by dealing with a white trader on commission. This was resented by the other traders as unfair competition.

Father White, at Piscataway, got along well with the new emperor who even sent his daughter to St. Mary's to be educated, put away his surplus wives, and desired to be baptized. The Jesuit letter of 1639 makes incidental mention of the earlier fratricide, but apparently nobody took it seriously. The baptism was postponed for a short time in order to provide for the most elaborate ceremony possible. Accordingly, a chapel was built at the Indian town of Piscataway and on July 5, 1640, the baptism took place, in the presence of the Governor and many of the important men of the colony, and with "nothing wanting in display which our means could supply." The baptism was followed by a Christian wedding with his remaining wife.

The publicity of the ceremony had its good effect and a

request was received from the "King of the Anacostans" for the establishment of a mission. Lack of personnel prevented compliance at that time and afterwards the increasing severity of the raids by the Senecas made it impossible.

The work prospered in the southern part of the Piscataway empire, though the Jesuits had to relieve the distress caused by the crop failure following the drought of 1639. According to the letter of 1642 almost all of the town of Port Tobacco, including its young "queen," had been converted. The Jesuits also became more proficient in the language, greatly to the advantage of their missionary work. By 1642 Father Rigby had even written a short catechism in the Piscataway dialect. It is not known whether this was ever printed.

The "Piscataway Princess" was placed under the joint guardianship of the Governor and Mistress Margaret Brent, a famous character in early colonial history, and sister of Giles Brent, a member of the Governor's Council and for a time acting governor. "The Little Princess" later married Giles Brent, who tried to have her succeed her father as empress in 1642. This was contrary to the Piscataway law of succession (brother to brother, and, lacking brothers to the eldest son of the eldest sister) and not in accordance with the policy of the Governor. The Piscataways therefore agreed that henceforth the Governor should nominate the Emperor.

Things did not prosper at Piscataway, however. The raids by the Seneca became more frequent, some of the converts were killed and much mission property looted. The mission was therefore abandoned shortly after the death of the Emperor in 1642, and missionary work concentrated at Port Tobacco and Patuxent, though Piscataway still remained the seat of the Emperor.

The Civil War in England had its repercussions in Maryland and the temporary Puritan ascendency in 1645 brought to a close the active Jesuit missionary work. Fathers White and Fisher were taken in chains to London but later released. Other priests took refuge in Virginia, where they were most unwelcome, but were allowed refuge.

It is quite possible that the work of Father White and his associates among the Piscataways during the short period of their mission (1639-1645) may have saved the infant colony of Maryland from a disaster such as the massacre that nearly wiped out the Virginia colony in 1622. The Piscataways had welcomed the settlers as protectors against the northern Indians, but with the increasing pressure of white settlement, the welcome was beginning to wear thin. The Nanticokes, Senecas and Susquehannocks were now hostile, and the Marylanders were too much involved in internal difficulties to pay proper attention to frontier defense. The Susquehannocks were reported to have offered the Piscataways an alliance to join with them in wiping out the English. Had the Piscataways waivered in their loyalty, Maryland would have had a difficult time. But in spite of unfair treatment by the settlers, the loss of their lucrative beaver trade and restriction of their hunting, the Piscataways remained friends of the English to the end. There were, however, many desertions to the Susquehannocks by the younger men of the tribe, who were impatient of the restrictions imposed by the increasing white settlement.

Indians and Settlers—During the years following Maryland settlement the Piscataway empire gradually weakened, caught between the pressure from northern Indians and the encroachment of the settlers crowding northward. Largely due to the protection offered by the friendly Piscataways, settlement along the Potomac side of the peninsula progressed rapidly and in less than a decade from the founding of the colony had reached the Piscataway Creek region. Probably the early settlers were mostly men of small means and indentured servants whose terms had expired. These included "transported felons" whose sentences had been reduced to service as indentured servants (transportable offences at that date included such crimes as game poaching and chicken stealing). In the first half of the century there were also a considerable number of Puritans whose emigration to Maryland had been encouraged by the Proprietor.

During these early years no provision was made for the protection of the Indians' land and, as settlement increased, friction between the two races was inevitable. The Indian had no notion of private property in land, and, particularly when compensated by a little in the way of trade goods, offered no immediate opposition to white occupation. Since the Indians did not fence their fields and the colonists allowed their cattle and hogs to range the woods, difficulties were bound to arise. Even after the Indians were ordered to fence their fields, which they did unwillingly, there are records of the settlers tearing down these fences in order to give free range to their stock. The hunting grounds of the Indians were also severely restricted.

The first attempt at protection of the Indians was made in 1662 with the grant of Calvert Manor to William Calvert. This covered an area along the south bank of Piscataway Creek from a point about two miles southwest of the present village of Piscataway, westward to the Potomac, and south-westward along the Potomac as far as Accokeek Creek. Inland it extended to about the position of the present Bryan's Point road. Included within its boundaries were the Indian village of Piscataway and the fort, garrioned from time to time by Maryland as a frontier post. Although the grant was made to an individual, the land was regarded as an Indian reservation and so described in William Calvert's will. There is no record of settlement or subdivision until after the Indians had left the area.

Just before the establishment of Calvert Manor, large areas along Piscataway Creek, and along the Potomac shore to the north and south, had been granted to individual settlers. These were not, at this time, occupied by their owners, but presumably rented to the newly arrived immigrants as tenant farmers. Indian villages within the grants, such as Accokeek (near Bryans Point), do not seem to have been disturbed but Indian fishing and hunting grounds were restricted.

Pressure from the white settlers also continued in other parts of the peninsula and in 1663 the "queen" of Port Tobacco complained that the settlers had occupied all the fertile land along the river, forcing the Indians to leave their town and plantations.

A final attempt to protect the Piscataway and other western Maryland Indians was made in 1669. It was ordered that the land between Piscataway and Mattawoman Creeks, including the Indian towns of Piscataway and Accokeek, together with "all land by the water and three miles into the woods above Piscataway to a total of 10,000 acres be laid out for his Lordships use." This included Calvert Manor, but the large tracts to the east and west were already in private ownership.

The order of the council creating this reservation specified twelve Southern Maryland tribes to whom the lands were to be allotted, including the Piscataways, Anacostans, Doegs, Mattawomans, Wicomicos, and other tribes. The Mattawomans also retained their old lands at the mouth of the Mattawoman Creek. The order creating the reservation did not exclude further settlement but provided that "no Englishman shall seat for the future within three miles of the Indians, without permission from the Governor."

The local authorities interpreted this liberally and settlement continued in the reserved area though no large grants were made until the Piscataway Indians had left the Province.

When a conflict arose, it was settled by a jury of neighboring white settlers who determined the damages, if any, to be paid to the Indian.

Indian Warfare

In the early days of Maryland settlement the Indian situation on the frontier was complex. Powerful tribes, the Susquehannock, Senecas, and Nanticokes, which, if united, could have wiped out the colony, warred among themselves and against the English and their Piscataway allies. The then powerful Susquehannock tribe was engaged in bitter warfare with the Senecas, and their allies of the Five Nations, principally the Oneidas. This was intensified as the fur trade developed and the Susquehannocks tried to block the river routes by which the Senecas shipped their furs. In the Chesapeake Bay region the Susquehannocks were also in conflict with the Nanticokes of the Eastern Shore.

Relations between Maryland and the Susquehannocks were worsening, due largely to trade disputes in Chesapeake Bay. The Susquehannocks tried to secure the Piscataways as allies and, early in 1642, a conference between them was held at Piscataway, attended by Henry Fleet as observer. The Piscataways remained loyal, however, probably due to the influence of the Jesuits.

War with the Susquehannocks broke out in 1642. The direct cause, according to Maryland sources, was the intrigue of Captain Claiborne, lately evicted from Kent Island, who tried to preserve his former monopoly of the Chesapeake Bay trade by instigating the Susquehannocks against the Maryland traders.

Fighting in the west seems to have been inconclusive and confined to the unsettled area north of Piscataway Creek. The Chesapeake Bay region suffered heavily from raids, including one on the Jesuit mission and storehouse near Patuxent, in which several servants of the mission were killed, the stores looted, and a priest taken captive.

The Piscataways, aided by the Maryland militia and rangers, gave protection to the settlers and no serious damage is reported. Maryland, always frugal in military affairs, wanted as many prisoners as possible for sale to the sugar planters of Barbados to defray the cost of the war. It therefore set a scale of bounties, one matchcoat for a "hairy scalp," but three for a "live prisoner in good condition." Maryland also promised that the women and children of Piscataways killed in war would be cared for and not made slaves of the English.

Finally the Susquehannocks wearied of fighting a war against both the Marylanders and the Senecas, and in 1652 a treaty of peace was made with Maryland. In 1661 this was expanded into an alliance and Maryland constructed a European-style stockaded fort for the Susquehannocks on the west shore of Chesapeake Bay at the northern border of the province. Until 1675, the Susquehannocks remained loyal friends and allies of the Marylanders and Piscataways.

War with the Senecas continued, with the Marylanders and Piscataways aiding the Susquehannocks. The principal fighting was between 1664 and 1666 in the unsettled wilderness region between the Falls of the Potomac and the head of the Patapsco River. The Susquehannocks and Piscataways are reported to have lost a considerable number of men, but the planters south of Piscataway Creek were protected from serious attack.

Having found its earlier sales of Susquehannock prisoners unprofitable, the Maryland authorities now left the prisoners to the Piscataways, paying a bounty for the right ear of enemies captured or killed. After Maryland made peace with the Susquehannocks, the raids of the Senecas increased in intensity both in Virginia and Maryland as the colonists and the Piscataways were now allies of the Susquehannocks. The Nanticokes were also hostile and were not finally subdued until 1668.

FRONTIER DEFENSE

The inadequacy of frontier defense during the first half century of Maryland settlement was a reflection of the social, cultural, and religious cleavage between the small planters of the frontier region, most exposed to Indian attacks, and the relatively safe, large landholders in the southern part of the province. The bitter feeling between the two groups deteriorated into intermittent fighting with the beginning of the Civil War in England and between 1644 and 1657 internal discord prevented any serious attempt at proper frontier protection. This cleavage persisted after the restoration of the Proprietor and there were sporadic rebellions of the frontiersmen of Charles County in 1680 and 1689. It was not until near the end of the century, when Maryland became a crown colony, that a proper defense system ended the Indian danger and permitted northward advance of the frontier.

The provincial assembly of Maryland was opposed to anything resembling a standing army, and provided only for a permanent staff of officers of some military experience, who were assigned two or three to a county. All able-bodied "Christian men," including indentured servants but not slaves, between the ages of eighteen and sixty five were subject to military training and service. The permanent militia officers had authority to "press" (draft) men for training and service. "Musters" for training were ordinarily held every three months and more frequently in time of danger. The number drafted varied from one in three to one in ten according to conditions. Each drafted man was required to bring his own musket, ammunition, supplies, and food, though those who escaped the draft could be required to assist in furnishing supplies and equipment. When on active duty food could be supplied but was charged to the soldiers' pay.

This "regular" militia was used for large-scale operations such as the Susquehannock War (1644-1652) and the expedition against the Susquehannock Fort on Piscataway Creek (1675), and, in the latter part of the century, to garrison the forts erected along the frontier eastward from the Falls of the Potomac. The defense of the small frontier plantations against the "hit and run" Indian raids was left largely to the planters themselves, aided by the Piscataways. During the first decade of Maryland history the outlying settlements suffered greatly, although some provision for frontier defense was made as early as 1637, when a small garrison was temporarily stationed at the Piscataway Indian fort.

The Governor and Council wished to establish a suitable frontier defense force, but the Assembly controlled by the larger planters in the south, objected to the expense and was not particularly interested in protecting the frontiersmen. In 1644, however, an act for the defense of the province enabled the governor to settle a garrison at the Indian town of Piscataway. The Assembly, frugal as ever, made no provision for expenses and the various hundreds were each assessed for a soldier and his keep. This might provide a garrison of perhaps a dozen men.

The only other action taken by the colony in the early years was to authorize the military officers in the frontier counties when an alarm was given to press not only men but horses, guns, ammunition, and all forms of supplies and equipment, even clothing and boots. Naturally, such a system was inadequate for protection against the hostile Indians. By the time the alarm had been given and an armed party collected, the damage had been done and all that remained to do was "to bury the dead with all the haste they can and so return from whence they came." Frontier settlers were murdered and plantations were being deserted in the frontier region "while the Grandees about St. Mary's and the middle of the county, being securely guarded...knows nothing about it."

This arrangement soon was improved to permit the drafting of frontier settlers for a few weeks at a time (later changed to weekly shifts) as "rangers." Small groups of these men, with the aid of friendly Piscataway Indians, patrolled the woods in the neighborhood of their homes in summer when leaves might conceal the hostile Indians. Besides patrolling the frontier the ranger had the duty of tracking down runaway slaves and servants.

The ranger had to provide his own musket, powder, and shot. He was mounted but had to furnish his own horse, though he was given an allowance for its keep. If he were a servant, one of his master's horses was pressed. Other articles of equipment were pressed, as needed, from the frontier planters.

The system of pressing all sorts of equipment gave rise to abuses. The militia officers appear to have delegated their powers to unscrupulous subordinates, and in some instances to have diverted pressed articles to their own use.

Matters were somewhat improved in 1676 when the power of pressing was taken from the militia officers. In each hundred of every county two "honest and sufficient men," known as "press-masters" were appointed with the sole power of pressing supplies and equipment. This, however, did not entirely satisfy the frontier planters who complained of "loose and idle fellows who many times abused their commission." On the other hand, militia officers complained that they did not receive sufficient supplies.

Ordinarily, claims for recompense of pressed articles had to be presented to the Provincial Court at St. Mary's, a hardship for the small frontier planter; but occasionally commissions were appointed with power to approve claims.

Raids by the Senecas were particularly numerous in 1664 and 1665 and the frontier settlers depended largely on the Susquehannocks and Piscataways for protection. Commanders of rangers were authorized to engage the services of "friend Indians" in order that they may more easily "find the skulking enemy" and to offer the reward of one hundred arms length of roanoke (shell currency) for any prisoner "alive or otherwise."

The nervous state of the frontier in the early 1640's is shown by a variety of orders to the frontier planters. Colonists were ordered to shoot on sight any Susquehannock, Nanticoke, or Wicomesee (a minor eastern tribe) Indian. This was difficult to obey "Forasmuch as the English cannot easily distinguish one Indian from another." Since peace treaties with the various hostile tribes were made at different dates, and only the Piscataways remained consistently friendly, the colonists naturally regarded all Indians as potentially hostile, and there were doubtless cases of mistaken identity. Colonists were also required to carry with them to "church or chappel or any considerable distance, a fixed gun and one charge at least of powder and shott."

It was also ordered that "No inhabitant or householder entertain an Indian under any color of liscence." When a friendly Indian had business with a planter he was to lay down his arms at a distance, advance, shouting, until he was within musket shot of the house and wait until the planter had loaded his musket, lit his match, and come out to parley with him. At a later date all friendly Indians were required to carry identification cards.

It has often been stated that the possession of fire arms by the colonists gave them a considerable advantage, but it seems doubtful whether the clumsy and inefficient matchlock of that era was superior to the bow and arrow for forest fighting, whatever its value in open European warfare. The matchlock was in use in Maryland until the end of the century, although the Swedes in Delaware had used the more efficient flintlock forty years earlier. Firing a matchlock took a relatively long time; fine powder had to be poured on the firing pan, the match, a cord soaked in a slow burning material, blown to insure a good spark, and brought to the firing pan by a pull on the trigger, igniting the fine powder which flowed down the touchhole to the coarse powder of the charge. Misfires were common, and the accurate range was only about 40 yards, not much more than that of the bow and arrow.

Attempts to prevent the Indians from obtaining firearms were not successful. Indian familiarity with firearms had begun with the hiring of Indian hunters by the richer planters, who trained them in the use of the musket. Soon a brisk illicit trade developed, for Indians would pay highly in beaver skins for guns, powder, and shot. Arms were also furnished by the province to the friendly Piscataways, and, after the alliance of 1661, to the Susquehannocks also. According to some, this encouraged the Senecas in their raiding, for the Piscataways lost a considerable number of muskets to them in the course of their border skirmishes. Maryland authorities complained that the Swedes and Dutch sold guns to the northern Indians. After the English occupation of New York the Iroquois of the Five Nations were given powder and shot by the province to protect the frontier from the French. Certainly by 1680, firearms had been so completely adopted by the Indians that the Piscataways could petition the Governor for an additional supply of guns and ammunition "as they had forgotten much about making bows and arrows."

DESTRUCTION OF THE SUSQUEHANNOCKS (1674-1676)

Following the suppression of the rebellion of the Virginia Indians in 1644 and the disruption of the Powhatan confederacy, Virginia was free from large-scale Indian warfare for the next thirty years. Settlement along the Potomac shore followed quickly. One of the furthest upstream land grants of the period was the Spencer and Washington grant of 1674, including the site of Mount Vernon, described as "lying near opposite Piscataway."

The Virginian settlers were thus in contact with the Maryland Indians, Susquehannocks above Piscataway Creek, Piscataways south of the Creek, and Doegs[2] southwest of Bryans Point. Raiding parties of Senecas harried the settlers on both sides of the river.

The Virginian settlers of the upper Potomac were of different type from the frontiersmen of the Maryland side. Men of substance, abundantly supplied with servants and slaves, they mostly lived on and cultivated their own grants. Friction with the colonial government, though present, was far less acute than in Maryland.

Among the early settlers was Giles Brent, who had moved from Maryland in 1646 and, in 1653, took up land, then the most northerly grant on the Virginia side, described as "opposite the Anacostan town of Aquakick."

Depredations by the Maryland Indians, though mostly minor, were a source of much friction between the two colonies.

[2]The Doeg Indians, possibly an offshoot from the Nanticokes of eastern Maryland, seem to have been relatively late migrants to the area. They settled on both banks of the upper Potomac. They were noted by Smith in 1608, but first mentioned in Maryland records in 1650. Their presence caused confusion of nomenclature, as midcentury Virginian records refer to both Piscataways and Doegs as Doegs. Earlier Virginia records refer to Indians on the Maryland shore of the Potomac as "Poscaticons and Moyancers" and "Nacostans."

Virginia authorities complained to London about the raids from Maryland and Maryland replied that it had no control over the Senecas whom it accused of all the raiding. Consequently, the Virginians organized a mobile militia which could come quickly to the aid of any plantation attacked.

By the spring of 1674 constant warfare with the Senecas had so weakened the Susquehannocks, that the Maryland authorities decided it would be politic to desert their allies and make peace with the Senecas. They, therefore, withdrew the garrison that had helped protect the Susquehannock fort on the west shore of Chesapeake Bay at the northern border of the province. The Senecas rightly interpreted this as a sign of weakness and increased their raiding along the Potomac. In the fall of 1674 they stormed the fort and massacred most of its defenders. The survivors, probably not many more than a hundred able-bodied men, with some women and children, fled southward into Maryland where they were most unwelcome, as it was feared the Senecas would pursue them. The Susquehannocks were therefore refused permission to remain in the settled part of the colony, but were told that they could settle at the Falls of the Potomac, which was equivalent to turning them over to the Senecas. Instead of going as far as the Falls, the Susquehannocks selected a site on the south bank of Piscataway Creek. This was within the William Calvert grant, which was still an Indian reservation, and nearly two miles west of the Indian village and fort of Piscataway. Here, during the early part of 1675, they constructed a European-style, stockaded fort, copied after their former fort on Chesapeake Bay.

Contemporary records of the events that followed are confusing. The brutality, treachery, and inefficiency of the colonists were so egregious as to call for later investigation by higher authorities. As a result, contemporary statements are contradictory. Everyone tried to blame someone else.

In the summer of 1675, a serious incident led to the siege of the Susquehannock fort, Bacon's rebellion, and the end of the Susquehannocks as an independent tribe. Thomas Mathew, a wealthy Virginia planter, had obtained goods from the Doeg or Piscataway Indians of Maryland for which he had never paid. To even the score, a party of Indians crossed the river and tried to steal some of Mathew's hogs. The party was intercepted by the local militia and several Indians were killed. In revenge, a second attack was made in which Mathew's herdsmen was killed. The local militia captains, George Mason and George Brent, with thirty men, crossed the river by night and at dawn attacked the Indian settlements, probably close to Bryans Point, surprised the Indians, and murdered fourteen unarmed Susquehannocks and ten Doegs or Piscataways, the latter having been called out by Brent for a parley.

The Maryland authorities promptly protested to Governor Berkeley of Virginia against this invasion of their territory and killing of friendly Indians, but nothing was done to compensate the relatives of the victims or to punish the Virginian aggressors. Governor Berkeley, however, ordered Colonel John Washington and Major Isaac Allerton to call together the militia officers of the region and make a full and thorough inquiry into the murders and raids. After such investigation they were to demand satisfaction and then, if they found adequate cause, could call out their men and attack the guilty nation. Instead of conducting any investigation, Washington inquired from the Maryland authorities as to "what number of men you will be pleased to order to our assistance." Accordingly, under orders from Governor Calvert, a military force of 250 horse and dragoons under the command of Major Truman was sent to assist Washington. The Virginia contingent may have been larger, for the total strength of the forces of the two provinces is given by some authorities as 1,000 men, but this figure may include levies of Piscataway and Mattawoman Indians under orders from the Maryland authorities. The Susquehannock defenders of the fort numbered not over 100 able-bodied men.

The Maryland contingent arrived before the Virginians and just after an Indian raid on the house of Randall Hanson on the Hansonton plantation "within three miles from the fort," probably at, or near, Bryans Point. The defenders killed nine Indians, but Hanson's overseer and some of his servants were also killed and the house burned.

Truman accused the Susquehannocks of this outrage, but the Susquehannocks blamed the Senecas and sent five of their chief men to Truman as hostages, carrying a medal given them by Calvert. Truman held the hostages until the Virginians arrived and a council was held as to their disposition. Accounts differ as to what followed.

The Maryland account quotes Washington as saying: "Should we keep them any longer? Let us knock them on the head. We shall get the fort today." At the same time a party brought in the bodies of the murdered colonists, and the Virginians became so clamorous that Truman, though believing the Susquehannocks innocent, felt obliged to yield. The Virginia account states that it was decided that Truman should march the hostages to the ruins of the Hanson house to determine whether the dead Indians were Senecas. He had only gone a short distance, however, when he ordered them killed, an order which his men obeyed unwillingly.

Both men later stood trial for this murder. Washington was acquitted before a court of inquiry in Virginia. His defense was that, although commanding officer, the operations were conducted in Maryland, and he felt obliged to defer to the insistence of Truman and the Maryland contingent. Governor Berkeley stated, however, that "If they had killed my Grandfather and Grandmother, my Father and Mother and all my Friends, yet if they had come to treat of Peace, they ought to have gone in Peace."

Truman was tried before the Maryland Assembly and Council, and pleaded guilty. He offered as mitigation the insistence of the Virginians and the fear of mutiny of his own men, both statements contradicted by the witnesses. The Governor's Council favored a severe penalty, but the Assembly, which mirrored the popular anti-Indian feeling of the time, refused to consent, and Truman was let off with a fine of ten thousand pounds of tobacco. He died a few years later and his tombstone bears the inscription, "The Memory of the Just is Blessed."

The murder of the hostages ended all possibility of persuading the Susquehannocks to evacuate the fort peacefully. All attempts at further parley were met with cries of "Where are our great men?" and a long siege began, Washington's estimate of "today" stretched to six weeks; a thousand colonial soldiers against a hundred Indians.

The fort was well situated for defense, since the landward side, except for a small strip of sand spit, was mostly swampy. It was, however, vulnerable from Piscataway Creek and a pinnace armed with even a small cannon could soon have blown it to bits.

The siege seems to have been very badly managed. The Susquehannocks made a number of "Bloody Sallys" in which they replenished their food supply by capture of the colonists' horses. Finally, having exhausted all their food, they escaped by canoe, first killing the sleeping guards who had been posted to give warning. The colonists lost at least fifty men in the course of the siege. The Susquehannocks loss can be estimated from a burial pit excavated within the fort stockade which contained twelve skeletons.

After the Susquehannocks escaped from the fort, they fled to Virginia, and raided the northern settlements. The killing of the overseer on Nathaniel Bacon's plantation was the spark that set off Bacon's Rebellion. They did an immense amount of damage; the settlements had pushed up as far as Hunting Creek, but after the Susquehannock raid they shrank back to Aquia Creek and ten years passed before the lost ground was regained. The Susquehannocks never forgot nor forgave the killing of their chief men, but as a tribe they were finished; they were forced to submit to the Senecas and were adopted by them. According to the Senecas, who should have been competent judges, the Susquehannocks were then a turbulent, bloody minded people who would never cease doing mischief to the English and the Piscataways as long as there was a man alive.

RAIDS AND DIPLOMACY, 1676-1685

Maryland's treatment of the Susquehannocks deprived the province of her best allies, leaving only the weak Piscataway tribe to guard the northwest frontier. The long defense of the fort by the Indians against superior numbers did not enhance the white man's prestige. The Senecas, urged on by their adopted former enemies, the Susquehannocks, redoubled their raids on the Piscataway Indians and the frontier settlements with increased ferocity. The colonists fought back confusedly, not always able to distinguish friend from foe, for the Maryland records for 1675 note: "Fought the Piscataways by mistake, they being our friends." The mistake was corrected the following year and it was ordered, or at least promised, that "In case the Piscataway Indians desire any men to assist them, it is resolved that forty or fifty men be appointed for that purpose." Whether they were sent is not known, but a small garrison was stationed at Piscataway Fort.

The fugitive Susquehannocks, doubtless aided by their hosts, the Senecas, next turned to raiding the Maryland frontier; and soon the fear of the Indians put the border region into a state of siege. The colonists were ordered to fortify their houses and always to keep a garrison of at least ten men in each of these forts.

Maryland authorities chose this time to neglect their Piscataway allies as they had previously deserted the Susquehannocks. An appeal by the Piscataways for further aid brought the answer from the Governor that as "an assurance of his Lordships favour to them he was willing and did propose to give them a testimonial in writing under his hand."

The planters of the western peninsula coveted the land still left to the Indians and plans were made to move the Piscataways, Mattawoman, and kindred tribes to the Eastern Shore, now deserted by the Susquehannocks and the project was finally dropped. In 1676 the Piscataways reported that the "Susquehannocks" had built a fort on the Anacostia River and the Emperor of the Piscataways offered to assist in attacking it. The Maryland authorities now turned to diplomacy and, in 1677, Colonel Coursey, with credentials from both Maryland and Virginia, was sent to Albany to try to make peace with the Iroquois Confederacy, including the Senecas.

The Iroquois were under the protection and control of the Province of New York. Sir Edmond Andros, then governor of the Province, appreciated their value as a bulwark against the French of Canada and their Indian allies, and therefore kept them well supplied with powder and shot. Occasional raids on other far away English provinces were not considered important. Coursey was instructed that in any agreement he was specifically to include the Piscataway Indians. He was even to go as far as to promise payment by Maryland for any damages claimed to have been done by the Piscataways.

It is difficult to understand the apathy of the Maryland government during these years. Apparently, the whole area north of Mattawoman Creek was abandoned, except for what defense the frontier planters themselves could supply, and murders and burnings were frequent. The Piscataways, in fear of the Susquehannocks, abandoned their part on Piscataway Creek and took refuge in Zachiah Swamp in the central part of the peninsula. The Susquehannocks, who had also defeated the friendly Mattawoman Indians, ringed the fort in Zachiah Swamp so closely that the defenders did not dare venture out to plant their corn.

The Susquehannocks refused to treat with emissaries from the Colonial government, but did not prevent a small supply of powder, shot, and corn being sent to the fort; nor did they intercept delegations of Piscataways to St. Marys to beg fruitlessly for direct military aid, nor occasional visits from Maryland officials to the Piscataway Fort. One of these reported that "They stand in daily fear almost to despair."

The Governor and Council wished to give military aid to the Piscataways—"it being a matter of absolute necessity in the opinion of this house."

The Assembly, controlled by the larger planters, unwilling to tax themselves to protect the frontiersmen, as usual, did nothing about it.

The Susquehannocks next built a fort beside the fort of the

Piscataways in Zachiah Swamp. A party of English was sent down to see what was going on, but the Susquehannocks refused to treat with them. In August 1681, they attacked the fort, took seventeen prisoners, men, women, and children. Contrary to the usual custom, the men, instead of being tortured and scalped, were accepted into the tribe.

In describing these operations, Maryland sources refer to the enemy only as Susquehannocks who were known to number less than a hundred warriors, and no mention is made of the Senecas who may have aided their wards. The Susquehannocks may also have been aided by deserters from the younger men of the friendly tribes, principally Piscataways and Nacostans.

Things were going so badly that, in 1682, Maryland again sent Coursey to New York to negotiate. Anthony Brockhalls, the acting Governor, proved to be more co-operative than Andros and agreed to keep the Iroquois, particularly the Senecas, from raiding in Maryland and Virginia. He would not, however, go to the extent of restricting their purchase of powder and shot. Maryland authorities appreciated the principal sources of their troubles, for, on this mission, Coursey was instructed to endeavor to bribe the Senecas to turn their Susquehannock wards over to the Maryland authorities "to be killed or transported."

The treaty of 1682, supplemented by a further agreement between the Iroquois (including the Senecas) and the Piscataways in 1685, ended the serious Indian troubles in tidewater Maryland. The Senecas are reported to have honorably returned prisoners taken during a raid when the peace was being arranged.

THE LAST YEARS OF THE PISCATAWAYS

The end of the Proprietorship in Maryland and the change to a Royal Colony, with Sir Edmund Andros as its first Governor, was marked by a great improvement in frontier defenses. A strong, well-garrisoned fort at Little Falls served as anchor to a line of block houses running eastward to the headwaters of the Patapsco, which was regularly patrolled by the militia from the fort. A similar system controlled the eastern part of the peninsula. Although sporadic incidents occurred, and the Senecas roamed the country above the falls, Maryland was henceforth free from serious Indian trouble.

The Piscataways were relieved of further danger of attack, but still had to meet the difficulties involved in the rapid increase in settlement. The best lands of the reservation between the Piscataway and Mattawoman Creeks were now occupied by the settlers, and the Indians forced to the poorer land as well as deprived of their hunting grounds.

There was much restlessness among the Piscataways, particularly among the young men. The Senecas jeered at them and told them they were nothing but old women and that they lived too near the English and had no chance to be men. Rumors spread by the Virginia traders that the Marylanders intended to kill them all, but Virginia would give them protection.

By 1694 the situation had got so bad that the Emporer came before the Council: "He signified that he had an unruly people to govern and therefore desired protection for himself and family in case he should be forced (through danger of his life) to leave them."

In 1697 the Piscataways, now known by their Iroquois name of "Conoys," after a short stay at Little Falls where the Maryland officials made them most welcome, left Maryland and settled in the wooded hill country of Virginia. They had made a treaty with the Senecas and, as the Emperor reported to the Virginia authorities, "we're now all one people." They retained their tribal identity and government, however.

The immigrants were not welcome to the Virginia authorities, and Andros, now governor of Virginia, repeatedly ordered the Stafford County authorities to force their return to Maryland. Maryland was also acutely conscious of the loss of valuable scouts and defenders and, facing the necessity of increasing its ranger forces, sent successive delegations to persuade them to return. The Virginia traders, however, welcomed their presence and spread reports that they would all be massacred if they returned to Maryland. Consequently, the Piscataways were evasive, continually promising to return, but postponing the date.

In 1699 the Piscataways, including the Indians of Accokeek, moved to Heaters Island, then known as Conoy Island, in the Potomac near Point of Rocks. They built a fort with eighteen cabins inside the enclosure and nine outside, suggesting a total population of not over three hundred. In April 1700, the Emperor and some of his "great men" appeared in Anapolis, saying that they had come to renew the treaties. The Emperor asked if he should come to live at Accokeek or Pamunkey, and he was told he could have either place. The next day the treaties were signed and the Emperor promised to come back within two months, with his family and as many Indians as he could persuade to accompany him. The Governor ordered ten barrels of corn to be delivered to them on their arrival. In July a message was sent to the Emperor that he was expected by October at the latest. In 1705 comes the last reference to the Piscataways in the Maryland Archives, "since the Piscataways failed to come."

There had been a bad outbreak of smallpox on the island and the Indians deserted it suddenly, even abandoning the corn in the fields. Soon after 1711 they moved to Conejholo on the Susquehanna. Their last appearance as a tribe was in 1793 when they attended a conference in Detroit and used a wild turkey as their signature. There were fifty of them left at that time.

In the region around Port Tobacco there is a group of people largely of Indian blood, known to themselves and their neighbors as "we-sorts," that is, neither white nor Negro. Presumably, these are descendants of the Mattawoman, or Wicomico, subtribes of the old Piscataway Empire who did not join the Piscataways in their wanderings. According to one legend, however, the Emperor and a few of his "great men" and their families did not go with the rest of the tribe after leaving Conoy Island, but returned to southern Maryland and the we-sorts are their descendants. If so, the Piscataway tribe is not yet extinct.

SOURCES

In revising Mrs. Ferguson's earlier publication, I have quoted extensively from her text. The material I have added has been from secondary sources, mostly not available to her at the time of writing. I regret that I have had neither sufficient leisure nor eyesight to explore personally that comprehensive source of colonial history, the *Maryland Archives*. The titles that follow are all recommended to those who desire to pursue any phase of the subject in more detail. For more detailed references, see also Mrs. Ferguson's earlier publication, *Mayaone and the Piscataway Indians*, Washington, D.C., 1937*a*.

Exploration and Settlement Before 1608. Hakluyt is the source for the history of the Roanoke Colony. A valuable reference is *The New World,* edited by Stefan Lorant, New York, 1946. This volume not only reprints the original text of the documents but reproduces in color the famous water colors accompanying White's description. Reprints of the original documents, but without illustrations, will be found in *Early English and French Voyages*, Henry S. Burrage, editor, New York, 1930, a volume in the valuable series of *Original Narratives of Early American History,* and also in Hakluyt.

A recent study of importance to the history of the Potomac region is *The Spanish Jesuit Mission in Virginia* by Clifton M. Lewis, S.J., and Albert J. Loomie, S. J., 1950. Fathers Lewis and

Loomie have not only reconstructed the history of the ill-fated mission from the contemporary records in the Vatican library, but by personal exploration of the region have presented convincing evidence of its location.

Potomac River, Before 1634. For early history of exploration of the Potomac, by far the best source is Captain John Smith, "A True Relation, 1608" and "Generall Historie of Virginia 1624," both contained in Smith's *Voyages and Discoveries*. The Arber Edition, Edinburgh, 1910, is of special value as it contains appendices giving reprints of early accounts, particularly that by Spelman, Pory, and Archer. Smith seems to have been an accurate and careful observer and is generally careful to distinguish his own observation from information received "by relation." The map accompanying the "Generall Historie," whether or not the work of Smith (see Alexander Brown, *The Genesis of the United States*, Vol. 2, p. 596, 1890); also W. C. Ford, "Captain John Smith's map of Virginia," *Geographical Review*, 1924, Vol. 14, p. 433), is a remarkable example of early reconnaissance cartography.

The narrative of the fur trader, Henry Fleet, is reprinted in Neill, *Founders of Maryland*, Albany, 1876. When trying to raise funds for his trading projects Fleet could be an atrocious liar, but his descriptions of his own voyages in the Potomac are probably authentic. His narrative is the only source on Piscataway history for the period between the close of Smith's History in 1624 and the settlement of Maryland ten years later.

Missionary Period. For the first few years of Maryland settlement, the principal source of Piscataway history is the Jesuit missionaries. Father White's *Briefe Relation* (1635) and parts of the annual letters of the English Province of the Society of Jesus are reprinted in *Narratives of Early Maryland*, C. H. Hall, editor, New York, 1925. Neill's *Founders of Maryland* also gives extracts from the Jesuit letters but they are not carefully selected. The Jesuit letters are well written, show good observation, and are probably essentially accurate.

Other than the Jesuit letters, only a few of *The Narratives of Early Maryland* contain matter of interest to Piscataway history. The anonymous *Relation of Maryland* (1635), reads like the output of a modern real estate promoter, but contains a map of the Province which is of interest because it shows the location of the Indian town of Piscataway, and omits Mayaone. Calvert's letter to Lord Baltimore (1638) contains important data on the early period of settlement. Alsop's 1665 description of Maryland in this volume is written in a turgid style and is largely concerned with the Chesapeake Bay region, but does give something of a picture of life in the colony at that time.

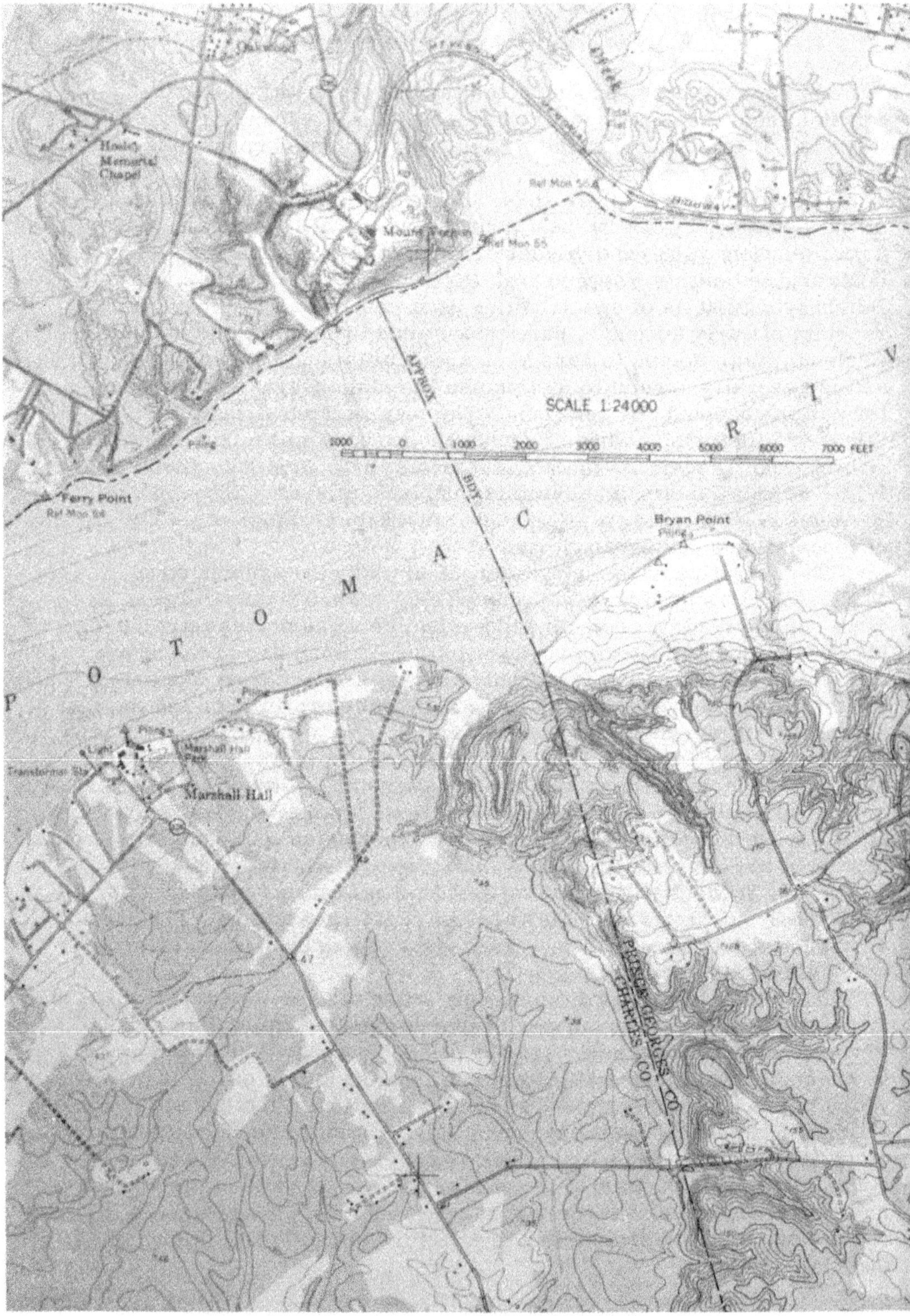
Memorial Chapel
Ref Mon 55
Ferry Point
Ref Mon 54
Bryan Point
Marshall Hall
P O T O M A C
R I V
APPROX BDY
SCALE 1:24000
1000 0 1000 2000 3000 4000 5000 6000 7000 FEET
PRINCE GEORGES CO
CHARLES CO

Fig. 2. Topographic map of the Accokeek Creek site area. (U. S. Geological Survey.)

Period of Settlement. For the remainder of Piscataway history the single major source is the *Maryland Archives*. Mrs. Ferguson's copies of the records of the Council and Assembly were quoted extensively in her earlier publication. I have not been able to make further exploration of this great source of information, but fortunately the work had already been done for me by Semmes in his monumental work, *Captains and Mariners of Early Maryland*, Baltimore, 1937. Chapters 17, 18, 19, 20, 23, and 24 contain most of the material relating to the Piscataways and I have supplemented Mrs. Ferguson's text with much data from these, nearly all of it derived by Semmes from the *Maryland Archives*.

Two papers by W. B. Marye, in the *Maryland Historical Magazine*, "Patowmack above ye Inhabitants," March, 1935, and "Piscataway," September, 1935, contain much valuable data on the region, derived largely from early land records.

Susquehannnock Fort. Bacon's Rebellion, which started with the escape of the Susquehannocks from the siege of the fort on Piscataway Creek, was later the subject of a long official investigation, and the interested reader can follow the confused and contradictory statements of eye witnesses reprinted in *Narratives of the Insurrections*, edited by Charles M. Andrews, New York, 1915. For shorter but more readable accounts see W. E. Washburn, *The Governor and the Rebel*, Chapel Hill, 1957, Chapter 2. T. J. Wertenbaker, in his study of Bacon's Rebellion, *Torchbearer of the Revolution*, Princeton, 1940, also describes the siege of the Susquehannock Fort. Semmes' *Captains and Mariners of Early Maryland*, Chapter 20, not only describes the siege but goes into considerable detail in the trial of Truman for the murder of the hostages. For a description of the location and excavation of the Susquehannock Fort, see Alice L. L. Ferguson, "The Susquehannock Fort on Piscataway Creek," *Maryland Historical Magazine*, Vol. 36, pp. 1-9, March, 1941.

Raids and Diplomacy. This section is almost entirely derived from Semmes, who gives references to original sources, chiefly *Maryland Archives*.

Last Years of the Piscataways. For the remainder of Piscataway history I have closely followed Mrs. Ferguson's earlier publication.

II

PRESENT AND PAST TOPOGRAPHY

Henry G. Ferguson

THE PENINSULA[1]

The Piscataway "Empire" in the early part of the seventeenth century occupied the western part of the western peninsula of Maryland as far north as the Falls of the Potomac, at the present site of Washington, D.C. (Fig. 1).

The peninsula, underlain by consolidated marls, clays, and sands of the Coastal Plain sequence (Cretaceous and Tertiary) is the deeply eroded remnant of a plateau. The present surface is capped by a mantle of gravel, consisting of water-worn fragments of the more resistant Paleozoic rocks of the Potomac and Shenandoah drainage system (known as the Brandywine gravel) deposited as an outwash apron of the ancestral Potomac, when the water level stood much higher, before the beginning of the glacial period.

THE SITE

The low terrace, which contains the Accokeek Creek site (Fig. 2), is a constructional rather than erosional feature and is of late preglacial or early glacial age. It borders the Potomac and the south side of Piscataway Creek, and, in the area of the site, ranges in height from close-to-river level to about 20 feet. At Moyaone, where it borders the Potomac in a low cliff 12 feet

[1]For a detailed study of the geology and geomorphology of a part of the western peninsula *see* John T. Hack, *Geology of the Brandywine Area and Origin of the Upland of Southern Maryland*, U. S. Geological Survey, Professional Paper 267-A, 1955.

high, it consists largely of sand containing nodules of manganiferous ironstone, and, at water level, rests on impervious clay of the Coastal Plain sequence. Elsewhere, particularly on the side bordering Piscataway Creek, are extensive interbeds of sandy clay. The low hill at Mockley Point is an erosional remnant composed of the same river sands, here capped by a few feet of windblown sand.

Landward from the site, the surface of the terrace rises gradually along the low ridge followed by the Mockley Point road until it blends with the wash slope from the upland. The surface of the terrace is mostly sand, overlain here and there by small patches of windblown material. Locally, principally east of the Mockley Point road, there is impervious clay a few feet below the surficial sand. This impedes percolation of the ground water and there are local swampy areas, parts of a once more extensive swamp, now reduced by drainage and plowing. Pebbles, cobbles, and rare boulders, mostly quartz and quartzite, washed down from the upland, have furnished the Indians raw material for projectile points and other stone artifacts. It is rare to find an unbroken pebble in the vicinity of the site.

The northeastern end of the site is bordered by the mouth of Piscataway Creek, now a broad, shallow estuary nowhere over 6 feet in depth and grading eastward into tidal flats, sand bars and marsh. Southwest of the site is a swampy area crossed by two creeks. The smaller, eastern creek rises in a spring at the base of the upland slope, and, except near the mouth where it enters the marsh, has no surface flow in dry weather. A similar small stream enters the western part of the marshy area. The latter, Accokeek Creek, cuts deeply into the plateau. Near its mouth it flows through swampy, wooded ground. Within the plateau the stream and its branches meander over the gravel surface of their valley bottoms, locally undercutting the valley walls. In places hummocky ground in the valley floor shows that this undercutting has caused small landslides.

The area of the Accokeek Creek site extends along the Potomac to Mockley Point and reaches Piscataway Creek at Clagett's Cove. Along most of the Potomac frontage the terrace ends in a low cliff of compacted river sand constantly being eroded by the river current. The Potomac, where it borders the site, is a broad, shallow cove in which an eddy reverses the current (note the direction of the "hook" of Mockley Point), and carries silt and sand derived from lateral erosion of the river bank into Clagett's Cove in Piscataway Creek, where there is a similar but smaller eddy.

CHANGES IN TOPOGRAPHY

There have been significant changes in topography since the Piscataway Indians deserted the site about 1630 (Fig. 4). These can be determined with a fair degree of accuracy. The same processes were active during the possible three centuries of occupation of the stockaded village, and their effects can, in large part, be evaluated; but no data are available to estimate possible changes during the many centuries of earlier occupation of the site.

It is obvious that a part of the stockaded village has been lost to the Potomac (Fig. 6). Some estimate of the amount of erosion can be made from personal observation supplemented by data from an old survey. During the thirty eight years we have had the place, a farm road, following the top of the riverbank, has had to be moved back three times, and I estimate that, at one point, at least as much as 30 feet has been lost. A survey along the riverbank was made in 1725. There is some doubt as to the accuracy of this survey and uncertainty as to the possibility of accurate adjustment to the modern topographic map, but it appears to indicate a retreat of the shoreline on the order of between 150 and 250 feet. It is therefore a fair assumption that the riverbank has retreated perhaps as much as 300 feet since the abandonment of the stockaded village about 1630.

This retreat takes place in two ways. The most obvious is the direct wave action during heavy storms, particularly at high tide or time of flood. The hurricane which passed over the area in 1956 caused waves that destroyed a line of locust trees along the bank, and at one point cut 20 feet into the bank (Pl. I). Spring floods, disastrous in the upper part of the Potomac, do not, in themselves, cause erosion in this part of the river, since the floods spread out where the river widens below Fort Washington and have never been known to rise to the terrace level.

Another process, perhaps more effective, since it is continuous, is the sapping of the bank by ground water flowing along the top of the impermeable clay at the base of the cliff, and carrying with it enough sand to cause occasional collapse of parts of the overlying bank. This process has also been effective along the river west of the site. The historic Indian village of Accokeek (not to be confused with the Accokeek Creek site), first mentioned in Maryland records of 1650 and apparently a town of some importance as late as 1700, can be identified from early land records as about 3,000 feet southwest of Bryans

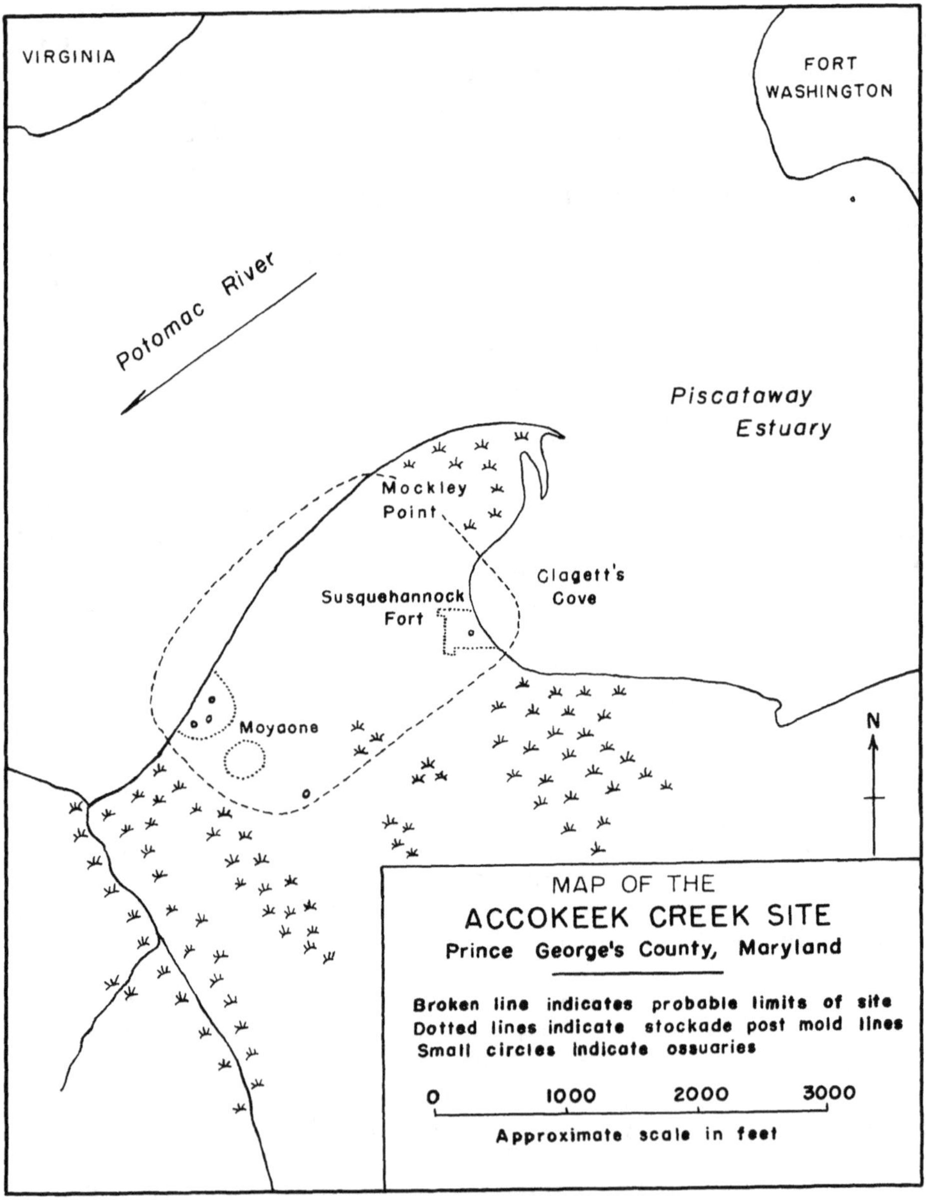
VIRGINIA
FORT WASHINGTON
Potomac River
Piscataway Estuary
Mockley Point
Susquehannock Fort
Clagett's Cove
Moyaone
N
MAP OF THE
ACCOKEEK CREEK SITE
Prince George's County, Maryland
Broken line indicates probable limits of site
Dotted lines indicate stockade post mold lines
Small circles indicate ossuaries
0 1000 2000 3000
Approximate scale in feet

Figure 3.

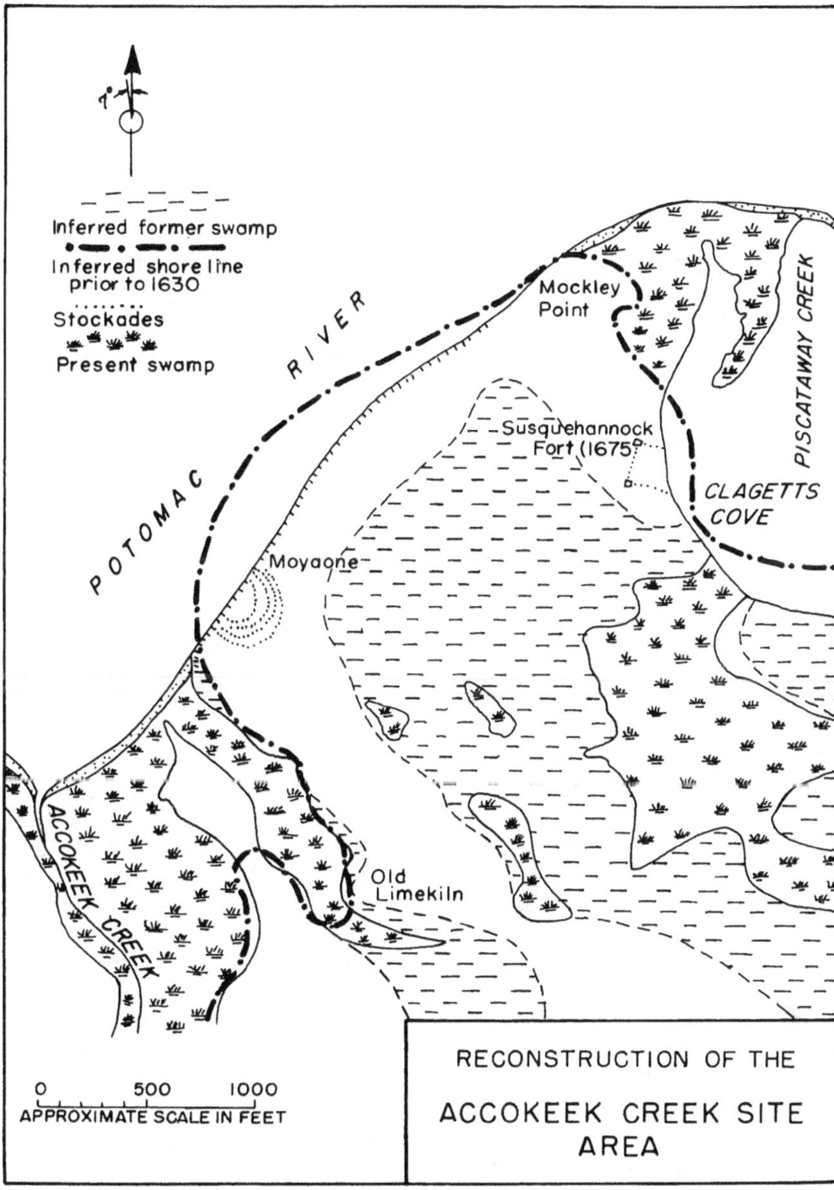
7°
Inferred former swamp
Inferred shore line prior to 1630
Stockades
Present swamp
POTOMAC RIVER
Mockley Point
Susquehannock Fort (1675)
PISCATAWAY CREEK
CLAGETTS COVE
Moyaone
ACCOKEEK CREEK
Old Limekiln
0 500 1000
APPROXIMATE SCALE IN FEET
RECONSTRUCTION OF THE
ACCOKEEK CREEK SITE
AREA

Figure 4.

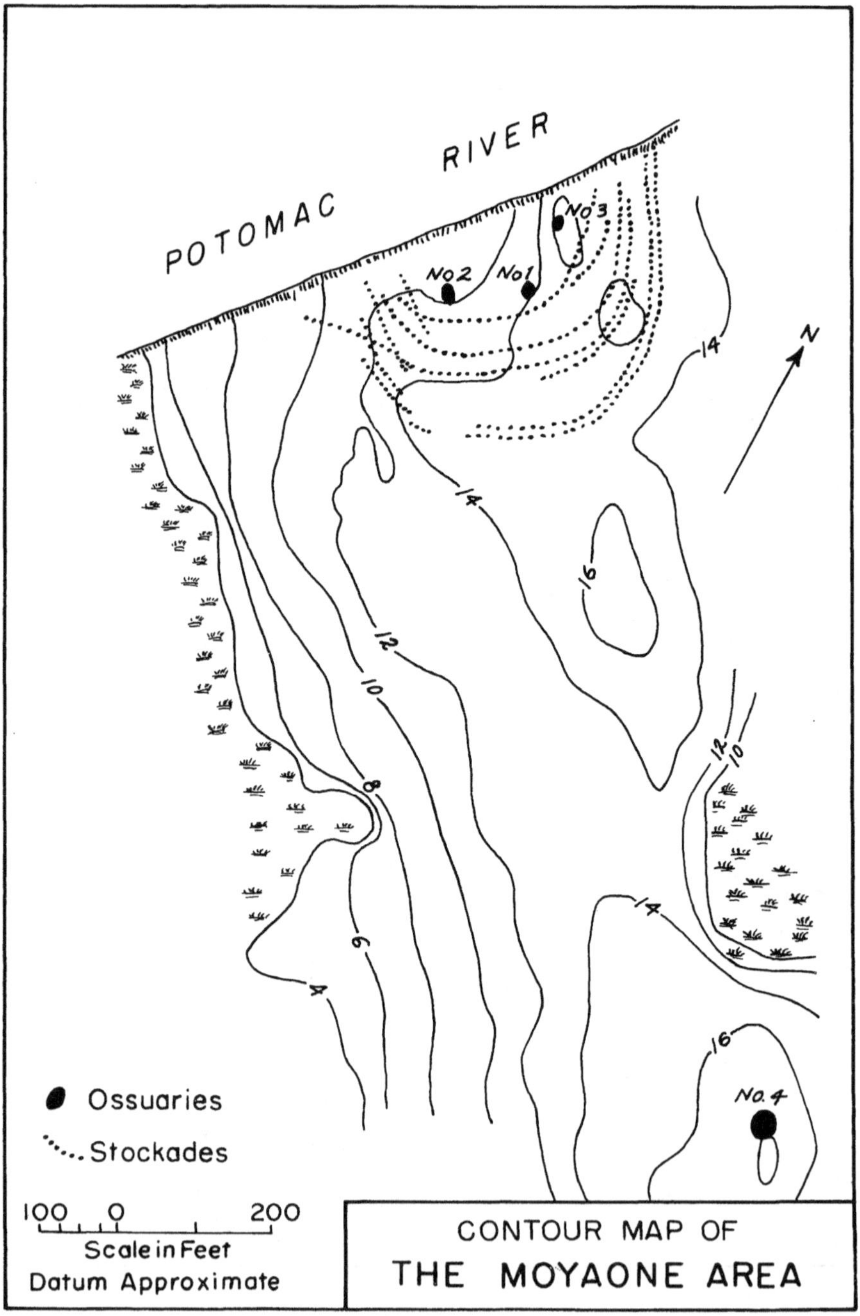
POTOMAC RIVER
No 3
No 2
No 1
N
14
14
16
12
10
8
12
10
14
4
6
16
No. 4
Ossuaries
Stockades
100 0 200
Scale in Feet
Datum Approximate
CONTOUR MAP OF
THE MOYAONE AREA

Figure 5.

Point. Potsherds can be found in the plowed fields, but a little test digging revealed no hearths or post molds. It is therefore inferred that, except possibly for the narrow belt of trees and brush between the fields and river, this entire village has been lost by erosion.

Piscataway Creek is relatively free from storm waves and not subject to the slumping process, so total erosion of the bank along its shore may have been much less. In Indian times, however, the water was much deeper. The Susquehannock Fort, built on unconsolidated river sand, probably close to the bank and only 3 or 4 feet above water level, would have been an easy prey to current-cutting by the eddy on the west bank of Clagett's Cove. The total erosion here since 1675 may not have been much more than about 50 feet.

In the extreme drought of 1932, the lowering of the water level in the Potomac caused the formation of a tidal bore in Piscataway Creek, with a wave high enough to flood parts of the bordering fields. If this is a recurrent phenomenon, it would have been effective in erosion of the fort.

Another major process affecting the site is the result of increased erosion due to clearing of the upland and, particularly, slopes of the small valleys for agriculture. Early records suggest that valley bottoms, now gravel strewn and brush covered, may have been wider and contained land suitable for cultivation, and probably the valley walls were much gentler. Surveys of the seventeenth century grants contain references to "old Indian fields" on the upland and valley slopes, and stone axes and hoes have also been found, so it is inferred that the process may have begun during Indian times. However, since neither the Indians nor the early Colonists used plows, the principal changes probably took place during the nineteenth and twentieth centuries.

Concomitant with erosion in the upland and covering of the higher reaches of the valleys with coarse gravel, has been the filling of the lower parts of the valleys with fine waste. Up to the time of the Revolution, the present village of Piscataway was an important tobacco shipping port (Fig. 1). Ships from England could sail far up the creek, though not quite to the present village. With the increase in sediment as more land was brought under cultivation, silting proceeded rapidly. Today the upper part of the creek is nearly choked by reedy tidal marshes, and the depth of water in the lower open portion is only a few feet (Fig. 2). The irregular coastline east of Clagett's Cove is the result of recent dredging for sand and gravel.

Open water in the area drained by Accokeek Creek, and the two smaller creeks to the east and west of it, must have persisted well into Colonial times, for oyster shells were burned in a lime kiln about 1,500 feet upstream from the mouth of the eastern creek (Fig. 4) and must have been transported by flatboat.

On the other hand, the swampy area east of the Mockley Point road is, in part, at the elevation of the terrace. At least on the higher ground it is not the result of aggradation, and though now reduced by drainage and plowing, has been in existence from Indian times. Its presence is mentioned in an account of the siege of the Susquehannock Fort in 1675. It owes its origin to the presence of a wide belt of impervious clay underlying a few feet of light, sandy soil. Water is held on the clay surface, and even in the drained portion, spring plowing must often be delayed.

A belt of dry land, bordering the river, must have extended from the stockaded village nearly to Mockley Point. The foundations of a house of Colonial date were uncovered in this area, but if there was Indian occupation, all trace has been lost by riverbank erosion. These inferred changes in topography are shown in Figure 4. Such a map, naturally, cannot be accurate in detail, but the evidence appears to be sufficient to justify the general outlines. Other, less significant changes may be mentioned briefly.

Traces of Indian occupation *in situ* are only to be found below the plowline, about 10 inches deep. Above this is a mixture of relics of both the Indian and White occupations, the latter including such objects as clay pipes, old bricks, hoes, bits of lusterware china, and similar refuse. Plowing has also tended to smooth out small irregularities in the topography. The post molds of the outer stockade are missing where the line should cross a group of Middle Woodland burials (Fig. 5). It is inferred that these were covered by a low, artificial mound, once crossed by the stockade and now leveled by plowing. It is possible that the flat ridge at terrace level, extending southward from the stockaded village, may have been steeper, but is now leveled by plowing. If so, the site of Pope's Creek occupation may have been destroyed. The only evidence for this is the abundance of sherds of Pope's Creek type on the slope west of the road, both above and below the plowline.

Little can be inferred as to topographic changes prior to the village occupation. The rarity of oyster shells in the refuse pits is evidence that during the period of village occupation the salinity has not changed greatly, and, consequently, the level of the Potomac has not been significantly lowered.

There is, however, a suggestion of a past period of greater aridity, when wind transport of material was a more important factor. Possibly river level was then lower and a greater area of the sandy bottom of the shallow cove was exposed to wind action. Evidence from burials at Mockley Point before and after the deposition of the windblown sand indicates that this dry interval occurred either near the end of the Mockley occupation of the site or not long after the coming of the Potomac Creek people, probably between 1100 A.D. and 1300 A.D. Further inference suggests that the dry period may have been a factor in this change. The small areas of swampy ground between the two larger swamps shown in Figure 4 (base map made about 1925) were probably also due to underlying clay and have now been eliminated by plowing, though the ground is still wet in the spring.

VEGETATION

The upland, near the site, is largely covered with second growth hardwood, interspersed with tangles of brush and honeysuckle. The general aspect is not seriously altered by the recent construction of scattered suburban residences. The region was closely logged off in the early part of the century, and relatively few large trees of the early generation have survived. A few areas are still farmed but long abandoned farms are now covered by a thick growth of pine, and those more recently abandoned, by blackberry and sassafrass brush.

Except that the woods were more open and the trees larger, conditions must have been much the same in Indian times. The browsing deer kept down the underbrush. That present day nuisance, the Japanese honeysuckle, was not introduced until 1806. Father White, in 1635, described the upland as "solid firme ground, with great variety of woode, not choaked up with undershrubs, but commonly so farre distant from each other as a coach and four horses may travale without molestation."

The lower terrace is largely treeless, wooded only in wet or swampy ground. It seems probable that this condition began with the beginning of clearing fields by the Indians and was intensified during nearly three centuries of European cultivation. Indian agriculture required a relatively large acreage per person. The fields were not fertilized and the sandy soil, though well suited for primitive agriculture, was soon exhausted,

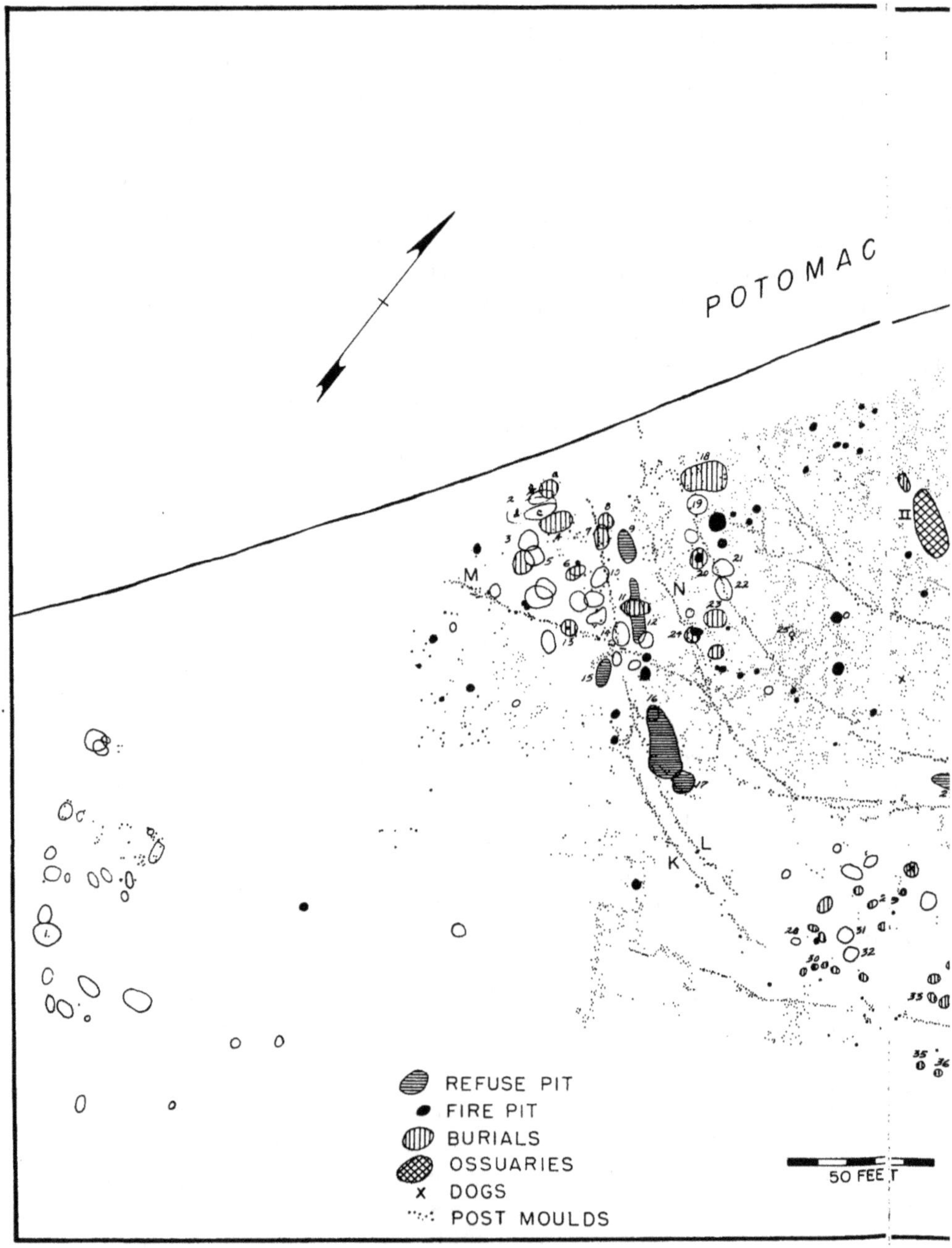
POTOMAC
REFUSE PIT
FIRE PIT
BURIALS
OSSUARIES
X DOGS
POST MOULDS
50 FEET

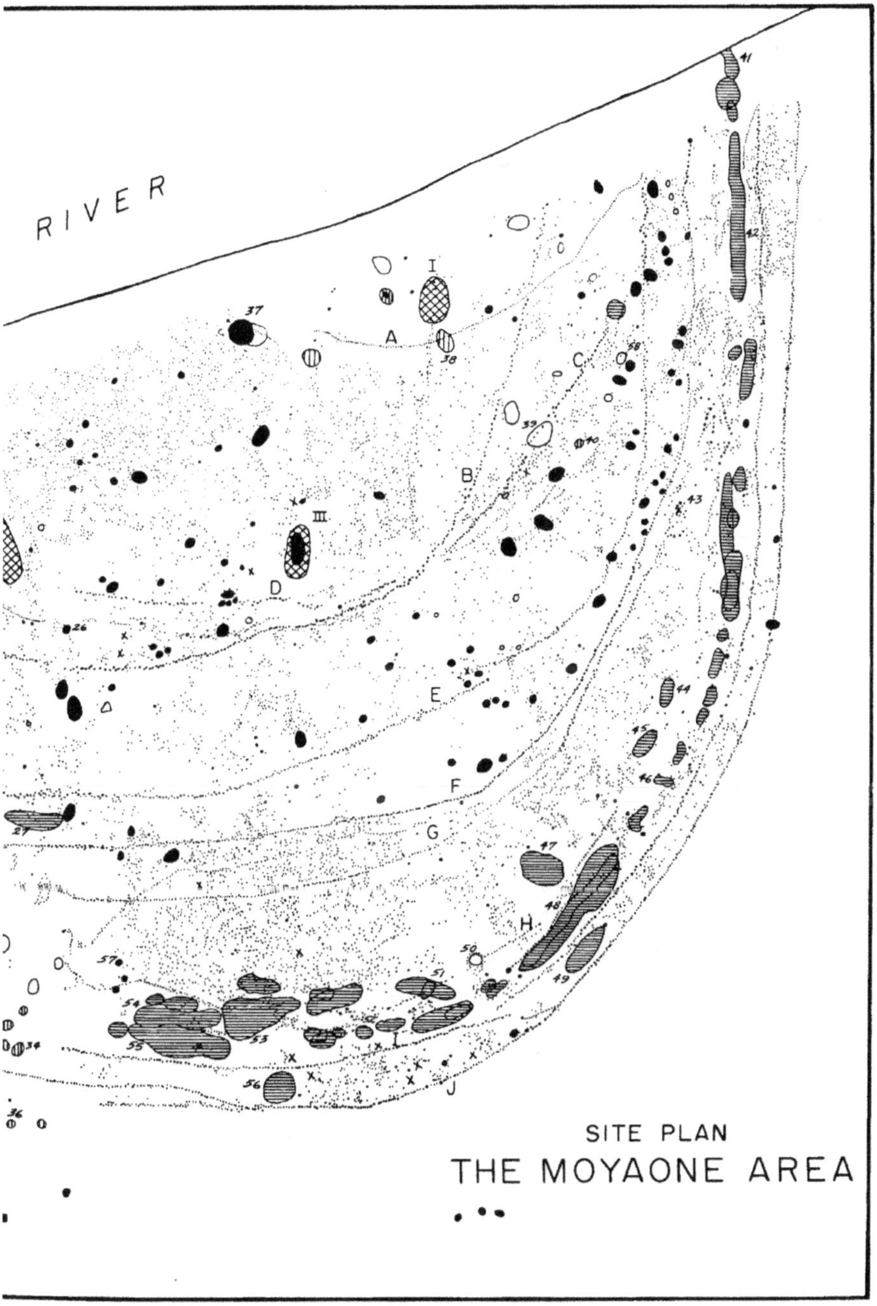

Fig. 6. Ground plan of excavations in the north section of the Moyaone area.

requiring the clearing of new land while the former fields were left fallow to regain their fertility.

An exception to the treeless condition was the presence of a large grove of honey locust trees along the river bank at the site of Moyaone. This was largely destroyed by erosion during the hurricane of 1956, but a few trees remain. This is the only grove of its kind in the neighborhood.

III

THE EXCAVATIONS AND FIELD WORK

Alice L. L. Ferguson

METHOD OF EXCAVATING

The site of Moyaone (Figs. 5, 6, 7) had been under white cultivation for about two hundred and fifty years with the plows biting deeper and deeper as modern machinery was developed. For at least fifty years it had been a happy hunting ground for collectors who came out from the city to gather arrowheads and whatever they could find. The result of all this was the complete destruction of the upper layer of the site. The dark color of the soil all over the site was the result of the dispersal of the charcoal and refuse from many shallow hearths. Only the material which had an original depth of more than 10 inches remained in place. The job was to strip back the disturbed top soil to this depth and get down to what remained in place (Pl. I).

A 50-foot grid was laid out over the area to be explored, and the daily surveying consisted of simple intersection based on the control posts. Whenever an area of special interest was found the 50-foot sections were subdivided into 5-foot squares. The area explored was much greater than had been originally intended but the extension of the grid was always a simple matter.

Whenever a stockade line was found it was followed, regardless of the development of the sections through which it passed. This caused a little more labor in rehandling minor dumps but more than made up for the additional work by the advantage of seeing and studying the stockade as a whole. It had the further advantage of clearly showing the extent of the job to be done.

All of the area inside the stockades of the village was stripped, working one 50-foot section after another. The method was laborious but complete. The work consisted largely of

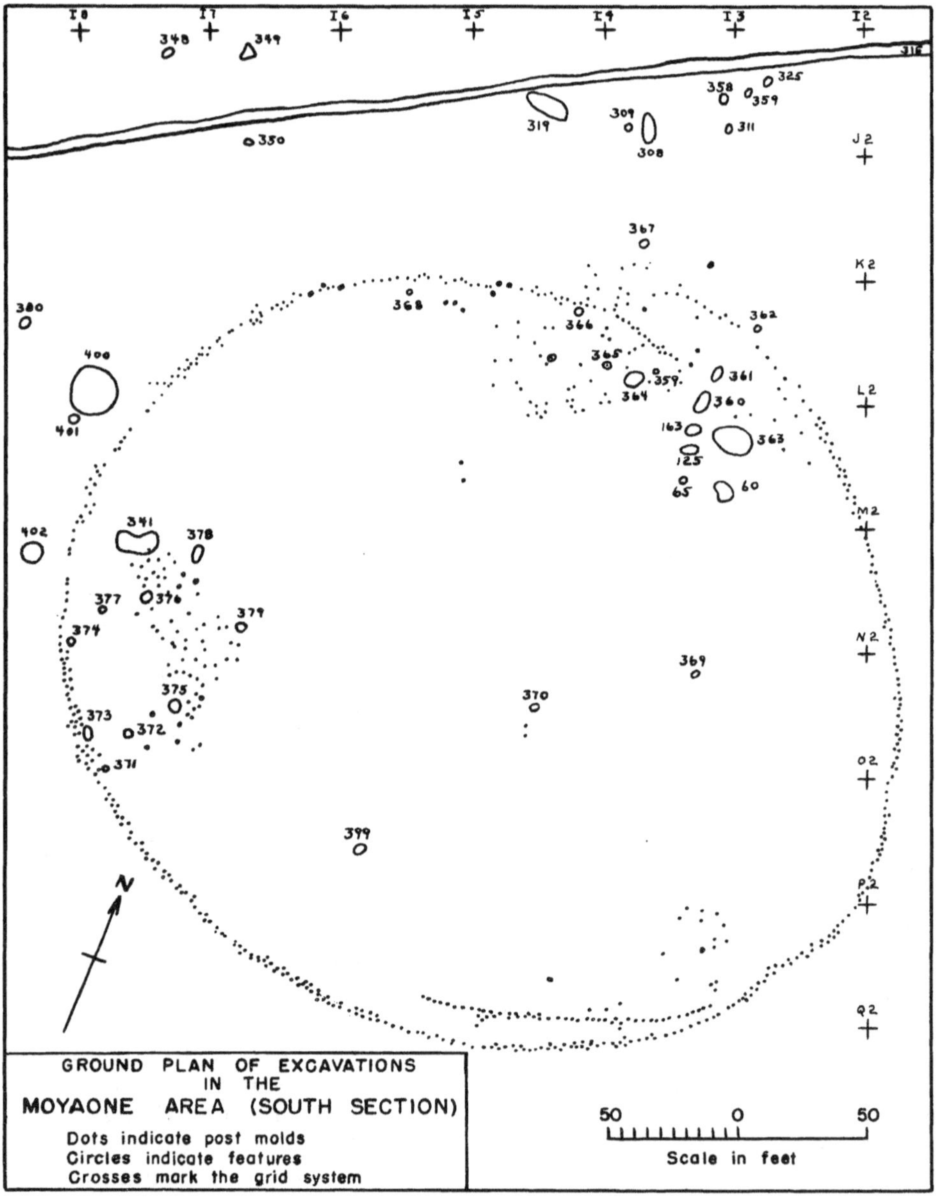
GROUND PLAN OF EXCAVATIONS IN THE
MOYAONE AREA (SOUTH SECTION)
Dots indicate post molds
Circles indicate features
Crosses mark the grid system
50 0 50
Scale in feet
N

Figure 7.

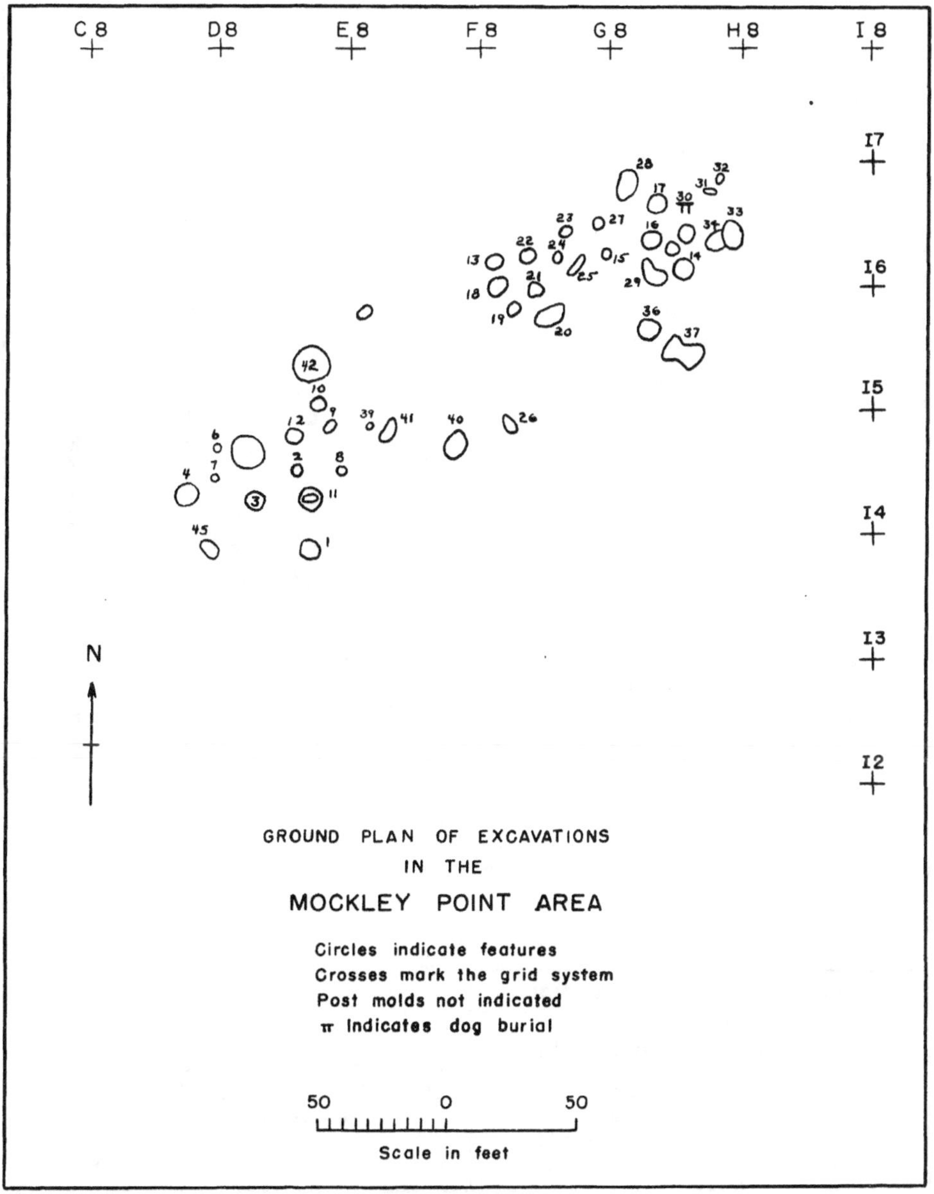
C 8
D 8
E 8
F 8
G 8
H 8
I 8
I7
I6
I5
I4
I3
I2
N
GROUND PLAN OF EXCAVATIONS
IN THE
MOCKLEY POINT AREA
Circles indicate features
Crosses mark the grid system
Post molds not indicated
π indicates dog burial
50 0 50
Scale in feet

Figure 8.

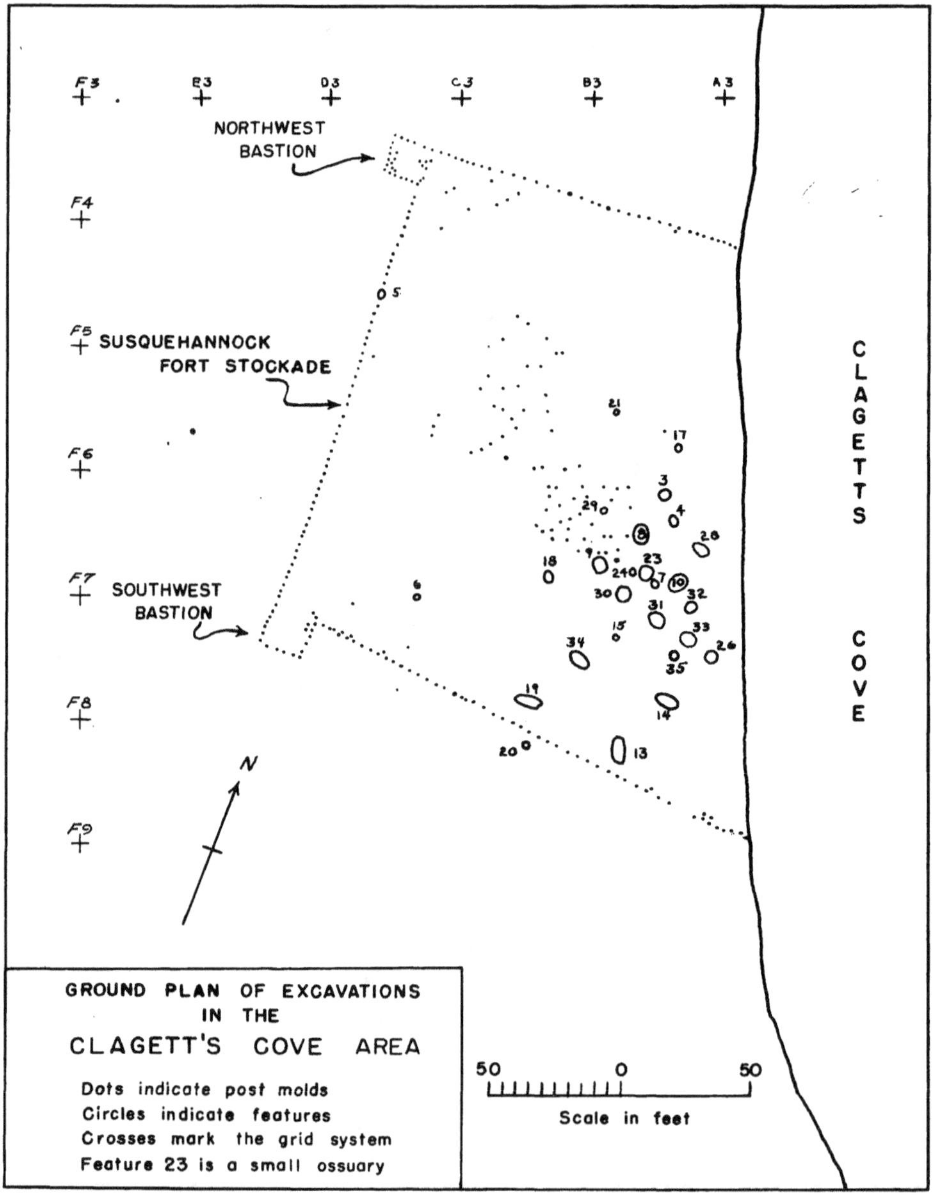
F3
E3
D3
C3
B3
A3
NORTHWEST
BASTION
F4
F5
SUSQUEHANNOCK
FORT STOCKADE
F6
F7
SOUTHWEST
BASTION
F8
F9
N
CLAGETTS
COVE
GROUND PLAN OF EXCAVATIONS
IN THE
CLAGETT'S COVE AREA
Dots indicate post molds
Circles indicate features
Crosses mark the grid system
Feature 23 is a small ossuary
50
0
50
Scale in feet

Figure 9.

watching for slight changes in the color and texture of the soil Pl. II). The pits were recognized by slightly darker soil with a looser texture and usually flecked with charcoal. The first sign of a pit was frequently that a spade cut a little more easily into the ground. The outlines of most of the pits were so clear that there was no trouble in recognizing and photographing them. Many of the pits at Moyaone extended well into the subsoil and a few of them reached as much as 6 feet below the surface. When the pits were found the stripping was abandoned in that part of the section until the pit was excavated. Every pit was cross sectioned and diagramed and all but a few of the very small pits were photographed. All artifacts found in the pits were kept and recorded separately but those found in the top soil in stripping back the refuse mantle were merely given the number of the section in which they were found.

Random test holes were tried at first but they were found to be of little value and were almost entirely abandoned. Outside the stockades a great deal of exploration work was done with trenches 2 or 3 feet wide. About every ten feet a test hole was sunk in the trench to check the deeper conditions. This method was used only in exploration and not always then, for the stripping was invariably found to be more satisfactory. Burial pit No. 33 was an example of what happened. It was found during stripping where a previous exploration trend had missed it by 3 inches.

Similar methods were employed in excavating the smaller sites at Mockley Point, and in the area of the Susquehannock Fort (Figs. 8, 9).

THE MOYAONE AREA[1]

Underlying a large area, much greater than the site of the stockaded village of Moyaone and including practically all the lower fields, was a stratum of mottled soil with occasional artifacts. All the pottery and artifacts from this stratum were of the previllage type. Although the earlier types of pottery were

[1]Note by H. G. F.—When Mrs. Ferguson excavated the site and prepared her manuscript, eastern archaeology, especially as based on pottery, had not reached its present state of refinement. The presence of at least two distinct cultures, the later of which was associated with the stockaded village, was evident, and in her description and references to the pottery she followed the nomenclature used by Holmes (1903, p. 153).

In order not to create confusion with the much more detailed classification used by Dr. Stephenson, I have changed this to a noncommital nom-

found in the top soil, it was much more abundant at greater depths, while the village pottery was never found below the refuse mantle except in pits. Obviously, the earlier settlements existed much longer than the village of Moyaone. The greatest concentration of previllage pottery was along the western boundary of the excavated area near Accokeek Creek but it was scattered all over the lower fields and covered about fourteen acres, an area so great that it was impossible to excavate it completely.

At Moyaone, the village-type pottery was essentially confined to the slightly more than two acres inside the stockades and it was not found in any of the deeper pits outside the stockades, except for Ossuary Number 4. It was only found locally on the surface or in a few shallow pits and hearths near the village. The earlier people left the ground so littered with their material that almost all the pits within the stockade lines had at least a few fragments of the previllage pottery mixed with the characteristic village types. In the northeast part of the village, near the river and away from the creek, the early pottery was less abundant and there were a few small pits with village pottery only. Toward the creek, to the west, the proportion was reversed; the village pottery became steadily more sparse and the previllage, more abundant until close to the creek and a little way back from the river, nothing but the previllage pottery was found.

One of the striking differences between the two cultures was the clay that was used in their pottery. The earlier people always used a surface clay that fired a reddish yellow. The village pottery was made from smooth gray clay which outcrops at the base of the cut bank bordering the river. These layers of clay are at present exposed only at low tide.

If, as suggested above there was a sloping bank, instead of the present low cliff, at the time of the earlier occupation, the river clay would not have been available. Even if the cut bank had been in existence, a river level two feet higher than the present would have covered the outcrop with river sand.

enclature, using "previllage" for the types characteristic of the earlier cultures, the "Early Woodland" and "Middle Woodland" of Stephenson's classification and "village" for the "Late Woodland," characteristic of the stockaded village. Where Mrs. Ferguson subdivided the "village" type, and division is approximately that of Stephenson's "Potomac Creek ware" and "Moyaone ware."

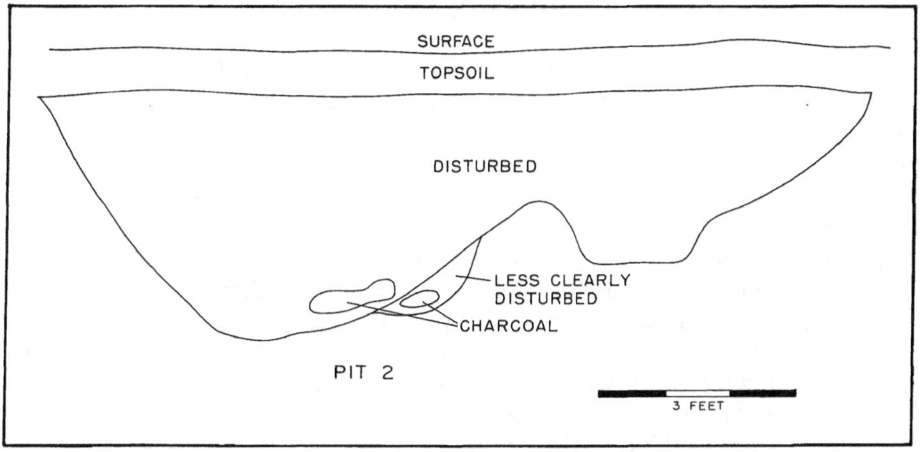

Fig. 10. Profile of pit Number 2, a deep pit near the west end of the stockades.

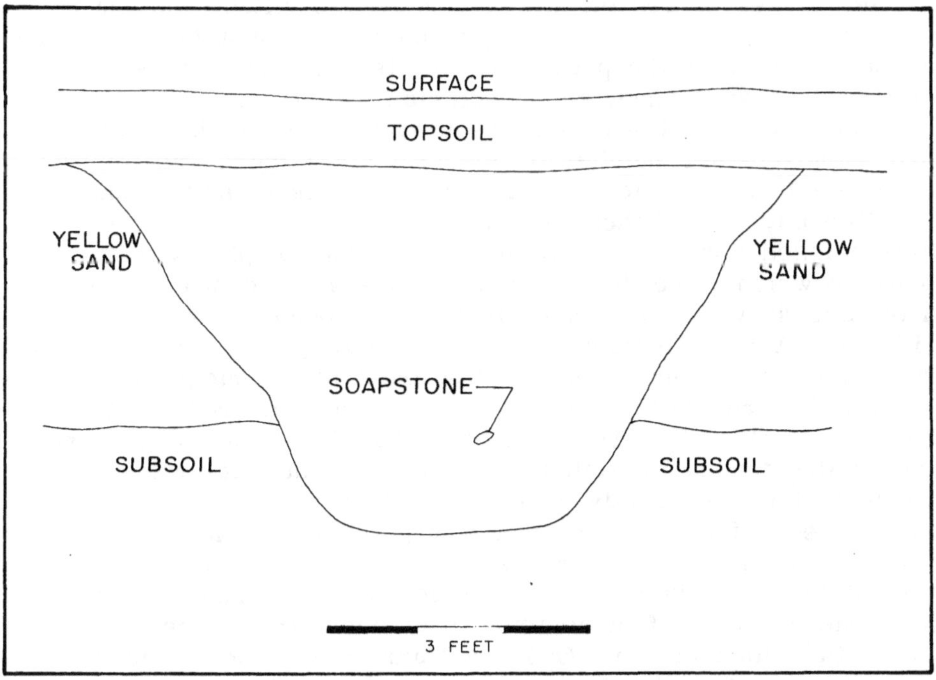

Fig. 11. Profile of pit Number 3, showing position of a large soapstone fragment.

THE PREVILLAGE SETTLEMENT

The record the previllage people left was difficult to follow. Their pottery was found in abundance along the west slope of the low ridge (Fig. 5) in a belt varying from 200 to 400 feet wide, extending at least 2,000 feet south from the river. This gives an area of about 600,000 square feet or about 14 acres. We found no post moulds or hearths that surely belonged to these people, and it was impossible to recover any definite limits to their settlement. There is a possibility that their main settlement was on the low ridge parallel to the present swamp and as the crest of the ridge eroded, some of the pottery from the hearths washed toward the creek and helped to make the heavy concentration found there. In spite of the large amounts of pottery and artifacts that were strewn around, very little about their mode of life was recovered.

Indian villages, depending as they did on hunting and crude agriculture, never could become very large; and it is doubtful to what extent agriculture was of importance, at least in the earlier stages of settlement. The Moyaone village was probably about as large a group as it was possible to sustain in a permanent location. If the previllage people made 90 per cent of the pottery that was found, the conclusion would be, not that there had been more of the earlier people at any time, but that there had been a lesser number on the site for a much greater period of time. Probably there were several waves of settlement.

The outlines of their pits were so obscure that we may have missed some of them. A small group of pits with vague outlines which were definitely theirs were found near the creek. They are shown on the map clustering around pit Number 1 (Fig. 6). A little pottery and a few arrow points were all that was recovered from them. At the crest of the ridge near Mockley Point were several of their pits which had probably been burial pits (Fig. 8). The iron oxide banding from the surrounding sand extended through these pits. The outlines were so vague that we frequently wondered if they were pits. Usually, a small piece of pottery or an arrow point was found deep down which gave much needed reassurance. Later and clearer burial pits of the previllage people were found on the ridge south of Moyaone at the 18-foot contour about one-third of the way between the stockades and Ossuary Number 4. One of these pits went down to 6 feet. The deep pits Number 2 and Number 3 (Figs. 10 and 11) in the river cemetery were also previllage.

In contrast to the later inhabitants of Moyaone, the

previllage people used soapstone bowls. Several examples were found of clay pots with soapstone fill[2] whose sides came up at the right angle from a flat base. Lugs were found on soapstone bowls, soapstone-fill pots, and also on some of the pottery vessels. The great mass of their pottery was firmly but coarsely built up in coils and imprinted with nets. Their pottery vessels were large, unwieldy, and very heavy. The previllage people must have been primarily hunters, and if they had agriculture, it was probably very crude and relatively unimportant.

They used stone mortars, cylindrical pestles, and grooved axes made from the local materials. A few of their knives, scrapers, spear points, and arrowheads were made of quartz but the greater majority were quartzite.

Owing to the vagueness of their pit outlines and the frequent association of their pottery and artifacts with mottled soil and iron oxide bandings, the conclusion is that their settlement here reached back into considerable antiquity and had spanned a long period.

MOYAONE VILLAGE

Post Moulds.—The plan of Moyaone as shown on the map of the excavation (Fig. 6) was largely developed by mapping the post moulds. A large part of the work of excavating consisted of searching for them. Whenever a post was driven in the ground to a depth below the present plowline and allowed to rot in place, it left its record in the soil. When the top soil and the refuse mantle were stripped off, the post moulds showed as dark circles in the light yellow of the subsoil (Pl. II, A, B, C). Cross sections of the ones that were mapped showed that, in contrast to tree root moulds, the post moulds were straight and tapered to blunt points from 4 to 24 inches below the plowline. These post moulds were the record of the Moyaone structures. The clearest, and for the most part the largest, were the post moulds of the stockades. Besides the stockades, which were built for strength, there were outlines of a great many little fences built of posts about 2 inches in diameter and placed at much closer intervals. These could not be followed for more than a few feet and may represent posts of houses or other structures such as racks used for drying skins and fish. Many of these posts have left their record in the earth and a long period of occupation with shifting structures has made the

[2]By "fill" Mrs. Ferguson means "temper" (RLS).

confusion which appears on the map. No definite outlines of such structures were traceable.

Some of the post moulds of the smaller stockades were not what are usually considered typical post moulds. They were apparently made by live poles which took root. When they were first uncovered they appeared as round post moulds like all the others. Digging down a few inches deeper, root marks began to appear and after digging a few inches still lower, the root marks spread out and became very clear. Some of the live poles apparently failed to take root for here and there were intervals of several feet with post moulds showing no indications of roots. Nothing could have given a better minor defense than a close line of growing honey locusts with their terrific thorns and it is possible that this is what they used. Honey locust is common along the river bank today and roots very early. Stockade lines, A and D, were of this type.

At intervals all through the excavations exceptionally large post moulds, apparently marker posts, were found. A large post mould, 12 inches or a little more in diameter, was found near each of the ossuaries. One of the post moulds near Ossuary Number III was 1.9 feet in diameter and tapered down to a blunt point 3.8 feet below the stripping level. Unusually large post moulds were found near most of the individual graves as well as near the ossuaries.

Stockade Lines.—The most striking thing in the village plan is the series of roughly concentric stockade lines. Like any other fence, the stockades, to be effective, would have to be repaired. If the site were occupied for any length of time it would be desirable at times to replace a rotting stockade with a new one. The stockades, as recovered and shown on the map, represent the maintenance of the village protection and, to some extent, can be considered the growth rings of the village.

No Indian village could grow indefinitely and Moyaone probably reached as great a development as economic security permitted. Agricultural land was necessary but even the big, easily cultivated fields around the village were limited. As the village population grew, the hunting ground tended to become less productive and more remote. An Indian village having reached its maximum size, unless it were depopulated by famine or war, would have to send its surplus population elsewhere. The village, of necessity, would roughly hold about the same population.

It is unlikely that a village like Moyaone would have had an unprotected river front. The river was the principal highway of Indian times and the river side of the village was the most vulnerable. Instead of the big arcs made by the existing traces of the stockades, the original plan may have been complete circles. At the Potomac Creek site, Dr. T. D. Stewart found concentric lines of stockades, like those of Moyaone, which made complete circles (Stewart, 1939). The two sites were very similar. Both were fortified villages on the edge of high river banks. If the stockade lines of Moyaone made circles, roughly half of the village has been lost to the river.

There was definite evidence of erosion in the village itself. The stockade lines went right up to the edge of the bank and a cross section of refuse pit Number 41 was exposed on the face of the cliff. It is always possible to pick up pottery on the beach at low tide and one of the largest axes found was brought up in a fish net some distance from the shore. It is likely that some of the later stockade lines represent a retreat from the eroding shore front rather than an enlargement of the size of the village.

The post moulds of the stockade lines were very evenly spaced at intervals of about 1 foot. They varied somewhat in size but were commonly from 4 to 7 inches in diameter while the usual diameter of the unidentified post moulds inside the stockades were only 3 to 4 inches (Pl. II, A, B. C). The historic records say that the stockade posts extended 10 feet or more above the ground and were laced with twigs and mats, which made them particularly arrowproof. Each of the stockade lines at Moyaone was interrupted occasionally by a gate 2.5 feet wide. All the stockades had gates to the east and south at relatively the same places. It appeared as though there had been continuity in the life of the village and that the villagers had established the habit of coming and going in those places, and when the stockades were rebuilt the gates were repeated in the same relative positions. Each gate was protected by a screen to prevent the enemy from seeing what was going on in the village and to make it impossible to shoot arrows through the openings. The final posts by the gates were larger than the others and in places they were further reinforced by a few small posts very near them either inside or outside the line. A few of these gates are shown very clearly on the map. The gate in the J stockade by the river and the gates in the center of the E and F stockades are especially clear.

All of the stockades were difficult to follow at their western ends. Some of them were deeply buried and others washed away completely. The 16-foot contour, where it crossed the stockades at pits Numbers 16 and 17, made a sort of dividing line. Above that contour to the south, the lines had washed away and had disappeared while below that contour to the north, the stockade lines were progressively more deeply buried as they approached the river.

On the map of the excavations (Fig. 6) the stockades are shown lettered from north to south. The oldest line was probably C including the small vestige just south of Ossuary Number III continuing over towards Ossuary No. II. The larger lines probably ran in the time sequence of C, B, E, G, F, I and J.

The B line was very clear in the center, but, like most of the other lines, it was faint and difficult to follow to the west.

The C line, where it was recovered, had large and rather poorly defined post moulds. It had been so nearly obliterated by the later life of the village, especially by the digging of Ossuary Number II, that it was concluded it was an early stockade. To the east, the C line crossed pit Number 39 which contained what probably had been a complete and very large pot of the previllage basket design.

The E line was unique in that it was clear from end to end and was without the patchy modifications which complicated the other lines. It crossed pits 18, 22, and 21, which probably had been burial pits of the previllage people in which the skeletons had completely disintegrated. It was also later than pit Number 20 which still contained a fragment of a burial. Near the eastern end little fire pits were superimposed on the post moulds of this stockade. It was deeply buried at the western end.

The F line was the clearest of them all. The post moulds were unusually large, nowhere less than 5 inches in diamter and many up to 8 inches. It was the easiest of all to follow except at the western end where the post moulds were deeply buried. There was no sign that this stockade had ever been burned. Probably M was the western continuation of this line.

The G line at the center and east had very small post moulds and appeared to have been eroded. The N line was probably the western continuation of the G line. As N left the M line and approached the river, it became steadily more deeply buried. None of the other stockades were found so far below the surface. It is possible that dirt from some of the near-by pits was piled over it but it is much more probable that soil from the higher ground to the south had washed over it. Owing to the signs of erosion in the main line and the great depth of N, this line is considered to have been earlier than F.

The I line was very clear and easy to follow until it was completely lost crossing the previllage burial area at the south end of the village. On the western side of this cemetery it was probably picked up again in line L. This L line crossed burial pits 7 and 10, and it also crossed the empty pit Number 14 which had probably been an earlier burial pit.[3]

The J line, with its probable continuation K, closely paralleled the I line. To the south, on the edge of the burial area, there was the vestage of an intricate gate. Both the I and J stockades had been burned. Neither of these lines would have been an effective defense unless they had crossed the burial area. They were too strong and consecutive, where they were recovered, to permit the thought that both stockades had been left open for 100 feet or more at the south. A possible explanation of the gap in the two lines might be that loose earth had been heaped over the burials and that the stockades had crossed the mound. In time the mound would have washed away to a considerable extent and plowing would have completed the leveling. This explanation is also suggested by the bowing out of the contour of this area.

Two stockades, A and H, do not fit into the general plan and their relation to the others is in doubt. Line A was different from all the others and may not have been built for defense. A continuous trench appeared to have been dug to a depth of about 2.5 feet and live poles, many of which took root were placed in it at intervals of only a few inches. The A line must have been planted very much as we plant a hedge today. The post moulds were unusually small, from 2 to 4 inches in diameter, and it must have been more like a hedge than a stockade. It may have been a fence enclosing a ceremonial area. We know that Ossuary Number I was inside this enclosure but unfortunately much of the rest of the area has fallen in the river. A suggestion of another line similar to it was picked up near Ossuary Number II. The A line was one of the late stockades. The village was already well established when it was built for it crossed burial pit Number 38 suggesting that enough time had elapsed to have forgotten the existence of this pit although the burial was still in good condition. The little broken continuation of this line to the west crossed pit 37*b*,[4] a previllage pit, but was itself crossed by pit 37*a*, a shallow fire pit with village potsherds.

[3]It seems likely that the break between stockades I and L at the cemetery area may have been due to the presence of an artificial mound above the burials. This, together with the connecting post moulds, would have easily been lost during two centuries of plowing and consequent erosion.—H.G.F.

[4]Letters indicated, throughout, do not appear on Figure 6.

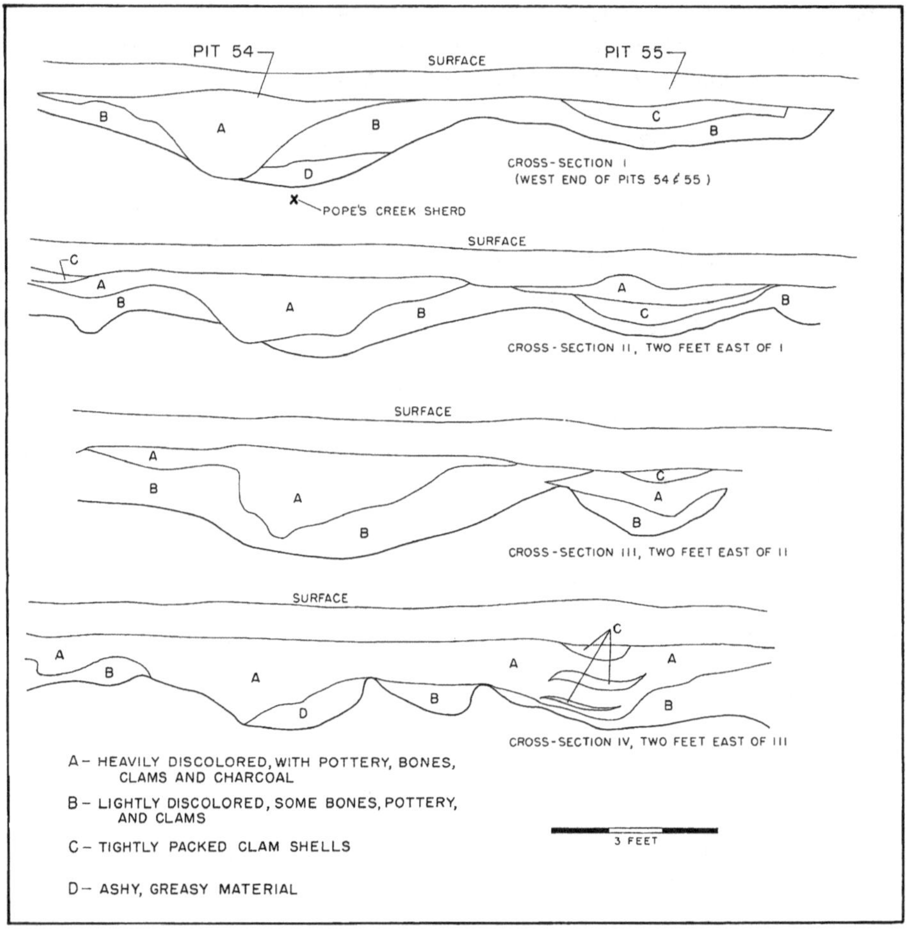

Fig. 12. Profiles of four sections of pits Numbers 54 and 55.

This A line also crossed the B line. I am under the impression that this A line came into the sequence probably between F and I.

The H line was crooked, weak, and fragmentary but it clearly crossed refuse pits 53 and 54. A possible continuation, just before it merged into the L line, crossed refuse pits 16 and 17. It was also interrupted by pit Number 50, a storage pit used for objects of value.[5] Since it crossed the refuse pits it would

[5]It is of especial interest to note that pit Number 50 is completely encircled by a row of postholes that appear to have been a part of stockade line H.

be later than I and J but if it had been a defense stockade it should have been straighter and more complete.

Inside the I stockade there was a line of refuse pits, almost continuous and in fact overlapping except across the burial area. It seems probable that these furnished earth for an embankment strengthening the stockades and then formed a convenient deposit of village refuse.

It is thought that F stockade with the unusually large post moulds was the boundary of Moyaone at a period of great strength and power. The village later expanded to the I line and there was a period of sustained prosperity during which the refuse pits were filled. This I line was burned and the post moulds were full of charcoal.

Post moulds of another stockade, distinct from the stockaded village were uncovered on the crest and southwest slope of the low ridge extending southeast from the village. This was about 150 feet from the outer stockade of the village and was circular, about 300 feet in diamter (Figs. 3 and 7).

Refuse Pits.—A striking feature on the map of the village is the long regular arc of the refuse pits, closely following the I stockade. An idea of the contents of some of these pits can be obtained from the fact that in Number 55 (Fig. 12), 288 unduplicated fragments of pottery vessel rims were found in 10 square feet and this pit was typical of all the others. Some of these refuse pits were huge. The Number 48 group was 53 by 10 feet of closely packed refuse and the Number 55 group was 35 feet by 21 feet. Although these large refuse pits almost completely encircled the village, they probably contained only a small fraction of the village waste accumulated during a relatively short period in the life of the village. Many of the refuse pits have probably slipped into the river with the loss of a part of the village through erosion. Part of pit Number 41 was found hanging on the edge of the cliff. The rest had disappeared. To a considerable extent the Indians undoubtedly did what many people would do now and pitched much of their trash in the river to be carried away with the next tide.

When the village expanded and built the I stockade, the inhabitants apparently heaped dirt against the inside of the stockade and made an earth rampart. If this had been done they would have used the nearest dirt, which would have resulted in an irregular and discontinuous trench just inside the stockade. An open trench like this would have been a nuisance in the village life, and it would have been natural to have utilized it by filling it in with village trash. The I stockade probably crossed the burial area in the center of the village, although no traces of it were found. The nearest refuse pits, the 55 and 53 groups, were unusually deep and some of the needed dirt might have come from there, or the rampart might have been omitted in that section. In any case the line of refuse pits did not cross the burial area although the line was continued again to the west on the other side.

The entire line of refuse pits belonged to the same period. Pottery fragments from Number 53 were matched to fragments from 46, 52, and 41; Numbers 51 and 54 had fragments that matched, and also 55 and 51, which would tend to prove that the pits in the main line had no perceptible time difference. It is thought that the refuse pits to the west, Numbers 16, 17, 9, and 12 were probably continuations of this main arc of refuse pits following the I stockade.

Refuse accumulations, which were found in only a few places other than the main line of pits, were probably not contemporaneous with the main line. These accumulations include Number 27 inside the F stockade; Numbers 44, 45, and 47 inside the H stockade and 49 and 56 between the I and J stockades. These pits were very shallow, only 6 or 8 inches below the plowline and were probably dumps rather than pits. They looked as if piles of refuse had spread from original surface dump piles. No matches were ever made between pottery fragments from these dumps and the pits of the main line.

If the theory of the expansion of the village is correct, dump Number 27 would be the earliest concentrated refuse in the village followed by 44, 45, and 47 then followed by pits of the main line with Numbers 49, 56, and probably 15 the three latest.

There was no apparent stratification in the refuse pits but to make sure, an arbitrary line was drawn horizontally through the middle of the large pits and all the material was classified as upper and lower. Apparently the pits were filled within a short period as no distinction could be found between material from the two levels, and matches were frequently made with pottery fragments coming from the different levels.

The only real difference between the refuse pits was in their size and depth. The usual depth was from 2 to 2.5 feet but a few like Numbers 53, 42, and 55 went down to 4 feet. They all showed below the plowline by a darker soil, almost black with a

[6]Since in this area the post moulds had been lost by erosion, the pits themselves, perhaps here less deep, might likewise have been lost.—H.G.F.

thick sprinkling of broken shells, charcoal, and small bone fragments. It was so seldom that any pottery could be restored from the heterogeneous pit fragments that all serious efforts to reassemble complete pots were abandoned except where similar fragments were found in little pockets or piles.

The heavily discolored soil carried the greatest amount of pottery, bones, and shell while the slightly discolored soil carried only scattering specimens. Frequently the largest and heaviest pieces would be found at the very base of the discolored soil.

The layers of thickly packed shells very rarely had anything else in them. At intervals all through the pits, there were streaks of grey soil with a very greasy texture which bubbled freely when touched with hydrochloric acid. There were also layers of almost pure ash.

Pit Number 55, one of the largest and most productive of this group (Fig. 12) yielded 3,546 fragments of pottery; 1,492 deer bones; 201 carapaces of turtles; 112 cheek shields of sturgeon; 10 dog bones and 1 complete dog skeleton, 27 racoon bones; 45 worked bones; 19 awls; 11 fragments of pipes; 28 arrowheads; 1 shell bead; 1 human skull; numerous bones of turkey, duck, squirrel, bob-cat, and a great many unidentified bones of birds and fish, besides abundant clam shells. Some of the other refuse pits like Numbers 53 and 42 were equally productive. No shell heaps were found on the site. If they ever existed they must have been lost by river erosion.

Fire Pits.—All through the excavations shallow little pits were found that were usually 1 foot to 1.5 feet in diameter, though some were larger, and reached a depth of from a few to 18 inches below the bottom of the top soil (Pl. II, E). They were full of charcoal and contained a little ash mixed with fragments of bone and pottery with occasional fire-spalled stones. These were probably the fire pits of the houses, and probably only those which extended to a greater depth than average were preserved. Below the plowline nothing was as disappointing in the excavations as the failure to recover the clear record of the houses with their fire pits. They must have been constantly shifting and the entire refuse mantle was probably made up very largely of the dispersal of innumerable small fire pits.

Storage Pits.—There were many small pits, larger and deeper than the first pits, and without any traces of fire. Most of them were about 2.5 feet deep from the bottom of the plowline and many of them had irregular discolorations of the sand suggesting the decay of vegetable matter (Pl. II, F). These may have been storage pits. A few of these pits had irregular floors of little stones at the bottom, and some of them were marked by small pebbles laid around loosely on the top. The remains of nuts were found in some, also a few potsherds, but very little else.

Food.—The refuse pits gave a good idea of the food supply of the village, other than agriculture. Eighty per cent of the identifiable bone fragments found in the refuse pits were the bones of deer. There was probably considerable seasonal variation in the Indian diet with the emphasis on deer during the winter months and fish and clams during the summer. Many turtles and crabs were eaten, and immense amounts of sturgeon and gar and many other fish whose bones have not been identified. Some of the pottery vessels had fish scales still sticking to the insides, and many of the pots were smudged with the remains of food burned to them. In contrast to the great accumulations along banks of the lower Potomac, very few oyster shells were found. If oysters formed part of the food supply, they must have been shucked where they were collected. One of the major articles of food was fresh water clams (*elliptio complanatis*). The halves of the clam shells were not broken and so few of them were calcined that they must have been steamed or eaten raw rather than baked, or they may have been allowed to open naturally be aging. Bones of all the animals now native in the locality were found in the refuse pits with the addition of several animals that are no longer known in Maryland such as elk, bear, wolf, and the Canada lynx. A great amount of turkey was eaten, some duck, squirrel, fox, bobcat, racoon, and even skunk. Dog bones were frequently found in the refuse pits and also a few human bones, some of them well charred. Disintegrated remains of walnuts were found and presumably all the native nuts were used. The fields outside the village were flat and sandy and very easily cultivated. Corn was in sufficient supply to be purchased by white traders, and in addition, beans and squash were probably raised.

Dogs.—The bones of 39 dogs were found (Fig. 6). These ranged from about the size of a fox terrior to a small setter. All of them were young, about three years old or younger. One of them was only a few months old and still had its puppy teeth.

Almost all the refuse pits had a few dog bones in them and there were also a few dog skulls. Many of the dog remains in the refuse pits were directly associated with clam and turtle shells, racoon bones, etc. In refuse pit Number 55 there was a skeleton of a dog a little larger than usual—on its back with the paws upward. It was one of several that suggested that they had died and had been thrown out rather than eaten. The complete dogs were usually found lying on their sides with their heads twisted sharply to one side. The skeleton of a very young dog in perfect conditon (No. 43) was found in a sharp corner of the G stockade near a gate, with a small arrow point between the vertebrae and the ribs and a larger point in the flank. He had probably escaped from his pursuers and crawled into a hole to die. Four complete dog skeletons were found in burial pits. They were definitely in the pits but at a higher level than the human burials, and probably were killed and placed in the pits just before the filling was completed.

Stone Piles.—Little stone piles were found in many places throughout the excavations both inside and outside the stockades (Pl. II, D). The piles that were found were probably merely the bases of the original stone piles. The upper parts of the piles had been scattered and it was noticeable that loose stones were always more abundant in the soil near the piles than anywhere else. Below the plowline, the stones of the piles were usually closely packed and sometimes up-ended and wedged into place. The piles varied in both size and depth. Some of them were so small that they were little better than a handful while one not far from the village, was more than 8 feet in diamter. The largest stone pile was about a quarter of a mile southwest of the village. It was 12 feet in diameter and the stones were tightly packed to a depth of 3 feet. A few pieces of village pottery were found in some of the stone piles but previllage fragments were absent. One stone pile had a large piece of soapstone from a broken vessle mixed in with the other stones. This was the only occurrence of previllage remains in a stone pile and it appeared to have been accidental. These stone piles had no pits nor anything that could be discovered under them but they were abundant near burial pits and ossuaries. Possibly they served the purpose of the "Pawcorances" described by Smith. "They have also certain altar stones they call Pawcorances but these stand from the temples, some by the houses, others in the woods and wilderness where they have had any extraordinary accident or encounter. As you travel by them they will tell you the cause of their erection wherein they instruct their children." (Smith, 1910, p. 77). Here, however, no large blocks of stone were available.

BURIALS

Two types of burial were excavated in the Moyaone area; individual burials, including a few group burials; and large ossuaries containing from 250 to over 600 individuals in a single pit. The use of ossuaries, admirably adapted to the conservation of a limited area of suitable agricultural ground, began during the period of the stockaded village. Occasional individual burials, however, seem to have taken place during the entire history of the village, and on the other hand, there were a few group burials of a few skeletons in a single pit, during the previllage period.

Everything that was found at Moyaone fitted into a record of a long history. One of the impressive facts discovered was a gradual change in the shape of the skulls. In many of the individual burials, the skulls were so dolichocephalic that they were in the Lagoa Santa class (Hrdlicka, 1937, p. 101). Gradually throughout Ossuaries I, III, and II the dolichocephalic skulls became less and less frequent until in the fourth ossuary they were almost absent. The physical type of any group of people, either by inheritance or mixture, does not change over night and if such a change occurred here, it could only be further proof that the history of Moyaone covered a long period of time.

Fifty-six individual burials were found. The condition of the bones ranged from a perfect skeleton with every bone present (No. 40) to those of which nothing remained but the tops of the teeth (No. 34). It is thought that many of the pits such as Numbers 31, 32, 5, and 3 were burial pits in which the skeletons had completely disintegrated. The pits were the same size and shape and had all the characteristics of near-by pits which contained bones in an advanced state of decomposition. In the pits where exceedingly fragmentary bones remained, as in Numbers 36, 30 and 7, the bones that were left were in normal relationship. There was no reason to believe that any of the bones had been disturbed for reburial in an ossuary. While one burial pit frequently intruded into another, no indication was ever found of the burial itself having been disturbed.

Individual burials were found here and there all through the village but there were two definite concentrations into cemeteries. The southern cemetery, in the center of the village stockade lines, was a unit to itself and showed more signs of a plan than the other cemetery. The burials were arranged in rough circles and there were no intrusive pits. There was a large post mould a foot across in the center of the area and near it was buried a middle-aged male (Pl. III, D) with a large scar on the skull (pit No. 29) surrounded by a group of 19 skeletons of which all that could be identified were female. In another pit, about the same distance from the post mould, was a double burial of a middle-aged, dolichocephalic female with a young adult female, probably brachycephalic. Around the post mould and these three burials was a circle of female burials predominately dolichocephalic. Other burials fringed this circle and those that could be identified were also females.

In the outer fringe of burials, Number 33 had a large fragment of a broken pot of previllage type crushed under her knee. (Pl. III, A). It was one of those pots marked by the imprint of baskets which were especially frail and difficult to reconstruct. The reconstructed fragment measured 14 by 10 inches. No other fragments of this pot were found in the pit, and it is thought that it was already a fragment when placed in the grave. Fragments of a similar pot were found in the corner of pit Number 35 where almost nothing was left of the skeleton.

There was a total of 20 burials in this cemetery and the burials averaged about 2 feet below plowline. There were also 7 empty pits which had almost certainly been burial pits. Forty-four fragments of previllage pottery were found in the pits which were possibly accidental intrusions when the pits were dug. A small stone smeared with red iron oxide paint and a few stemmed arrowheads were the only other artifacts found with these burials.

The strange thing about this cemetery consisting of one male surrounded by nineteen females was that there were only 186 potsherds, 170 of them previllage, found in surface stripping the 100 feet square of the burial area, while there was an abundance of potsherds in both the topsoil and the stripping of the ground immediately outside. There was also a striking lack of the usual post moulds within the cemetery. The stockades must have crossed this area. The burials with their orderly placing suggested burials of importance to the village; and a possible explanation might be that a low mound had been erected over at least part of the area, the erosion of which might account for the lack of potsherds and stockade lines.

The few measurements that could be made showed 2 hyperdolichocephalic skulls, 2 dolichocephalic, 1 mesocephalic, and 2 brachycephalic.

The cemetery to the west, near the river, was larger and very different. The southern cemetery suggested a unit, a burial of related people. The western cemetery was apparently a favorite burial place during a long period of years. One pit cut into another and the bones of 1 burial almost touched the bones of an earlier burial. Pit Number 8 had a burial at 3.4 feet and the pit was cut by pit Number 7, which had 3 burials at depths of 1.1, 2.1, and 3.5 feet. Pit Number 11 had 2 burials, one over the other. Pit Number 13 was another example of the confusion of this cemetery. One burial was at 3.9 and the other at 2.5 feet. These burials were on different sides of the pit and appeared to have been made at different times. Pit Number 6 had the fragmentary remains of 3 burials at depths of 0.7, 2.1 and 3.0 feet. Figure 13 shows the involved condition of this pit. The big pit, Number 18, was 3.5 feet deep and contained 7 identifiable burials. There had probably been other burials in it which had completely decomposed.

Pit Number 4 was 5.2 feet deep and contained charcoal and cremated bone (Fig. 15). The pit next to it, Number 2A, went to a depth of 5.8 feet and contained only solid masses of charcoal (Fig. 10). Number 2B, which cut into this pit, was 4.2 feet deep and Number 2 D cutting into both of the other, was deeper, 4.8 feet. High up in this pit, 2 D, were small remains of femora and a tibia at 2.5 feet, while lower at 3.3 feet was an arrow point which may have belonged to another and completely disintegrated burial. From pits like these with several burials in the same pit and one pit overlapping another, it was a small step to the custom of having one great burial pit or ossuary for all the burials.

We had by no means exhausted this burial area when we stopped digging. One of the important farm roads runs along the river bank. We closed the road twice to dig pit Number 18 and the Number 2 group, but the nearer we came to the river bank the greater was the danger of a cave-in and as we had to stop somewhere the road seemed the logical place. There is no doubt that a considerable part of this cemetery had slipped into the river and washed away with the steady erosion of the river bank.

For the most part, the burials in this cemetery were too fragmentary to permit measurements. Only 7 skulls were measurable. Of these, 1 was hyperdolichocephalic, 3 dolichocephalic, and 3 mesocephalic. There were equally as many males as females. Stray potsherds and arrow points were found in the burial pits but aside from several fragments of soapstone vessels in the deeper pits there were no grave goods.

Refuse pit Number 12 covered and crossed burial pit Number 11 which contained two burials and stockade lines E, L, M, and N also crossed the burial pits. If the conclusion is correct that the C and B stockade lines were the earliest, these five burials would have belonged to the C or B periods of the village and would have been just outside the village stockades at that time. The next stockade line in the time sequence, E, only crossed a very old pit, probably previllage, in which the burial had

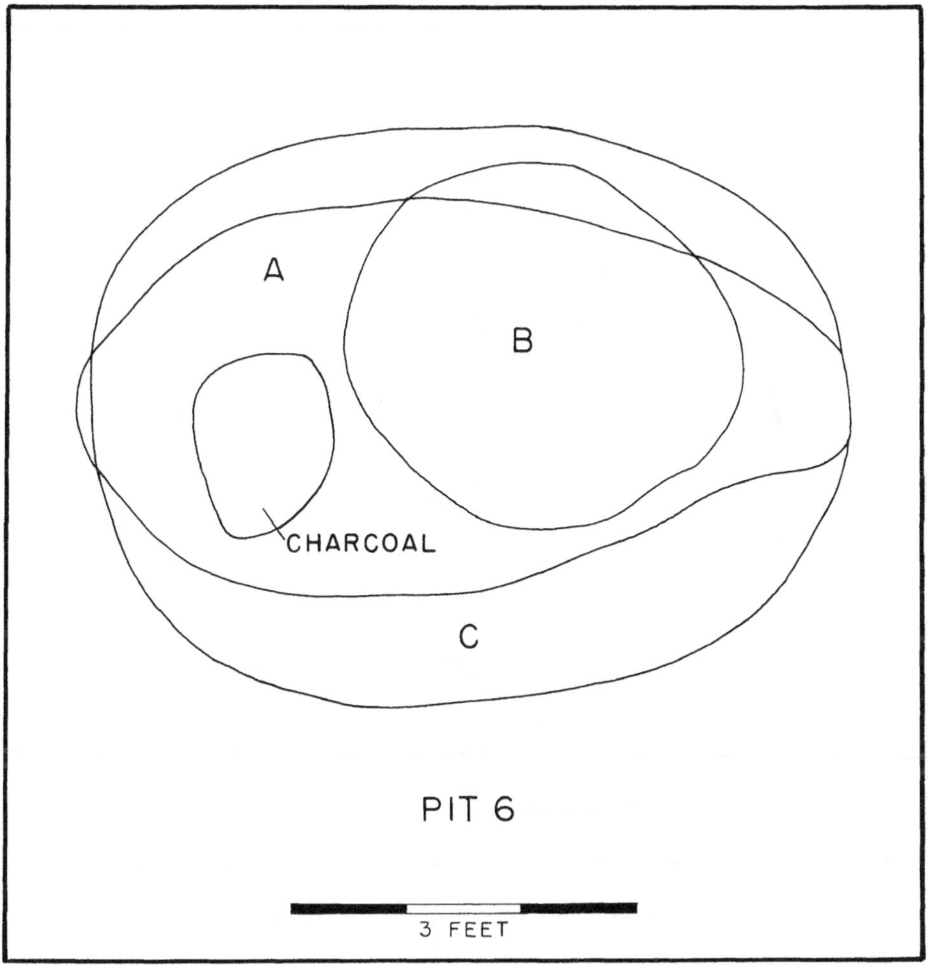

Fig. 13. Plan of pit Number 6 showing superposition of three pits.

disintegrated. By the time the G stockade was built with its continuation N, these burials had been completely forgotten. There was another important difference between the two cemeteries. The southern cemetery had only 16 small potsherds of the village type in the top soil and none in the burial pits, but this western cemetery had a little village type pottery mixed with the previllage type in the burial pits themselves.

The overlap of the previllage and village pottery in the burial pits was watched with considerable care. The empty pits

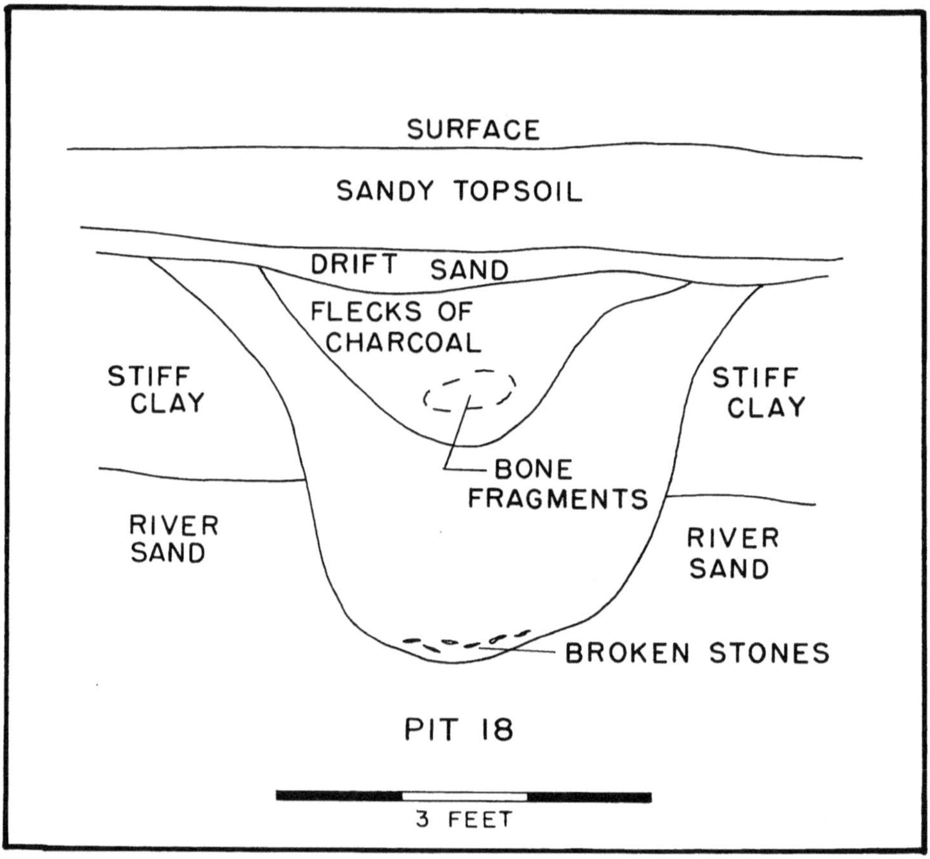

Fig. 14. Profile of pit Number 18.

which were supposed to have been burial pits and the majority of the individual burials in poor condition had only previllage pottery but a few of the nearly disintegrated skeletons had one or two small pieces of the village types with them. All of the better preserved burials and all the ossuaries had village-type sherds mixed with previllage. None of the latest types of village pottery, however, were found in individual burials or in Ossuaries Nos. 1 and 3.

While it is believed that the earliest burials were all individual, the custom of individual burial apparently persisted to a minor extent after the establishment of the ossuaries. Burial Number 40, the most perfect and recent-looking of all the

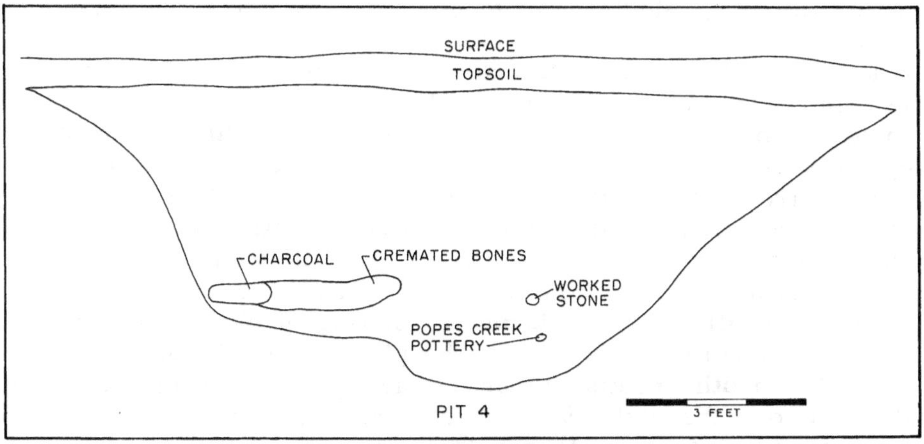

Fig. 15. Profile of pit Number 4.

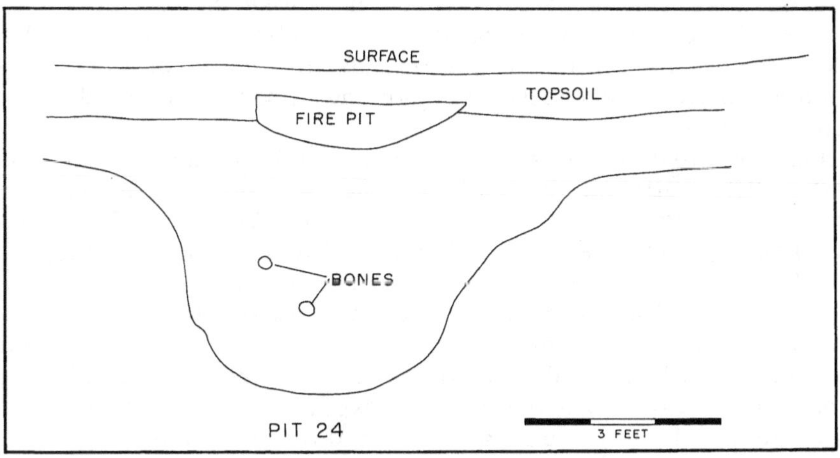

Fig. 16. Profile of pit Number 24.

burials, was an individual burial. He was identified by Stewart as Siouan and the difference in tribe may have been the reason he was excluded from the ossuary. Number 38 was buried just outside Ossuary No. I. It looked as though they had wanted to give him special consideration for he had elaborate grave goods and a fire pit of his own (Pl. III, B).

Number 38 was the most interesting of all the burials. He

was mesocranic, middle-aged to old, about 5 feet 8 inches tall and had a heavy muscular development. His hands were on the left knee and the entire left side of his face had been crushed. The upper surface of the skeleton had been scorched with fire so that the bones were very much discolored. This was probably done as part of the burial ceremony as there was considerable charcoal immediately above the skeleton. This was the only example found of fire being applied directly to an individual burial. Over each eye was a piece of previllage pottery a little larger than a silver dollar. Under his head was a neatly arranged pillow of 8 worked bones consisting of deer, elk, and 1 bone of trumpeter swan. Under the pillow were 2 abrading stones, 2 smooth grinding stones, a large quartzite knife, and a flaker. Under the right ear was a small, well-polished celt, and a broken axe was near his shoulder. Small potsherds and arrow points were scattered very near him. The right foot was missing. When the skulls were cleaned, it was a common occurrence to find bones, especially metatarsals, inside the skulls, possibly treasured possessions of the person in whose skull they were afterward found. The missing foot of Number 38 may have been divided among his relatives and friends and some of these missing bones could have easily been among those found in the skulls of later burials.

None of the burials showed any special orientation and they rested indifferently on the right or the left side. The average depth was 28 inches below the plowline but this varied considerably. The highest was just under the plowline and the deepest was 4 feet 3 inches. Eight burials were in pairs, but only one pair consisted of a male and female buried together. The others, as far as could be distinguished, were women, 2 of them young adults with children, and the others old women with middle-aged women. Twenty-one were loosely flexed, 3 tightly flexed, 3 flexed backward very much as though they were kneeling (Pl. III, D) and 3 were extended. Eleven of the burials were secondary. The bones were heaped together in a small space in no order.

Two cremated burials were found. In pit Number 4 there were about 5 quarts of small charred bones at a depth of 3.2 to 3.9 feet. About two-thirds of the fragments were human and the rest were animal bones (Fig. 15). The other cremation was in pit Number 362 some distance outside the stockades. It was a very small pit and only went down 3 inches below topsoil and had nothing in it but a shallow deposit of charred human bones. A few charred human bones, sometimes as much as a small handful were occasionally found in burial pits. Possibly members of the tribe dying at a distance were cremated and some of the charred bones brought back for a symbolic burial at home.

All the burial pits contained flakes of charcoal and most of them had well-defined patches of almost solid charcoal. An effort was made to record the positions of the charcoal in relation to the burial but no rule for its occurrence could be discovered. About half the burials had concentrated charcoal patches in the pits themselves and the other half had the fires close to the surface of the pits. Small fragments of fish and animal bones, mostly deer, were found in all fire pits close to the surface but not in the charcoal deep down in the pits. This suggests two burial systems; one a fire near the body, presumably ceremonial, and the other a feast after the burial was completed.

Most of the individual burials were in very poor condition and very few of the skulls were good enough to measure. Thirty-nine of the burials were too disintegrated to be measured in any way.

Ossuaries.—It was formerly thought that the custom of collecting the burials that had taken place during an interval of years and reburying them in a great common pit or ossuary was peculiar to the northern Indians, especially the Hurons. Recent years have proved the custom to be widespread among the Indians along the lower Potomac River. Graham has described the discovery and excavation of 4 ossuaries at Port Tobacco in Maryland (Graham, W.J., 1935) and in 1937, just before his death, he discovered others at Potomac Creek in Virginia. In 1936, Dr. Stewart and Dr. Wedel of the U. S. National Museum excavated two ossuaries on the site of Nacotchtank (Anacostia), now a part of the city of Washington (Stewart, T. D., and Wedel, W. R., 1937). In the summer of 1937, 4 large ossuaries were found on the site of Moyaone and the following summer another one was found at the site of the Indian town of Piscataway on Piscataway Creek (Ferguson, Alice, L. L., 1941).

The custom seems to have been a late development in the history of Moyaone. All the ossuaries at Moyaone had fragments of the decorated pottery characteristic of the village types; 2 of the ossuaries, Numbers II and IV, had fragments of the latest of the village designs.

Of the 4 ossuaries found at Moyaone, 3 were inside the stockades and the fourth was 1,000 feet southeast of the main village (Fig. 3). The ossuaries are numbered in the order of discovery but in the time sequence Number I was probably the earliest, Number III next, followed by Number II, with Number 4 the most recent.

Ossuary Number I had 288 skulls, Number II which was not completely excavated, probably had about the same number, and Number III had 248 skulls. This might suggest that the ossuary ceremony took place at regular intervals, perhaps at intervals of about a dozen years, as noted by Father de Breheauf for the Hurons of Canada (Jean de Breheauf, *Relations des Jesuits, Relation des Hurons*, 1636). On the other hand, Ossuary Number IV, at a distance from the village contained 618 skulls. This might indicate a longer interval, because the stockaded village could no longer afford space for the ossuary pit, or perhaps would suggest some sudden disaster.

It was found that the number of skulls was proportionately greater than the number of long bones. Many of the long bones were so badly broken in excavating that they had to be thrown away, but an effort was made to save the distal ends of the humeri and the proximal ends of femora regardless of their condition. In Ossuary No. I for example, it was found that while 261 right temporal bones were saved, only 161 left humeri and 180 left femora could be counted. There was an undoubtedly high infant mortality but only 24 skulls of children under six and 18 adolescent skulls were taken to the museum as against 159 adult skulls. This excess of skulls to long bones and the lack of children's skulls was true of all the ossuaries. It appeared that the skull was considered the most important part of a burial and that there was some other method of disposing of the bodies of young children.

Smith (1910, p. 75) says of the Virginia Indians, that the sepulcher of the kings was commonly near the image of the god in the temple. "Their bodies are first bowelled, then dried upon hurdles until they be very dry—and in the tombs which is an arch made of mats, they lay them orderly." Although Smith says that the ordinary people were buried in pits, no pits were found at Moyaone that showed any evidence of having been disturbed to remove burials. This would indicate that the first disposition of the bodies had been something other than burial. If the bodies were laid on racks it would be necessary to find something to do with them when there were too many and an ossuary would be the natural answer.

The ossuaries were very similar. Most of the bones were flung into the pit with no regard for order or sequence. In some parts, there were great numbers of long bones lying interlocked and side by side in thick layers suggesting that these bones had been gathered together in bundles before being placed in the pits. In places, particularly near the bottom of the pits, there were skeletons almost completely articulated, indicating that these were more-or-less complete bodies at the time the ossuary was filled. In addition to throwing the bones in the pit, there was apparently some heavy pressure on them, such as men walking or actually tamping. The depth and weight of the soil was never excessive, the greatest depth was only 4 feet from the surface, but many of the skulls on the bottom of the ossuaries were badly crushed.

A dark greasy soil was frequently found near the long bones and near the bottoms of the pits. A chemical test of this hard-packed, dark, greasy-looking soil, made by Dr. Parker Trask and Mr. John Gay of the U. S. Geological Survey, showed that while the normal soil at the top of the pits had .015 per cent of nitrogen, this greasy soil had .082 per cent indicating that some of the bones had been buried with the flesh still on them and that the flesh had disintegrated into this highly nitrogenous soil. The carbon analysis was confirmatory, .09 per cent in normal soil and .31 per cent in the dark soil.

There was a striking scarcity of artifacts in the ossuaries. All had a scattering of small potsherds and a few arrowheads but very little resembling mortuary offerings. Fire was used in connection with all the ossuaries except Number II and we are not sure that it was absent there as this ossuary was not completely excavated. Ossuaries III and IV had a charcoal mantle over the pit only slightly smaller than the pit itself and Number I had a fire pit to one side with many deer and fish bones scattered in the charcoal.

All the ossuaries that were completely excavated had some cremations but the number was variable. Ossuary Number I had fragments of only 3 cremated skulls and Number III had 4, while Ossuary No. IV had 7 deposits of cremated bones, representing a total of 30 identifiable individuals. The actual cremations did not take place in the ossuaries themselves for the charred bones and ash were in contact with bones that showed no signs of having been scorched. Charred bone fragments were occasionally found in skulls.

In all the ossuaries, metatarsal bones and, frequently, ribs had been placed in many skulls. Some of the skulls, particularly those of the female, were stuffed full of heterogeneous collections from the entire skeleton. It was very common to find infant bones in female skulls. One skull contained the complete skeleton of an infant and it was jammed so full that it had been broken from the inside. Only one male skull was found with a few infant bones; while on the other hand, bird and animal bones were occasionally found in male skulls but never in female. Where beads in any quantity were found, they were almost always near a child's skull. Father Lalemont's description of the Huron's of Canada states that bones were sometimes given to close friends of the deceased (Lalemont, 1642). Possibly bones were a symbol of a mystical attempt to share the life and character of others.

The first ossuary found and excavated, Ossuary No. I, suffered from a considerable handicap of inexperience in handling what was a very large job. The entire ossuary was first uncovered to the depth at which the bones began to appear. Then a wide trench giving ample working space was dug around the entire ossuary to 4.2 feet, the maximum depth of the bones. After this the edges of the bones were uncovered all the way around (Pl. III, E). It was an excellent method for photography but a poor system from every other point of view. The exposed ends of the bones dried out and were constantly being knocked off and the labor of digging the trench was both unnecessary and undesirable. The only advantage was the possibility of several people working simultaneously, an advantage which was more than balanced by the time already lost in digging the trench. In all the subsequent ossuaries, the surface soil was stripped back over the entire pit until there was danger of hitting the bones. After the stripping was completed, a small work trench was dug on the south side only. The south side was always chosen as it gave a better working light and better protection from spring and fall winds and from the sun. As the excavating progressed the dirt was tossed behind and the trench moved through the ossuary until the work was completed.

As each skull was excavated, it was placed in a two-quart fruit basket and a number written on the basket. The final number was the number of skulls excavated from that ossuary. Some of the skulls, particularly the skulls of children, were exceedingly fragile and were placed in their baskets in such a fragmentary condition that no attempt was made to reassemble them. The bones and skulls were given a few days to dry out and harden and then were cleaned, and as far as possible, repaired. At this point Hrdlicka and Stewart of the U. S. National Museum came to the rescue. Everything that gave any promise of being of interest was taken to Washington where Stewart, who had already studied the ossuaries of Port Tobacco, Anacostia, and Potomac Creek, very kindly worked over the material from Ossuary Number I. When the material from the other ossuaries has been studied, all of this will appear as a separate publication.

Ossuary Number I was 16 feet by 10 and 3.8 feet deep on the edges and 4.2 feet in the center. The band of bones averaged about 1 foot in thickness and there were 288 skulls. The skulls were so badly warped that only 48 of them could be reconstructed well enough to be measureable. There were places where 8 or 10 skulls were found together and areas where nothing was found but long bones. These deposits of long bones were more conspicuous in this ossuary than in the others. They were very suggestive of big bundles that had been collected and placed in the pit. As in the other ossuaries there were frequent suggestions of complete burials with the bones lying in the proper sequence. A few of the bones had marks on them suggestive of scraping or cleaning which would tend to indicate that the primary disposal had been something other than burial. The fragments of 3 cremated skulls were found widely spaced in the pit and were accompanied by a few fragments from other parts of the skeleton.

No beads of any kind were found in this ossuary and very few arrowheads and chips. There were 241 large fragments of pottery, almost all of them of the previllage type. The combination in this ossuary of predominantly previllage pottery with a few pieces of the village type was very like that found in some of the individual burials. It is thought that this was the oldest of the ossuaries.

At the bottom and in the center of the pit, 2 pipes were found (Pl. XXII, N). These pipes are unlike any others found on the site. They are similar to those from Pennsylvania described by Cadzow (1936, p. 58). They were apparently already broken when thrown into the pit. There was no fire pit closely associated with the ossuary. Several large post moulds were found in the immediate vicinity, but these may have been associated with earlier individual burials.

Ossuary Number II (Fig. 17) was 24 by 10 feet and 3 feet to the deepest point. The soil was a loose sand and easier to dig than any of the other ossuaries. Bones were found as little as a foot below the plowline. This ossuary has not been completely excavated. A total of 1,365 burials were excavated from the site as a whole including 155 from this ossuary. A great many people visit the site from time to time and an ossuary still *in situ* seemed more important than a greater collection of bones. A permanent building has been erected over the part of the ossuary that remains so that it offers a striking picture of this important Indian custom. This ossuary was chosen for the purpose because the bones are in exceptionally good condition,

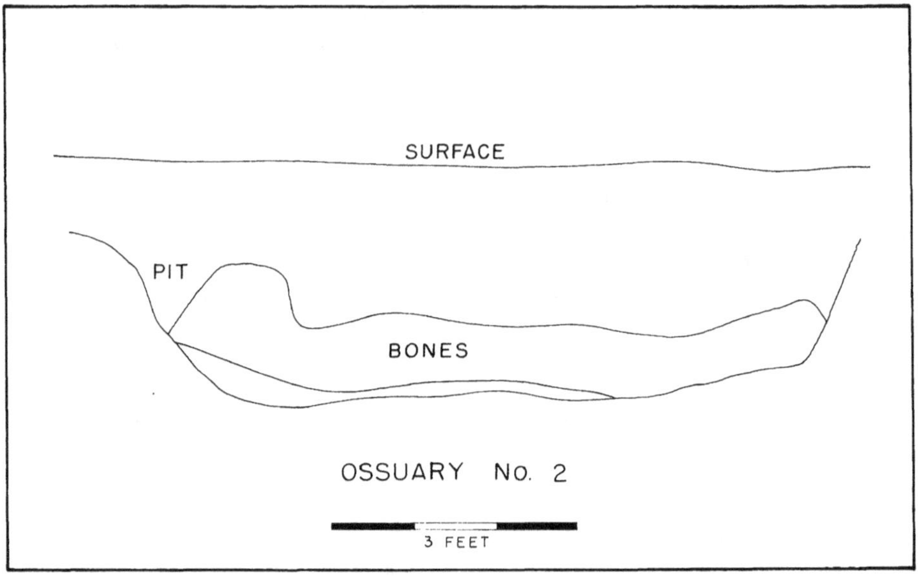

Fig. 17. Profile of Ossuary Number II.

and it is more easily accessible by automobile than any of the others. While only 155 skulls were excavated from it, it appears to have had about the same capacity as the others—probably a total of about 250.

No fire pit or traces of fire were found above or close to the ossuary. A large post mould close to the pit may have indicated the position of a marker post. A few small fragments of cremated bone were found in excavating, but no pockets of cremated bones were found in the part that was explored. Shell beads were frequently found both inside skulls and out. Fourteen very minute (1.5 mm.) copper beads were found in one skull. These beads were tested by George Schaller of the U. S. Geological Survey and were found to have only silver associated with the copper, implying a native source, presumably Lake Superior. This finding was especially interesting when compared with the trade copper found in the Piscataway Ossuary (Ferguson, Alice, L. L., 1941) which showed silver, arsenic, bismuth, lead, antimoney, and tin, which were suggestive of the Cornwall mines. What appeared to have been a complete necklace of shell beads came out of skull No. 29. Three arrow points were found, several chips and 125 very small fragments of pottery, but no pipes. It is believed that this ossuary was the third and the next to the last in time sequence.

Ossuary Number III was the smallest of the group (Pl. III, F). It was 8 feet by 17.8 and 3.5 feet to the deepest point. It contained 248 skulls and 4 cremations. At this point, the sandy topsoil was shallow and the lower half of the pit had been laboriously dug into stiff clay. The looser soil of the pit reaching down into the very hard clay formed a pocket which caught and held the surface drainage. The ossuary was excavated very slowly, mostly in the spare time of one worker, and it was not finished until the second season. In all that time the bones were never dry. The water had a strong iron content that had turned the bones an iron red, the color becoming richer and deeper as the bottom of the pit was approached. There were 30 small fragments of pottery, 1 triangular arrow point, and 2 pipes, but no beads or other artifacts. There was one considerable deposit of cremated bone fragments which has been counted as 4 individuals as 7 condyles of the lower jaw were identified among the fragments. One of the pipes was found with the cremated fragments. There was no indication of fire in the pit itself but there was a shallow fire pit directly over the ossuary. The bones had obviously been covered before the fire pit was started.

Ossuary Number IV had many points of difference from the other three. It was much farther back from the river, 1,000 feet southeast of the village (Fig. 3). It was deeper, 3 feet to the top of the bones and 4.8 feet to the deepest point, and much larger, 32 feet by 21 and contained 618 skulls. The river fields are almost flat, but at Ossuary Number IV there was a distinct knoll about 5 feet high with the ground falling away on all sides. The hummock is probably a remnant of the old river terrace covered by a thin mantle of windblown sand. It had been under observation for some time but several test pits had showed nothing. One day an unusually deep test pit was sunk and the ossuary was found. In this ossuary there had been a large fire directly over the bones and the bones themselves had been severely scorched on the upper side, differing from Ossuary Number III in which the apparent procedure had been to fill the pit with bones, then with dirt, and finally to have a ceremonial surface fire.

There were only 3 cremations in Number I and 4 in Number III. In this ossuary there were 7 separate deposits of cremated bones. The identifiable individuals in the deposits counted 3-3-5-6-7-5-1, which made a total of 30 individuals among the cremated bones.

All the ossuaries had fragments of pottery. With the surface soil as full of potsherds as it was in the village, any disturbance of the surface would have caused potsherds to slide into a pit which was being dug. This would account for the pottery in both Numbers II and III. The potsherds in Number I were too large to be accidental but they were fragments from a great many pots while in Number IV, in addition to casual potsherds like those found in II and III, there was a fragmentary pot which was easily reconstructed and also two small, perfect pots which could only have been placed there deliberately as burial offerings.

Shell beads were found all through the ossuary. Skull Number 102, an adult female with the atlas grown to the skull, had a shell bead necklace inside the skull. A great many beads were around it on the outside and, in addition, a very large shell bead had been placed deep in each eye socket. A male skull near by was almost equally rich in beads. As a rule, the same thing was true here as in the other ossuaries, most of the beads were found near children's skulls.

MOCKLEY POINT AND THE SUSQUEHANNOCK FORT[1]

Mockley Point.—Piscataway Creek is over a half mile wide at its mouth where it flows into the Potomac. On the north side of the creek is the steeply rising hill on which Fort Washington now stands. On the south side is Mockley Point, a hook of land which is gradually building out as the creek continues to fill with silt (Fig. 3). About an acre of the tip of the point is a partly wooded swamp. Back of the swamp is a knoll about 200 feet long rising about 8 feet above the flat fields around it, approximately 15 feet about sea level. For several years we wondered if the knoll were natural or artificial. It was found to be a natural formation of coarse river sand covered with clay, deposited during a period of very high water, and capped with

[1]Note by H.G.F.—Through the courtesy of our neighbor, Mr. Henry Clagett, some excavation was also done at Mockley Point and the area to the south, bordering Clagett's Cove, as far as the site of the Susquehannock Fort. The site appears to have been a ceremonial and burial area, rather than an inhabited village, at least until the occupation of the Fort by the Susquehannocks about 1674. The mound near the point was used as a burial ground by the previllage people, but apparently not by the inhabitants of Moyaone, if it can be assumed that the evidences of later occupation are to be connected with that of the Susquehannock Fort.

The following pages follow Mrs. Ferguson's text in the description of the site, except the Fort. To these I have added for completeness, a short description of the Fort, abstracted from her published paper (Ferguson, Alice L.L., 1941).

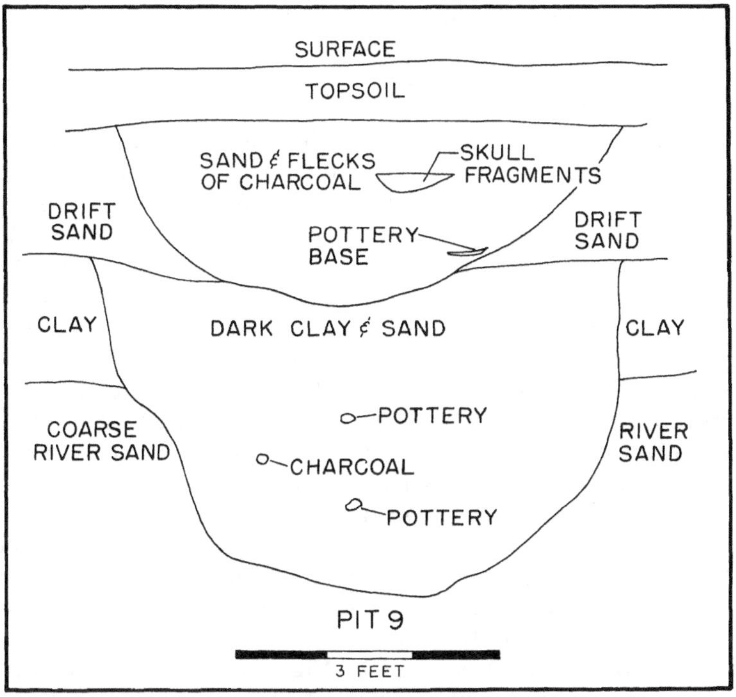

Fig. 18. Profile of pit Number 9, Mockley Point area, showing pit Number 9*a* cutting into the top of pit Number 9*b*.

fine wind-blown sand. There was no change in the color of the surface soil and nothing to indicate a site, but it was reasonable to suppose that a knoll that was conspicuous to us had also been conspicuous to the Indians and it seemed worth investigating. In the summer of 1939 it was excavated.

It contained the burial remains of successive Indian occupations. The burials appeared to have been made at considerable intervals and only a few of them could be classed as belonging to any one period. The only similarities among the pits were a complete lack of trade goods and a striking lack of chips and artifacts made of quartz, the most common stone in the vicinity.

An unusual number of grooved stone axes was found scattered around the knoll suggesting clearing of wooded ground, but there were no signs that anyone had ever lived at Mockley Point. The soil over the knoll was no darker than the surrounding fields. There was none of the scattered charcoal that comes from the dispersal of many little fire pits used for warmth and to cook the daily food. There were very few post moulds, and outside the pits there were almost no potsherds.

Of the pits excavated at Mockley Point (Fig. 8) 15 were believed to have been burial pits but they were so old that the bones had completely disintegrated. These pits had the size and shape of burial pits and were marked by slightly darker soil containing flecks of charcoal with occasional arrowheads and fragments of pottery and soapstone. In addition to these 15 empty pits, there were 7 like them except that they contained a few teeth or other bone fragments which could be identified as human. The outlines of these 22 pits were indistinct and they had iron oxide laminations running through them. These older pits were found close to the top of the knoll on the upper slope and are numbered 1 through 27 on Figure 8, with the exception of 3 stone piles, 3, 4 and 19, burial Number 5 and fire pit Number 16 which were more recent. All of the old pits with the exception of Number 18, began immediately below topsoil and were cut through the drift sand down to the clay. Number 18 went through the clay and down to the river sand. In developing pits 9 and 18 we accidentally discovered 2 others, *9b* and *18b*, whose tops were at the base of the drift sand and which cut through the clay and down into the river sand (Fig. 18). It is thought that these 2 pits were very early and that they were dug before the knoll received its cap of wind-blown sand. The few arrowheads and fragments of pottery found in these pits were similar to what was found in the other empty pits. It is quite possible that there are other concealed pits like these 2 that were not discovered.

In pit Number 9 a large flat base of a coiled pottery vessel was found (Pls. X, F and G). As much soapstone was found at Mockley Point as in all of the Moyaone excavation and the arrowheads were made of quartzite or felsite and were like the previllage examples. It is thought that all of these old pits belonged to successive occupations by the previllage people who lived in this vicinity for a very long time.

Going down toward the base of the knoll, on the south, pits 26, 27, and 41 were old pits. One corner of the old pit Number 41 was cut by a late pit. This *41a* was long and shallow and contained the skulls of 4 adults and an infant but almost no other bones. This shallow pit and the near-by pits 30 and 31 had been disturbed and most of the bones removed, possibly to be reburied in an ossuary. A total of 7 pits were found which had been disturbed. In all of these pits the remaining bones were firm and recent-looking and the pottery, while following the pattern found in the old pits, all had shell temper which made it weak and friable.

One of these disturbed pits, Number 5, had probably been one of the most important burials in the late history of the Indians. The burial was made on the crest of the knoll in the most commanding position available. There was a fire pit with the remains of a feast over almost all of the burial pit. A large post had been driven deep, right beside the pit and there were remains of a stone pile beside it. When the burial was disturbed, the ashes from the covering fire pit had poured down through the opening into part of the burial pit below. The only remaining bones, a foot, a tibia, a femur, and two humeri were left in unusual positions and looked as though they had been yanked and pulled at the time they were abandoned. The remaining bones were large and firm suggesting a late burial, an opinion which was confirmed by small fragments of pottery like the types which were found in the fire pit and the ash spill. One of the grave offerings, the celt with the corregated edge, had been left behind. The burial could have belonged to the period of the later ossuaries of Moyaone, but it could have also belonged to the episode of the Susquehannock Fort or to some visiting stranger. Whoever he was, the burial was important enough for his people to come after their hero at some later time and take a large part of him away with them.

Several pits were found here, just as they were at Moyaone, with small deposits of cremated bone but the only evidence of an actual cremation found anywhere in the excavations was pit Number 16 on the crest of the knoll. This was a fire pit full of black charcoal and the burnt bones of an infant. The few pottery fragments from the pit were heavily tempered with shell and the inference is that this pit was a late burial.

At the bottom of the slope, below the 11-foot contour, a group of 8 burials, Numbers 29, 32, 33, 34, 35, 36, 37, and 38 was found to be different from anything encountered elsewhere in any of the excavations. At Moyaone, at the Piscataway Creek Ossuary, and at the Susquehannock Fort the individual burials had been clean and orderly. These 8 appeared to have been given every possible indignity. Their bodies were thrown in the pits in distorted positions, their bones were broken and the pits were filled with refuse. The refuse normally would have come from habitations. It certainly was not carried very far. The inference is that it came from the nearby Susquehannock Fort or from feasts which took place nearby.

When it was first discovered, pit Number 29 appeared to be

a refuse pit. It was filled with charcoal and ash and had a profusion of clam shells and deer bones with some scattering of pottery, turtle and oyster shells, red fox, dog, and other bones. There were 4 burials in it, 3 women and a child of about seven years of age. The skeletons were loosely flexed with one skull directly above the next. The refuse went all the way to the bottom of the pit and had worked in between the joints of the skeletons. The skeletons had been articulated at the time they were buried but they were badly wrenched and many of the bones broken. The feet were turned back on the tibias and the skull of the second burial, Number 29*b*, was turned completely around on the spine with the upper vertebra jammed into the base of the skull, and the lower jaw broken and forced to one side. This 29*b* had a platform pipe, directly under her head (Pl. XXII, O, P). The pipe was so imperfect it would have been impossible to have used it.

A celt was found on each side of the head and a perfect spearhead by the feet. It was not customary to place things like this with a female burial but another check proved beyond doubt that all three adult skeletons were female. Under 29*b* was 29*c*. The bones of this skeleton like the others were firm and strong but the skull was crushed flat. With all the other bones in such good condition it looked as though the skull had been crushed deliberately. Under them all was a child. A gorget, a broken awl, and 2 pieces of worked bone were also found in the pit.

Burial Number 33 was the strangest of them all. The pit of Number 34, which was an extended burial, went down to 3.4 feet. The pit of this Number 33 went down to 4.5 feet cutting right through burial Number 34 at the base of his spine and obliterating all the lower part of the skeleton. Both pits were full of refuse but there was more trash in the 33 pit than in 34. The hands of Number 33 were close together and over his head as though they had been tied to a post and he had been buried in a semiupright position with his chin 18 inches higher than his knees which were the lowest part of the burial. The legs were dislocated at the knees and the lower legs folded forward and up. There were scratches on his skull made by some very sharp instrument applied with a great deal of pressure. There were also seven triangular arrowheads inside his rib basket. Owing to the nearness of Number 33 to the Susquehannock Fort it seems possible that this torture was done by the Susquehannocks and that it occurred sometime in 1675, or earlier.

Near Number 33 was pit Number 37 which contained charcoal, ash, and a profusion of clam shells, but no trace of any other food. There were fragments of human bones at the bottom. Pit Number 39 was thick with refuse and human teeth were mixed in with it. Number 40 seems to have been a storage pit. There were stones at the bottom, a great many nuts, and a little pottery but no traces of fire. At Moyaone, quartz was the predominant material used for arrowheads and stone tools. Here at Mockley Point quartz was practically never used, although quartz pebbles were abundant. It looked as though these people had come from a place where there was very little quartz and had gone to a considerable trouble to find chert, slate, and other materials to which they were more accustomed. Decorated bone was found at Mockley Point but not at Moyaone. Pipes were common at Moyaone, but the only one found at Mockley Point was a defective platform pipe which was very different from anything found at Moyaone. The pottery was also different. With the exception of a few fragments of the latest village type pottery found in Number 5 and fire pit Number 16 there was no decoration on the pottery and nothing like the Moyaone designs were found anywhere either in the stripping or in the pits. Most of the Mockley Point pottery was either the early previllage or a pattern similar to some of it, but done in a shabby manner with the shell temper.

There was no direct evidence that the people of Moyaone had anything to do with Mockley Point. The area between the Moyaone stockades and Mockley Point was completely barren, except for a few previllage potsherds and rare arrow points. There were no indications that the life of Moyaone had extended in this direction beyond the stockades. It was quite different on the south side of the Mockley Point mound facing the Susquehannock Fort. The few post moulds that were found were all on the south side. Below the 11-foot contour, around the refuse burials, they occurred with some frequency; and below the 10-foot contour, going toward the fort, there were not only post moulds but a dog burial, the small fire pits Numbers 43 and 44, and many chipped stones and arrowheads.

The tentative conclusion is that Mockley Point was used as a burial place by the previllage people at several widely spaced periods and not used again until a long time afterward, possibly during the eighteen months when the Susquehannocks lived in their near-by fort.

Susquehannock Fort.—During the excavation of the mound at Mockley Point and the adjoining pits bordering Clagett's Cove, we had accepted the statements in historical literature that the site of the Susquehannock Fort was on the north bank of the creek, near where Fort Washington now stands. The dark area shown in the air photographs bordering the south bank of the creek had interested us, though, and we had done a certain amount of exploration, including the discovery of a small ossuary containing eleven skulls and much trade material, arrowheads, and pottery below the plowline. It was not until the spring of 1938 that Professor Wertenbaker of Princeton University arrived at our farm with a copy of the 1677 map he had found in the British Public Records Office. With this map he located the site of the Susquehannock Fort as readily as though it had been set down on a road map, not on the north side of the creek but on the south side, at Mockley Point where Piscataway Creek joins the Potomac opposite Mount Vernon (Wertenbaker, 1940).

In 1939 we began to look seriously for the fort, but it was not until the following year that intensive trenching revealed the post moulds of the stockade. The Algonkin stockades that we knew were all circular, but this one had straight sides that turned at right angles with rectangular bastions at the corners like the ones shown on Professor Wertenbaker's map (Fig. 9).

The shore lines of both the Potomac and Piscataway Creek have changed greatly, and are still changing. On Piscataway Creek the bank by the site of the fort is steadily being eaten away and the big trees are being undermined and falling in the creek. The air photograph shows a shoal extending from Mockley Point down past the fort. This line of shoal probably approximates the old shore line. The topsoil on that part of the Clagett farm is very thin and due to long-continued plowing and the steady erosion, all that remained of the fort were the deep post moulds and a few pits. The post moulds showing the lines of the fort stockade were not complete. The west side of the stockade was all there as well as almost all of the south and north sides, but the east side was completely lost in the creek. If the fort had been a perfect square about 70 feet had been lost from the north side. It is of some interest that the fort was oriented precisely in the cardinal directions. The west side measured 175 feet; the south side, 185 feet; the north side 120 feet. In addition, a bastion 19 feet square was attached to the northwest and southwest corners. Apparently the south side was complete except for the corner bastion, but all of the east side and about one third of the north side had been eroded away by Piscataway Creek.

The post moulds indicated a very strong stockade. The smallest were 5 inches in diameter and most of them were 7 and 8 inches. Where the stockade turned the right angles into the bastions, the corner post moulds were even larger, some of them 10 inches in diameter. The entire stockade had been burned. On the west side the charcoal was nearly 3 inches deep and paralleled the stockade in a band 10 feet wide inside the fort. Here and there inside the stockade were small areas of solid charcoal suggesting structures that had been burned. It was the diffusion of the charcoal from the burned stockade and buildings that caused the darkening of the soil shown in the air photographs.

Within the stockades the most important find was a small ossuary, or common burial pit, containing 42 burials, 7 of which were young children. Ossuaries usually have more skulls than long bones but in this ossuary the skulls and bones checked very closely. The burials at the top of the pit were complete skeletons doubled up into separate heaps. At the bottom of the ossuary were 2 nearly perfect pipes, one of them a white clay pipe and the other a Susquehannock pipe like the ones Dr. Cadzow found in Susquehannock burials in Pennsylvania (Pl. XXII, A). There were also 3 Jew's harps, 7 copper hawk bells, 8 iron brackets, an iron hoe, a copper finger ring set with glass, a snuff box, fragments of a pair of scissors, and a flattened lead musket ball.

Only about 1 foot from the ossuary was a small shallow pit containing 2 iron hoes, an upright Dutch gin bottle, 2 small iron pots, and a mass of almost completely disintegrated stuff that looked as though it might have been textile. Altogether there were 26 pits excavated within the fort and 1 outside, including the small ossuary, the burial pits, refuse pits, and storage pit, containing the European trade goods.

IV

THE ARTIFACTS

Robert L. Stephenson

The Accokeek Creek site has been so thoroughly excavated as to nearly exhaust the possibilities for collecting additional data or materials. Presumably, nearly all of the recoverable specimens have been removed from the ground and the total, including those gathered from the surface over the years, has become rather impressive. An estimate of 150,000 to 200,000 specimens would perhaps not be far from correct, to include all the material collected from this site. This quantity is indeed unusual for a site in the Middle Atlantic Seaboard area. Even the controlled sample of less than half of this material, considered in the present analytical study, is indeed large. There are 72,131 specimens considered for analysis in the present study. This includes all of the artifacts from Mrs. Ferguson's excavations that are of known provenience within the site. Most of this group bear individual provenience markings as to the specific features or excavation squares from which they were recovered. The remainder of the analyzed group have no individual markings but had been kept in separately marked containers indicating the area within the site from which they were excavated.

Not included in the analyzed group are many thousands of potsherds and other artifacts that have been collected from the site over the years by various individuals, as well as a large group of specimens discarded by Mrs. Ferguson during, or shortly after, her excavations. For the most part these were not available for study, but some small groups in private collections or museums and the large group of discards were available. In all cases where these were known to exist the artifacts were examined and compared with the analyzed collection. In no case did the materials in the private collections, the museums, or the discard pile differ in kind or in style from the materials in the analyzed group. It is reasonable to assume, then, that the artifacts discussed in the following pages provide as fully representative a sample of the variations of style and technology as could be hoped for from a site of this kind.

TABLE I

TABULATION OF ARCHEOLOGICAL FEATURES EXCAVATED

Feature	Mockley Point	Clagett's Cove	Moyaone		Total
			North	South	
Post moulds*. . .	112	679	16,298	155	17,244
Stockade lines . .	. . .	1	16	2	19
Refuse pits	. . .	12	70	7	89
Storage pits . . .	. . .	1	19	3	23
Fire hearths . . .	5	4	137	11	157
Stone piles	6	1	36	6	49
Ossuaries	. . .	1	3	1	5
Burial pits	31	5	59	3	98
Dog burials. . . .	1	. . .	18	. . .	17
Miscellaneous pits	2	4	30	. . .	36

*Does not include post moulds in the stockade lines.

METHODS OF ANALYSIS

The analytical processes applied to these specimens in the present study deserve some explanation. The specimens, having lain in storage in open containers for 12 years since excavation, required complete recleaning, and the gross quantity of material made simple mechanical handling a formidable task. The use of tables, benches, shelves, and other space so generously made available in the three "cabins" or "museum buildings" at the Hard Bargain Farm in the summer of 1952, provided ample layout space for cleaning and initial sorting. That fall, when the artifacts were transferred to Ann Arbor, the Museum of Anthropology made available a large room with several long rows of tables in the "Old Maternity Hospital," an annex of the Museum.

The generosity in making this space available for so long a period can hardly be overemphasized since the analysis went along so sporadically. Interruptions, including a two-year absence from the work to assume the direction of the Missouri Basin Project of salvage archeology, and academic work at the University of Michigan made utilization of the space unusually prolonged.

The comparative approach to the analysis was used throughout because stratigraphic data from this site were not adequate to substantiate any other type of analysis. During the excavations every effort was made to secure some indication of cultural levels but without success. Some of the refuse pit materials suggested hints of overlapping of one pit on another but even here mixture was so extensive as to eliminate from consideration the use of stratigraphy as a basis for the analysis. Seriation was considered, especially since Evans and Holland (1955) both had had such apparent success in using this method with large groups of similar materials from 96 and 42 sites respectively, in Virginia. The Accokeek Creek site specimens, though, were all from one site. To be sure, it is a multicomponent site with separable find-spots, but still it is one single site. To seriate these artifacts might have provided some information as to the ordering of the find-spots but this would have been largely an artificial ordering as the units were contiguous and there was mixing of the material within and between the units, not only after final occupation but between occupations. The comparative approach, while based to a considerable extent upon subjective judgement, provided the most reasonable method of analysis available. Moreover, it has the advantage of making maximum use of other researches in similar material and stratigraphy in other sites.

Analysis of the Pottery.—There were 58,298 specimens of pottery vessels and vessel fragments in the analyzed group, including 5 restored vessels, and over 100 restored vessel sections. These vessels, vessel sections, and sherds were ultimately classified into 8 pottery wares which include 16 pottery types. The specimens that did not fit into these wares were sorted into 7 miscellaneous pottery groups.

The first step in the ceramic analysis was the washing, cleaning, and rough sorting of the pottery into 52 groups, which were called "varieties." These varieties were not considered to be types in any sense, but were merely sorting groups that, upon brief visual and tactile inspection, differed from each other in some combination of attributes that, at the time seemed significant.

The second step in the analysis was a general search of the literature and available museum collections for comparable material from other sites. The third step was a resorting of the varieties in the light of the material referred to in the literature and in the comparative collections. This reshuffling of the varieties and re-evaluation of what seemed to be significant attribute combinations, resolved the pottery into 32 varieties. The fourth step was another, and more intensive search of the literature.

The fifth step was to formulate two concrete definitions as guides to further analysis. One was the delineation of what would constitute a valid and useful pottery ware for the purposes of this study. The other was the delineation of what would constitute a valid and useful pottery type for purposes of this study. Specifically "the concept of a pottery ware," as used here, may be defined as a group of pottery specimens distinguishable from all other pottery specimens on the basis of a single, identifiable set of past attributes (including temper) and combining, under a single name, the several clusters of other attributes of the specimens that are identified with the component types included within that ware. "The concept of a pottery type," as used here, may be defined as a group of pottery specimens within a pottery ware, that may be distinguished from all other pottery specimens within that ware on the basis of a single, identifiable set of attributes of surface treatment or technologically distinct decorative styles, or both. The "ware," then, is defined on the basis of paste. The "type" is defined on the basis of the surface treatment and decorative technique. These definitions may, or may not, apply to other pottery wares and types in other archeological areas. They do serve well for the pottery from the Accokeek Creek site and provide a basis upon which to compare that pottery with similar pottery elsewhere.

It may be pointed out that these are pottery wares and types, not sherd wares and types. Throughout all stages of the analysis, rim sherds, body sherds and basal sherds, while kept separated, were given equal consideration. All pertinent attributes of the pottery vessel were taken into account. The collection from this site was extensive enough that this could be done since the mass of sherds, reconstructed vessel sections, and whole vessels provided portions of all parts of individual vessels of each of the wares and types.

At this point in the analysis the concept of "varieties" was abandoned as a working tool. It had served its purpose and was no longer useful. The sixth step was to sort the pottery into wares and types. The inevitable residue of sherds that did not fit well into any of the formal types were grouped by attribute combinations into several miscellaneous pottery groups, each of which was assigned a lettered designation. Up to this point the pottery was examined by visual and tactile inspection of attributes and comparison of the materials with those from other sites. There was no reference to individual specimen provenience within the site nor to the association of specific sherds with archeological features. Neither was there any statistical treatment. The sherds were not even counted.

The seventh step incorporated provenience and association analysis and some rudimentary statistical treatment. Each sherd was recorded, by type, as to the feature or excavation unit from which it had been recovered. These pronvenience data, forming a sort of catalog, were transferred to large sheets of paper that had been marked off according to excavation units and features. Total numbers and percentages of each pottery ware, type, and group were then computed for each feature and for each excavation unit in order to demonstrate associations or lack of associations.

The wares, types, and groups of pottery established by the above sequence of methodological steps are specifically intended for the purpose of systematizing the pottery from the Accokeek Creek site and of illuminating the temporal and spacial significance of this material within this one site. The typology thus formulated may well be useful for other sites within the area and between this and other areas. As will be seen later in the present report, such has already been the case to a limited extent in that these pottery types are used as one of the bases upon which to define the culture area of which the Accokeek Creek site is a part, to associate this site with other sites, and to suggest a temporal sequence for both the site and the culture area. Never-the-less, it was the narrower, specific use of the typology at the Accokeek Creek site that dictated the formulation of the wares and types.

The names of the wares and types used in this study are, in part, new to the literature. Previously published names applicable to these materials, though, have been retained when possible. The only deliberate synonymy occurs in the use of the term "ware" to apply to the same concept to which Evans (1955) applied the term "series." This was done more to accommodate personal preference than anything else and probably either term is equally acceptable. With this exception no changes in terminology have been made from those already fixed in the literature. Only new names have been added to apply to the pottery not previously named in the literature.

Analysis of Tobacco Pipes.—The analyzed specimens within this category include 420 pottery tobacco pipes, of which 5 are whole specimens and 231 are more than half complete. Seven stone tobacco pipes were also present, of which only 1 is complete. The stone specimens were simply described and compared with similar specimens from other sites.

An attempt was made to relate the pottery tobacco pipes to the pottery vessel types and wares by typological analysis comparable to that used for the pottery vessels. The specimens were sorted into varieties and resorted into types. The types were based upon attribute clusters of form, paste, and decorative technique. Four of the 5 types were named according to the pottery vessel types they most closely resembled on the basis of nearly identical characteristics of paste and decorative technique. The fifth type was named from the historic tribe with which such pipes have elsewhere been associated. Within 3 of the 5 types, aberrant examples are noted as variants.

Analysis of Projectile Points.—The chipped-stone artifacts included within this category are those that presumably served as points for projectiles to be propelled through the air by bows, atlatls, or the human arm alone, such as arrows, darts, or lances. Some of these specimens may have served other purposes such as cutting, scraping, perforating, piercing, or incising tools; some may have been hafted on short or long handles, or simply used without handles. Many probably served several of these purposes. Lack of any evidence of the sort of haft used, though, necessitates lumping them all under the function that all of them may have served and that most of them must have served.

The sample from the Accokeek Creek site included 2,849 complete, or nearly complete, projectile points. The analytical procedures for categorizing these artifacts were, in general, the same as those used in the analysis of the pottery. The specimens were cleaned, sorted into varieties, compared with the literature, resorted, and again compared with the literature. Then a definition of a projectile point type was formulated, for the purposes of this study. Specifically, "the concept of a projectile point type," as used here, may be defined as a named group of projectile points that are distinguishable from all other projectile points on the basis of a consistently similar cluster of attributes of outline form, technique of manufacture, length-width-thickness ratio, and over-all size. Within each type there is a range of variability of any, or all, of the attributes, and that range is stated as centering around a generalized norm. With this definition formulated, the concept of varieties was dropped and the specimens were sorted into types with those that did not fit well into the formalized types being described as miscellaneous groups. Provenience analysis and some rudimentary statistical treatment was then made. Helpful suggestions from colleagues necessitated some revisions of the types and groups thus formulated. Ultimately, 9 types and 14 groups emerged that appear to have validity, at least for the Accokeek Creek site material. There is some gradation within the extremes of the ranges of variation of the several types. This does no violence to the validity nor the usefulness of the concept as used, but, instead, suggests possibilities of developmental sequences within types or contemporaneity of related types. Some of the groups appear to be only aberrant variations of one or another of the formal types, but others are distinctly "foreign" to the several types described.

Analysis of Other Material.—The remaining specimens from the Accokeek Creek site were sorted into groups on the basis of the materials from which they were made, that is, other chipped stone, ground and polished stone, shell, antler, bone, and the like. Within each of these groupings, categories of tools and implements were distinguished and the specimens within each were described. These were compared with materials from other sites and implications drawn. Table II, page 131, lists all of the materials from the site with quantities indicated.

STEATITE VESSELS

Predecessors of the pottery vessels—numerous fragments of stone bowls—were recovered from the site. There are 41 rim sherds, 240 body sherds, 29 basal sherds, and 6 vessel sections in the collection. These fragments represent medium-sized, thick, low-walled vessels carved from large blocks of soft, gray-buff steatite (or soapstone). This soft stone is easily carved, even with stone tools, has a soapy texture, and often contains numerous, small, shallow, natural cavities 3 mm or less in diameter. Vessel exteriors are usually marked with abundant tool marks (Pl. IV, D, E, F). These are small or large gouges of an uneven tool or are fine striations made by scraping the surface after the rough shaping was finished. In some cases exterior surfaces are partly or completely ground smooth, thus obliterating the tool marks (Pl. IV, A). Vessel interiors are usually scraped or ground smooth (Pl. IV, H) but in some, scraping striations and gouge marks are visible.

The form of these vessels is quite distinctive. The lip is usually rounded, but some are flat and lip thicknesses range from 5-18 mm. There is no rim as the body extends to the lip and rim sherds can only be distinguished by the presence of a portion of the lip. The vessel walls are thick, ranging from 9 to 26 mm. Vessel shapes are elongate ovals, round, or rectangular with rounded corners in outline, with low walls of 10 to 15 cm in over-all height. Some expansion from the base and slight constriction toward the lip is often present. The base is usually flat with rounded or "heeled" juncture of base and body, but a few bases are rounded. Bases range from 7 to 27 mm in thickness, sometimes being thinner than the vessel walls (Pl. IV,H).

Decoration is entirely absent but spatulate or hemispherical lugs are usually present (P. IV,B). These are placed, singly, on opposite sides of the vessel. The spatulate lugs are large, about 6 cm wide, 3 cm long, and 2 cm thick, and placed near the lip of the vessel. Hemispherical lugs are smaller, about 2.5 cm in diameter, and are placed either near the vessel lip or about one-third of the way up the vessel wall from the base. Mending (or suspension) performations are frequent and occur on all parts of the vessel (Pl. IV,G). Sherds and vessel sections suggest moderate-sized vessels of 10 to 20 cm diameter and 10 to 15 cm depth.

POTTERY

Marcey Creek Ware

(Marcey Creek Series, Evans, 1955, p. 54)

This ware is defined on the basis of 39 rim sherds, 186 body sherds, 49 and basal sherds and 3 reconstructed vessel sections from the Accokeek Creek site, and upon descriptions of 2 of its component types in the lieterature. The type Marcey Creek Plain, the only component type of this ware recovered from the Accokeek Creek site, has been described by Manson (1948, p. 225) and by Evans (1955, p. 55). The type Selden Island Cord Marked was described by Slattery (1946, pp. 262-66) and by Evans (1955, p. 56). Evans (1955, p. 54) combined these 2 types into a "Marcey Creek Series" which is essentially the same as the Marcey Creek ware described here. Some additional data are added, though, from the Accokeek Creek site material.

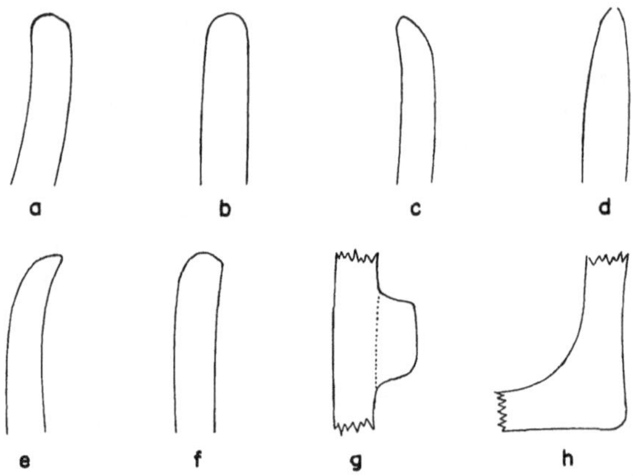

RIM, LUG, AND HEEL PROFILES OF MARCEY CREEK WARE
Interiors to left.

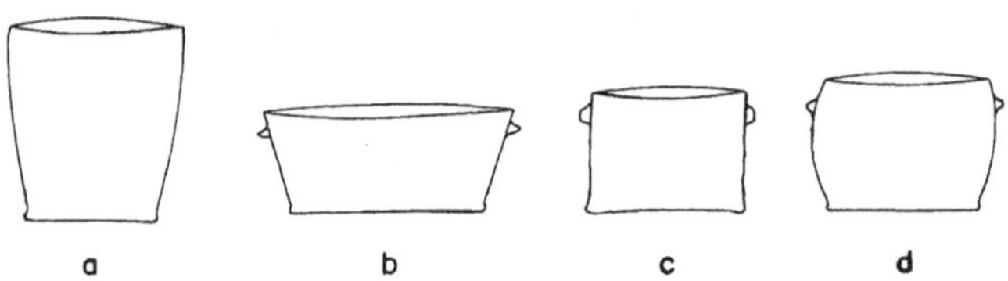

VESSEL PROFILES OF MARCEY CREEK WARE

Fig. 19. Profiles of Marcey Creek ware.

The Marcey Creek ware is a pottery group consisting of vessels manufactured by the coiling technique with hand-smoothed or paddle-malleated surfaces and composed of a fine-grained, reddish to gray-tan clay, tempered with fine to coarse lumps of crushed steatite. Temper constitutes 30 to 80 per cent of the paste giving the sherds a soapy feel and a softness not otherwise a property of the clay. Vessels are of medium size, thick, with flat bases, basal heel protrusions, straight-sided or expanding-sided bodies, and straight rims. Vessel shape is distinctive and depths are usually less than diameters. Maximum diameters are usually at the orifice (Fig. 19).

The ware derives its name from the Marcey Creek site on the Potomac River in Arlington County, Virginia.

Marcy Creek Plain

(Manson, 1948, p. 225; Evans, 1955, p. 55)

Summary Definition

The type Marcey Creek Plain is a coiled pottery with hand-smoothed surfaces, made of compact, reddish to gray-tan clay, tempered with crushed steatite, and having a soft, soapy texture. Surfaces are smoothed, with no decoration, but are often lumpy and uneven. Vessel form is cylindrical or semiconical, tending toward globular with flat bases and heel protrusions. Lugs are usual. Vessel size is medium with depth usually less than diameter.

Type Description

Method of manufacture.—Coiling: occasional lack of coil welding, and breaks along coil lines, are often visible (Pl. V, F). Coil widths are 15 to 20 mm. There is some suggestion in a few sherds that the vessel was modeled by hand rather than coiled.

Paste.—Temper is composed of coarse-to-fine lumps of crushed steatite ranging from mere flecks to particles 10 mm in diamter but usually about 2 to 5 mm in diameter. The temper constitutes 30 to 40 per cent of the paste but in rare instances up to 80 per cent.

Plastic is a fine-to-medium-grained, compact, cohesive clay with rare extraneous inclusions.

Hardness in Moh's scale is 1.5 to 2.0. Very soft.

Texture is coarse to fine and smooth. The steatite temper gives the sherds a soapy feel not otherwise a property of the clay. Some sherds with large temper particles are very coarse in texture while others with finely pulverized temper are of extremely fine, compact texture.

Color.—Exterior surface color ranges from dull gray through buff and tan to red and reddish brown. Buffs and reddish-tans are dominant.

Interior surfaces are usually the same as the exterior but sherds of reddish exteriors are often more tan or gray on the interior.

The core is usually the same color as the interior and exterior but sometimes darker, tending to brown.

Firing.—Low temperature and an oxidizing atmosphere is apparent and smudge marks are rarely present.

Surface treatment.—Exterior surfaces are smoothed by hand and often exhibit a wavy or lumpy appearance due to uneven smoothing over large temper particles (Pl. V H, I). About one third of the sherds are very evenly smoothed and in these the temper is finely pulverized and not abundant. Basal sherds often bear impressions of a coarse, open-weave matting.

Interiors are identical to exteriors except for the basal interiors which are crudely smoothed and never exhibit mat impressions.

Vessel form (Fig. 19).—Lips are rounded or slightly wedge-shaped, and usually thinner than the body. One lip is slightly everted. A minority are nicked.

Rims are vertical to slightly inverted. One is slightly everted.

Bodies are oval or cylindrical to semiconical. Some large, flat sherds suggest a minor, rectangular form but this is uncertain as no corner sherds are present.

Bases are flat with heel protrusions around the entire base. Heels are usually very pronounced and sometimes cause a slight concavity of the base (Pl. V A-E, G).

Thicknesses of vessel walls are 7 to 14 mm: of bases are 9 to 15 mm.

Lugs are occasionally attached to the rim area 20 to 40 mm below the lip. These are hemispherical and range from 18 to 30 mm. in diameter.

Decoration.—None except occasional lip nicking.

Other.—Mending performations are frequent and occur on all parts of the vessels.

Vessel size.—Medium. Sherds and small sections of vessels suggest diameters of 15 to 28 cm. and depths of 10 to 20 cm.

Sample size.—39 rim sherds, 186 body sherds, 49 basal sherds, and 3 reconstructed vessel sections.

Temporal position.—Early Woodland

Pope's Creek Ware
(New ware name)

This ware is defined on the basis of 179 rim sherds, 2,078 body sherds, 87 basal sherds, and 3 reconstructed vessel sections from the Accokeek Creek site, and descriptions of its principal, if not its only, component type in the literature. It is identical to the pottery discussed by Holmes (1903, pp. 153-55)

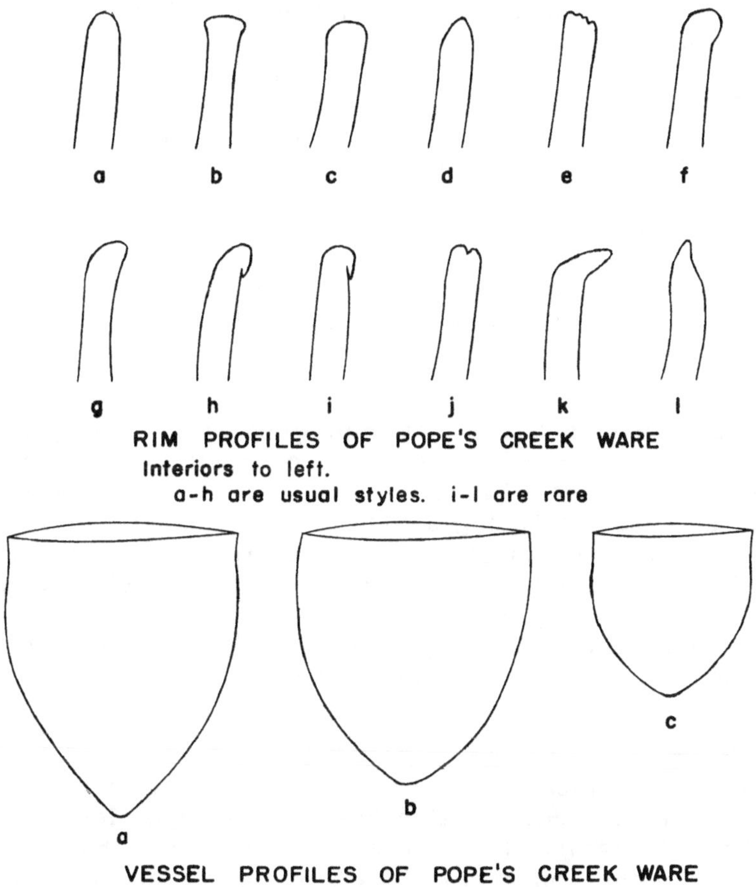

Fig. 20. Profiles of Pope's Creek ware.

and has been referred to extensively in the literature. The single component type found at the Accokeek Creek site is also the dominant type found by Holmes and others, elsewhere—"Pope's Creek Net Impressed." This type, however, is usually accompanied by a small number of sherds of the same ware characteristics but with cord-marked, exterior surfaces. The sherds of this latter sort, found at the Accokeek Creek site, were not numerous enough to provide adequate data on which to form a type and are listed as Miscellaneous Pottery Group A.

The Pope's Creek ware is a pottery group consisting of vessels manufactured by the coiling technique with paddle-malleated surfaces, and composed of a coarse reddish tan to gray-brown clay. The temper constitutes a major percentage of the paste and is a coarse ferruginous sand with some inclusions of small, rounded gravels and other lithic particles. Temper is so abundant as to give the sherds a distinctively friable texture. Vessels are large, thick-walled, conical containers with simple rims (Fig. 20). Interiors are distinctively scored.

The ware derives its name from the Pope's Creek Shell Midden on Pope's Creek in Charles County, Maryland.

Pope's Creek Net Impressed
(Holmes, 1903, pp. 153-5)

Summary Definition

The type Pope's Creek Net Impressed is a coiled pottery with paddle-malleated surfaces, made of reddish-tan to gray-brown clay, tempered with large quantities of medium-grained, ferruginous sand and having a distinctively friable texture. Exterior surfaces are impressed with open netting and interiors are distinctively scored. Vessel form is conical with simple rim and conical or semiconical base. Lugs are occasionally present and incised decoration is rare. Vessel size is large with diamters slightly less than depths.

Type Description

Method of manufacture.—Coiling and paddle malleating. Rarely is lack of welding noticeable but breakage along coil lines is usual. Such breakage often makes the convex face of the coil resemble a rim lip. Coil widths are 10 to 20 mm. Basal sherds often appear to have been modeled by hand from lumps of clay with the coils beginning 4 to 10 cm above the basal point.

Paste.—Temper is composed of medium to coarse sand representing 50 to 70 per cent of the paste. This sand readily rubs off between the fingers and often a whole sherd may be crumbled away in this manner. Inclusions within the paste of some sherds are composed of coarse, water-smoothed, quartz pebbles; angular, crushed quartz; or other lithic material. They range from 1 to 14 mm in diameter and are seldom abundant in a sherd. They appear to be accidental rather than intentionally a part of the temper.

Plastic is composed of a medium-grained, moderately compact clay.

Hardness in Moh's scale is 2.0 to 2.5. Medium.

Texture is coarse, rough, and extremely friable. The sherds break easily and crumble readily.

Color.—Exterior surface color ranges from dark browns, grays, buffs, and tans to yellowish-orange, and reds. Dark reddish browns and tans are dominant.

Interior surfaces are often the same as exteriors but usually are darker and often black.

The core is usually the same as or somewhat darker than the exterior. Sherds of black interior are often black to about the center and change to a reddish brown or tan for the exterior half of the sherd's thickness. Rarely is a real "core color" distinguishable.

Firing.—Low temperature and an oxidizing atmosphere is apparent. Smudge marks are rare on exteriors. Interiors are often smudged to an even black.

Surface treatment.—Exterior surfaces are roughened all over with various sorts of loose, open, net impressions (Pl. VIA-C, E, F). The most common net used is of a medium mesh, of 3 to 6 cords per inch, with knots at each juncture of crossed elements. A second variety of net has a coarse mesh with knots, and 1 to 2 cords per inch. A third variety of net is of fine mesh, knotted, and with 8 to 12 knots per inch. Exteriors of bases are often smoothed or bear haphazard, overlapping, net impressions. Apparently the net was wrapped about the hand or a paddle and carefully applied by patting or rocking. Impressions of coarser nets appear to have been applied on wetter clay than were those of the finer nets as they are impressed deeper and more distinctly.

Interior surfaces are usually scored or combed with short, deep, patterned strokes (Pl. VID, G, H). The scoring tool appears to have had 4 to 8 teeth. Diagonal strokes of 3 to 8 cm in length are met by vertical or horizontal strokes, forming irregular, geometric patterns. Basal portions are not scored. In some sherds the scoring is done in long, sweeping strokes diagonal to the rim. About 20 per cent of the sherds are simply roughened on the interior and 10 per cent are partially smoothed. Rarely do rim sherds have net impressions over the lip and extending into the interior some 3 to 10 cm below the lip.

Vessel form (Fig. 20).—Lips are rounded, flattened, or slightly wedge-shaped. They are usually thinned and rarely everted with small folds of clay overlapping the lip exterior (Pl. VI C). Four per cent of the lips are nicked or punctated along the top.

Rims are vertical to slightly everted. Two per cent are constricted.

Bodies are conical. The upper portions of the body are nearly cylindrical while the lower portions taper evenly to a conical or semiconical base.

Bases are conical with 80 per cent being extremely pointed and 10 per cent tending toward semiconical (Pl. VIE,H,I).

Thickness of vessel walls range from 6 to 18 mm, but most are 9 to 11 mm. Bases ranged from 15 to 28 mm. Rims are usually 5 to 10 mm. This is a thick pottery.

Lugs are rare but appliqued, conical lugs are attached along the rim of a few vessels.

Decoration.—Usually none. About 5 per cent of the rims have 2 to 5 horizontal, broad-trailed incisions that appear to be finger marks trailed over the damp, plastic clay (Pl. VIB). These are 10 to 12 mm wide and 1 to 2 mm deep. Another 5 per cent of the rims have concentric chevrons, incised with a pointed tool, with apex pointed down from the lip (Pl. VIC). There are 4 to 8 chevrons per design unit. One everted rim has a row of deep punctations 10 mm below the lip. One rim has incised crosshatches similar to the chevrons.

Other.—Mending perforations are frequent and occur on all parts of the vessel.

Vessel sizes.—Large. Sherds and small sections of vessels suggest diameters of 25-35 cm and depths of 30 to 45 cm. Maximum diameters are usually at the orifices.

Sample size.—179 rim sherds, 2,078 body sherds, 87 basal sherds, and 3 reconstructed vessel sections.

Temporal position.—Early Woodland.

Accokeek Ware
(New ware name)

This ware is defined on the basis of 1,093 rim sherds, 8,223 body sherds, 398 basal sherds and 12 reconstructed vessel sections from the Accokeek Creek site. No previous description of the ware has been published, although it is related, typologically, to the Stoney Creek, Prince George, and Albermarle series of Virginia (Evans, 1955, pp. 39,60,69,126). A single type—Accokeek Cord Marked has been delineated within this ware.

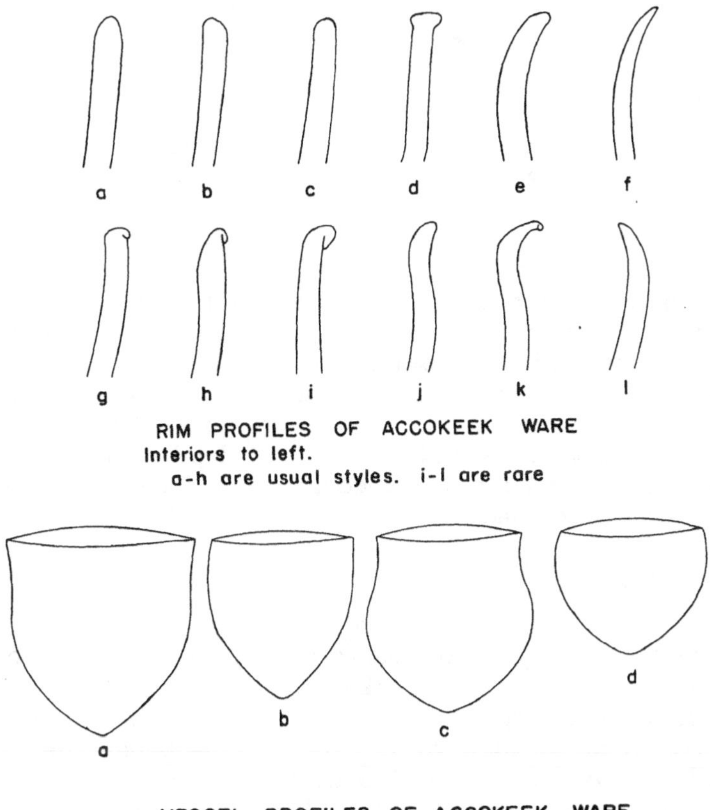

Fig. 21. Profiles of Accokeek ware.

The Accokeek ware is a pottery group consisting of vessels manufactured by the coiling technique with paddle malleated surfaces and composed of a coarse to medium textured, buff, tan, orange, or reddish-brown clay. The temper comprises 20 to 50 per cent of the paste and is a coarse to medium-fine sand often combined with lesser amounts of angular, crushed quartz. The sand temper gives the sherds a moderately friable texture, but a wide range of texture from coarse, soft, and friable to fine, hard, and but slightly friable is present in the ware. Vessels are large to medium in size, of medium thickness, with conical or semiconical bases, and straight, moderately everted, or moderately inverted rims (Fig. 21). Vessel interiors are smoothed.

The ware derives its name from the Accokeek Creek site on the Potomac River in Prince George's County, Maryland.

Accokeek Cord Marked
(New type name)

Summary Definition

The type Accokeek Cord Marked is a coiled pottery with paddle-malleated surfaces of buff, tan, orange, or brown clay, tempered with coarse to medium fine sand and often minor amounts of crushed quartz. It has a wide range of textures from coarse and soft to medium fine and hard, and is always somewhat friable. Exterior surfaces are impressed with cord-wrapped paddle marks haphazardly applied and interiors are smoothed. Vessel form is conical or semiconical with conical or semiconical base and straight, slightly everted, or slightly inverted rims. Vessels range from large to medium with diameters about equal to or slightly less than depths. Lugs are occasionally present and incised decoration is rare, though rim areas are often smoothed.

Type Description

Method of manufacture.—Coiling and paddle malleating. Rarely is lack of welding noticeable but breakage along coil lines is usual. Such breakage often makes the convex surface of the coil resemble a rim lip. Coil width appears to be about 8 to 12 mm. Some basal sherds appear to have been modeled by hand from lumps of clay with the coils beginning 4 to 10 mm above the basal point.

Paste.—Temper is composed of coarse to medium fine sand comprising 20 to 50 per cent of the paste. Predominantly this sand is of medium sized grains and makes up about 30 per cent of the paste. This is often combined with lesser amounts of angular, crushed quartz, quartzite, and rarely granites, gneisses, and other rocks. Particles of this minority temper are 1 to 10 mm in diameter and appear to be intentional inclusions in the paste.

The plastic is composed of a fine-grained, moderately compact clay, often ferruginous in content.

Hardness in Moh's scale is 2.0 to 3.0. Medium.

Texture ranges from moderately coarse, rough, and quite friable to moderately fine, smooth, compact, and but slightly friable. It is always sandy to the feel.

Color.—Exterior surface color is usually a shade of reddish tan or gray brown but ranges from dull black through brown, red, orange, and gray to tan and buff.

Interior surface color is usually the same as the exterior or slightly darker. About 30 per cent of the sherds, especially those of light-colored exteriors are smudged black on the interior.

Core color is usually the same as, or a little darker than, the exterior but some 15 per cent of the sherds have wide, black cores that extend nearly to the surfaces.

Firing.—Low to moderate temperatures and an oxidizing atmosphere. Smudge marks are rare on the exteriors and interior smudging is even and well controlled.

Surface treatment.—Exterior surfaces are roughened all over with cord-wrapped paddle impressions (Pl. VII). In a great majority of the sherds paddle impressions are deep and made on fairly plastic paste. Horizontal, vertical, and diagonal cord marks, or more often combinations of these, suggest application by patting. The general tendency is for the impressions to be applied at a diagonal, downward to the right from the rim. Seldom are the cords wrapped closely together around the paddle but are spaced 1 to 8 mm apart. This gives the impression of narrow, corded grooves separated by wider lands and where the paddling is criss-crossed, a check-stamped appearance results. Cord marking usually extends from lip to base but many of the rims were subsequently smoothed and 40 per cent of the basal sherds appear not to have been cord-marked for a distance of 3 to 7 cm above the basal tip (Pl. VII, H).

Interior surfaces are smoothed. Some sherds, though, have uneven interior surfaces suggesting use of the hand as an anvil in conjunction with the paddle.

Vessel form (Fig. 21).—Lips are of a variety of forms. They are usually straight and rounded or flattened but slightly everted lips with bits of clay overlapped on the exterior and cord marks along the top are common. Minor variations are wedge-shaped, thin lips either straight or everted; inverted lips: "T"-shaped lips; or thickened lips.

Rims are vertical to slightly everted. Rarely are they inverted or markedly everted. Rim areas generally blend into the body 5 to 10 cm below the lip.

Bodies are conical to semiconical ranging rarely to globular. Upper portions are usually cylindrical from rim to about midpoint or expand slightly outward from the rim. Lower portions usually constrict to a point at the base or round out to a semiglobular base.

Bases are conical, semiconical, or rarely rounded. The usual base is an extreme cone (Fig. 21).

Thickness of vessel walls ranges from 4 to 14 mm but 90 per cent are 6 to 8 mm. Bases are 9 to 21 mm thick. Rims are usually about the same as the body.

Lugs are rare but in a few specimens large, globular, cord-marked lugs are attached to the sides of the vessels along the rim area.

Decoration.—Usually none but 20 per cent of the rim sherds are smoothed, over cord marking, in an area 10 to 80 mm wide extending to the lip with cord-wrapped paddle impressions on top of the lip or extending 3 to 5 mm below the lip. A few sherds that are only partly smoothed in this area illustrate that the smoothing was done by rubbing the fingers or other similar tool over the cord-marked area. On 5 per cent of the rim sherds, long triangles suspended from the lip, horizontal zig-zag lines, vertical or horizontal straight lines, crossed lines, or short random lines, are incised over the cord marking (Pl. VII J). Incising was done with a round-pointed tool. Four sherds have rows of punctations made with an irregular-pointed tool (Pl. VII, B).

Other.—Mending perforations are frequent and occur on all parts of the vessel.

Vessel size.—Large to medium. The sherds and vessel sections suggest diameters of 25 to 40 cm and depths of approximately the same range. A few vessels appear to have been smaller than this.

Sample size.—1,093 rim sherds, 8,223 body sherds, 398 basal sherds, and 12 reconstructed vessel sections.

Temporal position.--Middle Woodland

Albemarle Ware
(Albemarle series of Evans, 1955, p. 39)

This ware is defined on the basis of 39 rim sherds, 685 body sherds, and 14 basal sherds from the Accokeek Creek site and a description of the Albemarle series in the literature. Evans' Albemarle series equates fully with Albemarle ware as described here and three of the five component types are represented in the Accokeek Creek site collections. It seems useful to restate the basic description of the ware here, in terms consistent with the other wares described, as a somewhat fuller statement than Evans provided. The small quantity of specimens of the component types of this ware in the Accokeek Creek site collections, however, add little to the full descriptions of the types as provided by Evans. Therefore, the ware will be described and each of the three types present here will be defined but the detailed descriptions will be omitted with mere reference to Evans' descriptions except where something can be added from the Accokeek Creek site material.

The Albemarle ware is a pottery group consisting of vessels manufactured by the coiling technique with paddle-malleated surfaces and composed of an orange-red to gray-red clay. Temper constitutes less than half the paste and is composed of angular bits of crushed quartzite, granite, gneiss, quartz, greenstone, or medium-grained sand. It has a compact, medium fine, clayey texture, is hard and has a distinctive, angular fracture.

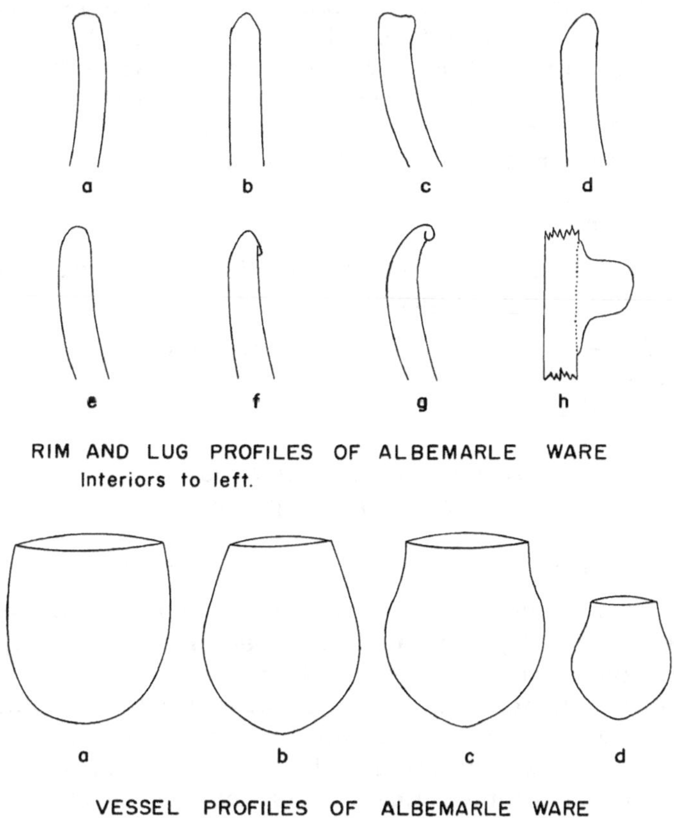

Fig. 22. Profiles of Albemarle ware.

Vessel size is large to medium with rounded or semiconical bases, and straight, slightly everted, or slightly inverted rims (Fig. 22).

The ware derives its name from Albemarle County, Virginia, in the eastern foothills of the Blue Ridge Mountains, in the central part of the state.

Albemarle Cord Marked
(Evans, 1955, p. 41)

Summary Definition

The type Albemarle Cord Marked is a coiled pottery with cord-wrapped paddle malleated exterior surfaces, smooth interior surfaces and of a reddish orange to tan clay, tempered with crushed granite, quartz, or other rock, of large angular particles. It has a compact, medium fine, clayey texture and a distinctive, angular fracture. Vessels are of large to medium size, uniformly thick with rounded or semiconical bases and simple rims. Lugs are often present, but decoration is absent on the Accokeek Creek site specimens (Fig. 22).

Type Description

No variations from Evans' description are noted in the Accokeek Creek site specimens.

Sample size.—28 rim sherds, 474 body sherds, and 14 basal sherds.
Temporal position.—Middle Woodland.

Albemarle Net Impressed
(Evans, 1955, p. 43)

Summary Definition

The type Albemarle Net Impressed is a coiled pottery with knotted, net-wrapped-paddle malleated exterior surfaces, smooth interior surfaces and of a reddish brown or orange to tan clay, tempered with crushed granite, quartzite, quartz, or other angular rock. It has a distinctively angular fracture. Vessels are large to medium size, uniformly thick, with rounded or semiconical bases and simple rims. Lugs and decoration are usually absent but rare incised decoration and smoothed rim areas occur on the Accokeek Creek site specimens (Fig. 22).

Type Description

No appreciable variations from Evans' description are noted in the Accokeek Creek site specimens except the presence of diagonal, broad-line incising of crossed lines along the rim on 2 sherds.

Sample Size.—9 rim sherds, and 160 body sherds.
Temporal position.—Middle Woodland.

Albemarle Fabric Impressed
(Evans, 1955, pp. 41-43)

Summary Definition

The type Albemarle Fabric Impressed is a coiled pottery with coarse, fabric impressions on exterior surfaces, smooth interior surfaces, and of a reddish or orange to tan clay, tempered with crushed granite, quartzite, quartz, or other rock. It has a compact, medium fine, clayey texture, and distinctively angular fracture. Vessels are large to medium size, uniformly thick, with rounded or semiconical bases and simple rims without lugs or decoration (Fig. 22).

Type Description

No appreciable variations from Evans' description are noted in the Accokeek Creek site specimens except that the exterior surface treatment is consistently impressed with a plain, coarse, twined fabric of fine weft and coarse, wide, rigid warp resembling basketry. This is listed by Evans as a minor variation within the type.

Sample size.—2 rim sherds and 51 body sherds.
Temporal position.—Middle Woodland.

Mockley Ware
(New ware name)

This ware is defined on the basis of 818 rim sherds, 6,885 body sherds, 268 basal sherds, and 8 reconstructed vessel sections from the Accokeek Creek site. No previous description of the ware has been published. Three component types—Mockley Cord Marked, Mockley Net Impressed, and Mockley Plain—have been distinguished.

The Mockley ware is a pottery group consisting of vessels manufactured by the coiling technique with paddle-malleated

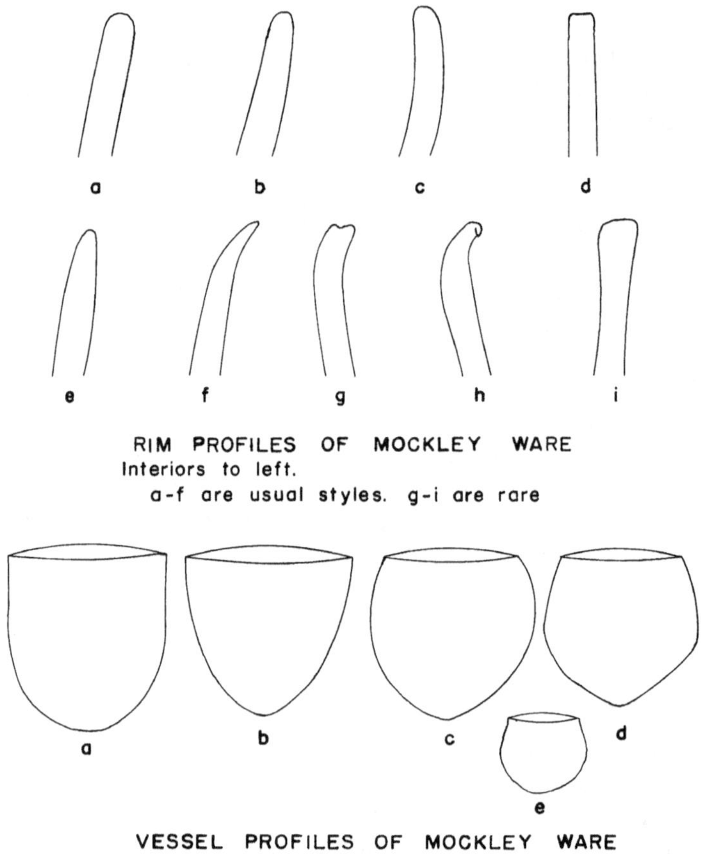

Fig. 23. Profiles of Mockley ware.

surfaces and composed of a medium to fine-textured buff, tan, orange, or brown clay. The temper is predominantly of crushed shell, alone, or combined with varying amounts of angular or rounded particles of hematite, limonite limestone, clay, or other soft material. The temper gives the ware a very clayey texture and produces a distinctively laminated appearance in the sherds. Temper constitutes 20 to 30 per cent of the paste, but the shell and some other particles are often leached out, partially or completely, leaving the sherds honeycombed with thin, flat, or angular holes. The shell fragments do not have a burned appearance but are a clean white and range from finely pulverized particles to large flakes and lumps 7 to 10 mm in diameter. Vessels are of large to medium size, of medium thickness, with semiconical or rounded bases, and straight, moderately everted or moderately inverted rims (Fig. 23). Vessel interiors are smoothed.

The ware derives its name from the point of land on the northern extremity of the Accokeek Creek site—Mockley Point.

Mockley Cord Marked
(New type name)

Summary Definition

The type Mockley Cord Marked is a coiled pottery with cord-wrapped paddle malleated surfaces, of buff, tan, orange, or brown clay, tempered with crushed unburned shell, and varying amounts of angular or rounded particles of limonite, hematite, clay, limestone, or other soft material. It has a noncompact, medium fine, clayey texture, and distinctively laminated structure. Vessels are of large to medium size, uniformly quite thick, with rounded or semiconical bases, and straight, flaring, or slightly inverted rims (Fig. 23).

Type Description

Method of manufacture.—Coiling with paddle malleating. Lack of welding is rare but coil breakage is frequent (Pl. VIII, A). Coil widths are 12 to 16 mm. Coils are usually flattened in welding so that the interior portion overlaps the coil below and the exterior portion overlaps the coil above. Often, though, the coils are simply pressed together. Stretching and patching are sometimes noticeable.

Paste.—Temper is principally a clean, white, unburned, crushed shell apparent as angular or flat particles ranging from almost powder-fine to as large as 5 mm in diameter, and comprising 20 to 30 per cent of the paste. Other inclusions are angular or rounded particles of hematite, limonite, clay, and soft limey concretions. These appear to be accidental inclusions in the paste. A majority of the sherds contain the shell temper as finely crushed, unburned particles along with small amounts of the other inclusions. A minority contain only shell, and in these the shell is usually present as large flakes or as angular, laminated lumps. In a majority of the sherds both the shell and the other inclusions have been partly, or completely, leached out leaving large and small, flat, angular holes. Burned shell is present in less than 1 per cent of the sherds.

The plastic is a fine-grained, compact clay that appears to be noncompact due to the leaching of the temper. The combination of the shell temper and the compact clay plastic gives a distinctive structure of contorted laminations to the pottery that is very evident in cross-sections of the sherds.

Hardness in Moh's scale is 1.5 to 2.0. Soft.

Texture is very clayey, soft, and crumbly; often porous and always of contorted lamellar structure.

Color.—Exterior surface color is usually a rusty reddish or orange to reddish-tan. A minority of the sherds are almost black through brown, buff, and tan.

Interior surface color is usually the same as the exterior but some sherds are of darker shades of the exterior color.

Core color is usually the same as the exterior. A minority of sherds, though, have a darker core extending nearly to the 2 surfaces. Exterior, interior, and core usually show white flecks of shell temper.

Firing.—Low temperature and oxidizing atmosphere. Smudge marks are rare on the exteriors but interiors are sometimes evenly smudged.

Surface treatment.—Exterior surfaces, are malleated with a cord-wrapped paddle. Impressions are vertical, horizontal, diagonal, rarely criss-crossed, or combinations of these (Pl. VIII, A-G). Predominantly the marks are of a medium to coarse cord, wrapped loosely about the paddle, 3 to 10 mm apart and moderately deeply impressed. A minority of 15 per cent of the sherds are marked with a fine cord, wrapped tightly about the paddle, never criss-crossed or overlapped, and applied vertically to the rim. These are lightly and carefully applied almost appearing to be marks of a fine fabric but a plasticene impression readily distinguishes them as cord marking. Occasional paddle-edge impressions appear at random near the base. About half the basal sherds are smooth.

Interior surfaces are usually smooth, rarely striated or rough, but occasionally uneven as a result of hand or other tool use in conjunction with the paddle (Pl. VIII, H).

Vessel form. (Fig. 23).—Lips are usually rounded or thinned to a wedge-shape, a minority of 4 per cent are flattened, nicked, or everted.

Rims are predominantly vertical or slightly flaring. Rarely are they slightly inverted.

Bodies are hemispherical to conical or straight-sided. Usually they are straight from the rim to the midpoint and taper toward the base.

Bases are semiconical or rounded. Two conical bases were found.

Thickness of vessel walls is 8 to 11 mm. Rims are 6 to 10 mm thick. Bases are 10 to 19 mm thick.

Lugs are absent.

Decoration.—None, unless the occasional, paddle-edge impressions occurring singly and at random near the base may be considered to be intentional decoration. In one vessel, though, these impressions were applied horizontally about the rim and along the interior of the lip.

Other.—Mending perforations are frequent and occur on all parts of the vessel.

Vessel size.—Large to medium. Sherds and vessel sections suggest diameters of 20 to 35 cm and depths of 20 to 40 cm. Depth is usually greater than diameter and maximum diameter is usually at the orifice.

Sample size.—248 rim sherds, 2,278 body sherds, 109 basal sherds and 3 reconstructed vessel sections.

Temporal position.—Middle Woodland.

Mockley Net Impressed
(New type name)

Summary Definition

The type Mockley Net Impressed is a coiled pottery with knotted net-wrapped paddle malleated exterior surfaces, of buff, tan, orange, or brown clay, tempered with crushed, unburned shell and varying amounts of angular or rounded particles of limonite, hematite, clay, limestone, or other soft material. It has a noncompact, medium fine, clayey texture, and a distinctively laminated structure. Vessels are of large to medium size, uniformly quite thick, with rounded or semiconical bases, and straight, flaring, or slightly inverted rims (Fig. 23). Rare decoration is by incising along the rim.

Type Description

Method of manufacture.—Same as Mockley Cord Marked (Pl. IX, C and Pl. X, F, G).

Paste.—Same as Mockley Cord Marked.

Color.—Same as Mockley Cord Marked.

Firing.—Same as Mockley Cord Marked.

Surface treatment.—Exterior surfaces are malleated with loose, open, knotted net impressions applied on damp paste leaving clear markings. Nets appear to have been wrapped about the hand or paddle and carefully impressed over the vessel with little overlapping. Predominantly the knots are 4 to 6 mm apart (Pl. IX, C-F), but finer mesh nets with knots 2 to 3 mm apart are not uncommon (Pl. IX, A, G). In a small minority of cases the knots are 8 to 15 mm apart (Pl. IX, B). In the sherds with fine mesh net the threads are not distinct and the knots leave a pimpled appearance. Impressions are usually 1 to 2 mm deep. These net impressions closely resemble those on the types Pope's Creek Net Impressed and Albemarle Net Impressed.

Interior surfaces are the same as Mockley Cord Marked (Pl. X, G).

Vessel form.—Same as Mockley Cord Marked.

Decoration.—Over 95 per cent of the sherds are without decoration. A few sherds have wide, crosshatched or diagonal, incised lines along the rim, evidently made with a blunt tool. Incisions are 2 mm wide and 1 to 2 mm deep.

Other.—Same as Mockley Cord Marked.

Vessel size.—Same as Mockley Cord Marked.

Sample size.—531 rim sherds, 4,456 body sherds, 132 basal sherds, and 5 reconstructed vessel sections.

Temporal position.—Middle Woodland.

Mockley Plain
(New type name)

Summary Definition

The type Mockley Plain is a coiled pottery with smoothed exterior surfaces, of buff, tan, orange, or brown clay, tempered with crushed, unburned shell, and varying amounts of angular or rounded particles of limonite, hematite, clay, limestone, or other soft material. It has a noncompact, medium fine, clayey texture, and a distinctively laminated structure. Vessels are of large to medium size, uniformly quite thick with rounded or semiconical bases and straight, flaring, or slightly inverted rims. Decoration is absent.

Type Description

Method of Manufacture.—Same as Mockley Cord Marked.

Paste.—Same as Mockley Cord Marked.
Color.—Same as Mockley Cord Marked.
Firing.—Same as Mockley Cord Marked.
Surface treatment.—Exterior surfaces are plain and smoothed over the entire area. A few sherds appear to have been net- or cord-roughened, and smoothed over. Smoothing is usually even and well executed.

Interior surfaces are the same as Mockley Cord Marked.
Vessel form.—Same as Mockley Cord Marked.
Decoration.—None.
Other.—None.
Vessel size.—Same as Mockley Cord Marked.
Sample size.—39 rim sherds, 151 body sherds, and 27 basal sherds.
Temporal position.—Middle Woodland.

Townsend Ware
(Blaker, 1950, p.11)

This ware is defined on the basis of 89 rim sherds, 213 body sherds, 3 basal sherds, and 2 reconstructed vessel sections from the Accokeek Creek site and descriptions and discussions in the literature (Blaker, 1950, pp. 11; Schmitt, n.d. p.27; Evans, 1955, pp. 44,124-25). It is similar to the Chickahominy series that Evans described for Virginia but the ware and the type names used by Schmitt and by Blaker seem more appropriate for the Accokeek Creek site sherds for the same reasons that Evans established the new series and type names. The Virginia material rarely had decoration whereas the Accokeek Creek site sherds are abundantly decorated. Also slight differences in vessel shape, surface color, and core structure distinguish them from the Chickahominy series and suggest closer identity to the material described by Blaker and Schmitt as Townsend ware.

The Townsend ware is a pottery group consisting of vessels manufactured by the coiling technique with paddle-malleated surfaces and composed of a reddish-tan or buff paste. Temper constitutes but 10 to 20 per cent of the paste and is unburned, crushed shell usually, in part, leached out. The ware has a medium texture, is clayey, and tends to crumble with an uncontorted, lamellar structure. Vessel size is usually large with rounded or semiconical bases and straight, slightly everted, or slightly inverted rims. Orifices are usually circular or, rarely, pentagonal (Fig. 24). Decoration is by incising in short strokes with a blunt or, rarely, sharp-pointed tool.

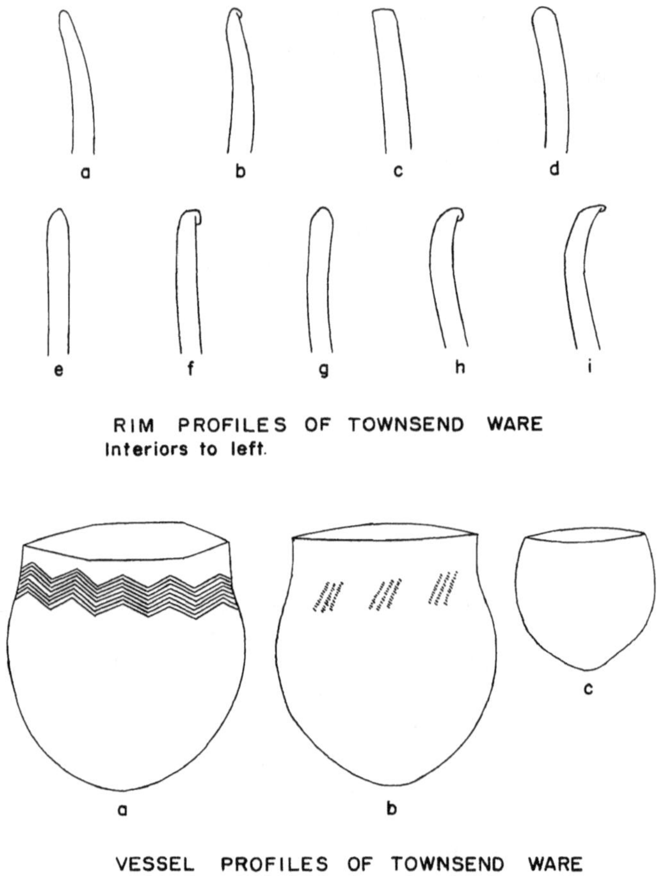

Fig. 24. Profiles of Townsend ware.

The ware derives its name from the Townsend site near Lewes, Delaware. The two component types represented in the Accokeek Creek site material--Rappahannock Fabric Impressed and Rappahannock Incised—derive their names from the Rappahannock River area of coastal Virginia.

Rappahannock Fabric Impressed
(Schmitt, n.d., p. 27)

Summary Definition

The type Rappahannock Fabric Impressed is a coiled pottery with coarse fabric impressions on exterior surfaces, smooth interior surfaces, and of a reddish-tan to buff clay, tempered with unburned crushed shell. It has a moderately compact, clayey texture. Vessels are of large to medium size, moderately thin, with rounded or semiconical bases, and straight, slightly everted or slightly inverted rims. Diameters are usually less than depths and maximum diameters are usually about midway between rim and base.

Type Description

Method of manufacture.—Coiled with paddle malleated exterior surfaces. Occasional coil breaks may be seen.

Paste.—Temper is predominantly irregular, lumpy or flakey particles of crushed, unburned shell, usually leached out of, at least, the surfaces of sherds leaving irregular, flat-sided holes. Shell is not finely crushed and particles are 4 to 10 mm in diameter. Small amounts of fine sand and some bits of hematitie are present in a few sherds. Temper constitutes but 10 to 20 per cent of the paste.

The plastic is composed of a compact, fine-grained clay.

Hardness in Moh's scale is 2.0 to 2.5. Medium.

Texture is medium and moderately compact, very clayey and often rather crumbly and porous. Structure of the paste is lamellar without contortions.

Color.—Exterior surface color ranges from reddish through orange, brown, buff, gray, and tan with reddish-tan or buff predominant.

Interior surface colors are usually the same as the exteriors but some are darker and a few are smudged black.

The core color is usually the same as the exteriors but no well-defined core area is present.

Firing.—Medium temperature and an oxidizing atmosphere but often not well controlled, resulting in spotty smudge marks.

Surface treatment.—Exterior surfaces (Pl. XI) are roughened all over with impressions of a coarse, twined textile of fine weft and coarse, rigid, wide warp (Mason, 1901, p. 117; Miner, 1936, pp. 184,186). This is often locally called "basket impression" (Schmitt, n.d., p. 27), as the fabric appears to have been a twined basketry fragment held in the hand and impressed over the vessel surface. Rigid warp elements are usually parallel to the rim and shallowly impressed. Distance between warp elements is 7 to 8 mm. Basal and rim sherds are sometimes smoothed over after fabric-impressing.

Note: basketry is not actually a fabric but should be included along with fabrics under the broader term of textiles (Miner, 1936, pp. 181-92). Perhaps this pottery would be better named "textile impressed." The term "fabric impressed," though, is so firmly imbedded in the literature (Holmes, 1903, p. 73; Evans, 1955, pp. 41,44) that it has been retained here in the interests of consistency.

Interior surfaces are evenly smoothed.

Vessel form (Fig. 24).—Lips are usually rounded but sometimes are flattened, often lightly nicked and with a small, irregular fold of clay overlapping the exterior.

Rims are vertical or inverted; rarely everted.

Bodies are rounded or semiconical.

Bases are rounded or semiconical (Pl. XI, B).

Thicknesses are uniformly thin over the whole vessel. Walls range from 5 to 8 mm with rims the same or a mm thinner and bases 2 to 3 mm thicker.

Decoration.—Usually none except for nicked lips, but one vessel has groups of three cord-wrapped dowel impressions placed diagonally in a band about the rim (Pl. XI, A, Fig. 24).

Other.—Mending performations are rare but are present.

Vessel size.—Large. Diameters appear to range from 30 to 45 cm and depths seem to be about the same or slightly greater. Orifice size is usually less than maximum diameter. One small vessel 10 cm in diameter and 7 to 8 cm deep is present.

Sample size.—12 rim sherds, 213 body sherds, 3 basal sherds, and 2 reconstructed vessel sections. Undecorated body sherds of both types of Townsend ware are included together here as they are indistinguishable.

Temporal position.—Late Woodland.

Rappahannock Incised
(Blaker, 1950, p. 11)

Summary Definition

The type Rappahannock Incised is a coiled pottery with coarse fabric impressions on exterior surfaces, smooth interior surfaces, and of a reddish tan to buff clay, tempered with unburned, crushed shell. It has a moderately compact clayey texture. Vessels are of large to medium size, moderately thin, with rounded or semiconical bases, and straight, slightly everted, or slightly inverted rims. Diameters are usually less than depths and orifices are sometimes pentagonal or hexagonal. Decoration is by incising with a blunt tool in short, patterned strokes (Fig. 24).

Type Description

Method of manufacture.—Same as Rappahannock Fabric Impressed.
Paste.—Same as Rappahannock Fabric Impressed.
Color.—Same as Rappahannock Fabric Impressed.
Firing.—Same as Rappahannock Fabric Impressed.
Surface treatment.—Same as Rappanhannock Fabric Impressed.
Vessel form.--Same as Rapphannock Fabric Impressed.
Decoration.—Incising with a blunt tool (Pl. XII). Incisions are U-shaped in cross-section, 1.5 to 2.5 mm wide and 1 to 2 mm deep. Rarely a fine-pointed tool is used or punctations are applied with a blunt tool. Designs are in bands around the rim as chevrons, triangles, diagonals, horizontals, stepped lines, crosshatching, and punctate-filled triangles, all carefully executed.
Other.—Same as Rappahannock Fabric Impressed.
Vessel size.—Same as Rappahannock Fabric Impressed.
Sample size.—77 rim sherds and 1 reconstructed vessel section. Body sherds are included in the count of the type Rappahannock Fabric Impressed as body sherds of the 2 are indistinguishable.
Temporal position.—Late Woodland.

Potomac Creek Ware
(New ware name)

This ware is defined on the basis of 4,836 rim sherds, 28,904 body sherds, 997 basal sherds, and 51 reconstructed vessels, or vessel sections, from the Accokeek Creek site and descriptions of the dominant type in the literature (Manson, MacCord, and Griffin, 1944, pp. 406-9; Schmitt, n.d. p. 26; 1952, p. 63). The ware as represented by the Accokeek Creek site material readily fits the published descriptions of the dominant type—Potomac Creek Cord Impressed. Some additional data, though, may be added to this type description as a result of the unusually large sample from this site. Also a companion type—Potomac Creek Plain--may be distinguished within this ware.

The Potomac Creek ware is a pottery group consisting of vessels manufactured by the coiling technique, with paddle-

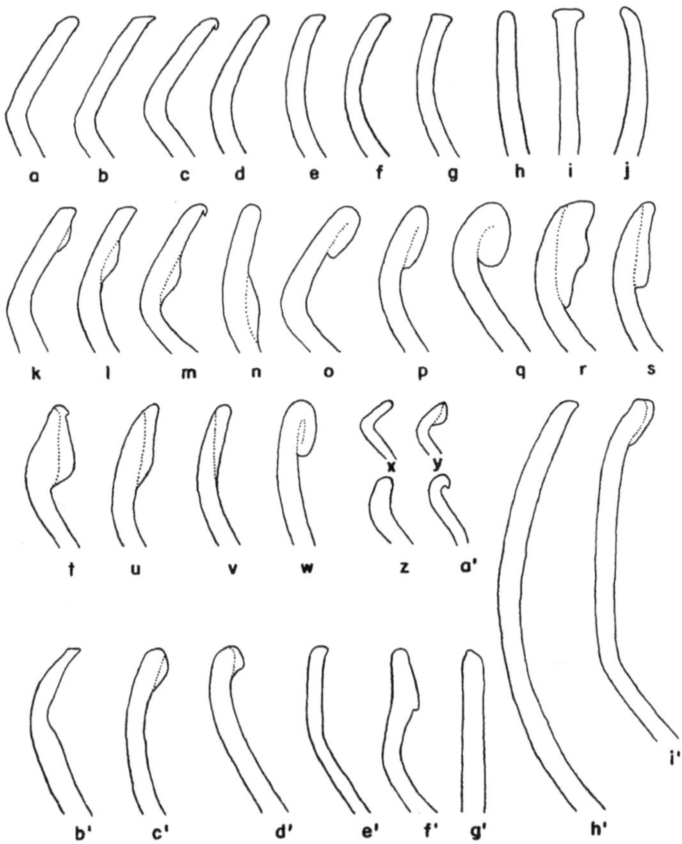

Figure 25.

malleated surfaces, and composed of black to brown or tan to buff clay. Temper constitutes 20 to 35 per cent of the paste and is predominantly crushed quartz often with lesser amounts of other crushed stone or medium-grained sand. It has a fine to medium texture, is hard and generally thin but does not break easily. Vessel size ranges from medium large to small, with globular bodies, flaring rims, and rounded bases (Fig. 26). Orifices are smaller than maximum diameters and rim construction occurs on most vessels. Decoration, when present, is any of several varieties of cord impression or, rarely, is incised or punctate.

The ware derives its name from the Potomac Creek (or Patawameke) site on the Potomac River in Stafford County, Virginia.

Potomac Creek Cord Impressed
(Schmitt, n.d., p. 26; 1952, p. 63;
Manson, MacCord, and Griffin, 1944, pp. 406-9)

Summary Definition

The type Potomac Creek Cord Impressed is a coiled pottery with cord-wrapped paddle malleated exterior surfaces, smooth interior surfaces, and of a black or brown to buff or tan clay, tempered with crushed quartz or, rarely, other crushed, hard rock or coarse sand. It has a compact, fine-grained texture, is hard, with thin vessel walls. Vessels are of medium size with rounded or, rarely, semiconical or flat bases, and constricted rim areas with distinctively flaring rims. Decoration is always present, consisting of any of many variations of cord impressions applied around the rim. Rims are often thickened by application of a strip of clay (Figs. 25, 26; Pls. XIII-XVIII).

Type Description

Method of manufacture.—Coiled with paddle malleating. Coils begin at the apex of the base and continue up to the lip. Lack of welding is rarely noticeable but breakage along the coil lines is sometimes seen, especially in the rim area (Pl. XV, B, C, N, O).

Paste.—Temper is predominantly of angular, crushed quartz with occasional inclusions of other crushed, hard rock or coarse sand. Temper particles are 1 to 4 mm in diameter but usually about 2 mm. A minority of the sherds is tempered with coarse to medium sand but with small amounts of crushed quartz. Temper constitutes 20 to 35 per cent of the paste and is usually quite noticeable in the sherd.

The plastic is a fine-grained, compact clay, well prepared and with few extraneous inclusions.

Hardness in Moh's scale is 3.0 to 4.0. Hard.

Texture is consistently medium with a few of the sand tempered sherds being medium coarse and slightly friable. Typically it is hard and smooth textured with a slight grittiness to the feel. Never feels clayey.

Color.—Exterior surface colors are usually dark brown to black but range through light brown, gray, tan, reddish, buff, and light cream. The lighter colored sherds are more elaborately decorated than the darker ones.

Interior surface colors are usually the same as the exterior or slightly lighter. Some vessels of dark exterior color

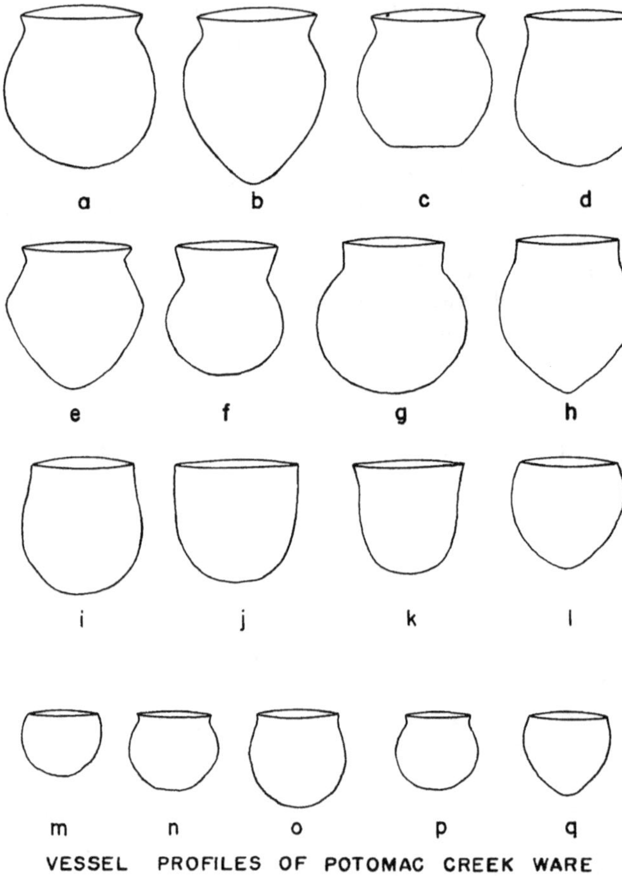

Figure 26.

have light interiors and those with light exteriors sometimes have black interiors.

Core colors are usually distinctive, comprising some three-fourths of the sherd thickness. Core colors are as varied as exterior surface colors. In sherds of light surface color the core is about a shade darker, but in the sherds of dark surface color the core is several shades lighter.

Firing.—High temperature, usually in a reducing atmosphere producing allover surface smudging or uneven smudge clouds. A minority of the sherds are evenly fired in an oxidizing atmosphere with no smudge clouds.

Surface treatment.—Exterior surfaces are uniformly malleated with a cord-wrapped paddle from base to rim, generally diagonally to the rim but some paddle marks are vertical, horizontal, criss-crossed, or combinations of these (Pls. XIII, XIV). Cords used on the paddle are loosely twisted, of 1.0 to 1.5 mm in width and wrapped tightly about the paddle. Some cords are finer and a few are coarser than this (Pl. XV, G, H, M). Impressions are distinct and 0.5 to 1.5 mm deep, but some are partly obscured by smoothing. Rim areas especially tend to be smoothed (Pl. XVII, G, L). Carbon incrustation is common over exterior surfaces.

Interior surfaces are smoothed to almost polished in a few cases. Smoothing striations are sometimes present near the base.

Vessel form.--Lips are usually rounded, flattened, or wedge-shaped. Cord impressions often appear on top of the lip, and small bits of clay are occasionally pressed down over the exterior lip edge resulting from lip flattening or cord impressing (Fig. 25).

Rims are predominantly flared. The angle made by the junction of rim and body is distinct and of 15 to 45 degrees forming a constricted neck in most vessels. A minority of the rims, though, blend gently with the curve of the body and rarely are rims straight or slightly inverted (Fig. 26; Pls. XIII, XIV). Rim height is 20 to 105 mm but usually 35 to 50 mm. Often the rim is thinned toward the lip and an extra band of clay is applied around it producing a thickened rim of from 1 to 3 times the body thickness. This "false collar" or applique strip is not always substantially welded to the rim and often separates from the rim (Pl. XVI J). Another less frequent, rim thickening technique is to fold the upper portion of the rim down over the lower portion (Pl. XV G, H; Pl. XVI F). In some instances the rim is thickened by application of a narrow, thick coil of clay around the central area of the rim without thinning the rim (Pl. XV E).

Bodies are predominantly globular, expanding evenly from base to midportion and contracting evenly to the rim juncture. A minority of 10 per cent has a maximum expansion well above the mid-portion and contract to a semiconical base. No angular shoulders are present and all body contours are smooth-flowing curves (Fig. 26).

Bases are predominantly round, blending smoothly with body contours. A minority have semiconical bases and a rare few have almost flat bases (Fig. 26).

Thickness usually ranges from 4 to 7 mm and is usually uniform within all parts of a single vessel, except for the artificial rim thickening mentioned above. Vessels of sandier temper range from 6 to 10 mm in thickness. Rare extremes of thickness range from 2 to 20 mm.

Lugs or other adornments are absent except for the rim applique mentioned above.

Decoration.—Technique: decoration is confined to the rim area and applied by impressing single or multiple cords horizontally, diagonally, vertically or criss-crossed about the rim from the lip to the body juncture (Pls. XV, XVI, XVII). Cords are usually impressed deeply in the damp clay, from 0.5 to 4.0 mm deep, but are most often about 2.0 mm deep. Cords range from fine, tightly twisted 2- or 3-ply cord of about 0.5 mm in diameter to coarse, heavy, loosely twisted cords of more than 2 mm in diameter. These were: (*a*) single cords applied individually around the rim and pressed into the damp clay, (*b*) a cord-wrapped dowel rolled vertically about the vessel rim, or (*c*) a cord-wrapped dowel used to stamp the design along the rim. A small minority of the sherds are incised with a blunt or sharp tool (Pl. XVIII G, I,J), and a few are punctated with a round, hollow tool (Pl. XVIII, A, C, D, F). Incising and punctating never occur together but either may be combined with cord impressions and many of the incised decorations are obviously imitations of the cord-impressed decorations. Designs: predominantly designs consist of several horizontal cord impressions encircling the rim. These may be single cord impressions or cord-wrapped dowel, stamped impressions. Usually there are 4 to 8 such impressions, rarely less, but sometimes as many as 28. Often short, cord-wrapped dowel impressions are applied diagonally or vertically alone or over the horizontal impressions, some forming crosshatching and others arranged in zoned designs. The more complex designs appear on rims of smaller, lighter colored vessels, often of smoothed exterior surfaces. Six sherds have complex designs inside the rim (Pl. XVN; XVIG), as well as on the outside and 23 rims have deeply notched lips (Pl. XVIII H).

Other.—Mending perforations are frequent and appear on all parts of the vessel (Pl. XII F).

Vessel size.—Predominantly medium with a few ranging to medium large or medium small. Depths range from 13 to 30 cm, usually 20 to 25 cm. Diameters range from 12 to 28 cm but usually 2 to 4 cm less than maximum depths. Orifices are usually less than maximum diameters.

Sample size.--4,672 rim sherds, 28,904 body sherds, 997 basal sherds, 4 wholly restored vessels, and 41 reconstructed vessel sections. Body and basal sherds of both component types of the Potomac Creek ware are lumped together here as they are indistinguishable.

Temporal position.—Late Woodland.

Potomac Creek Plain
(New type name)

Summary Definition

The type Potomac Creek Plain is a coiled pottery with smoothed exterior and interior surfaces, and of black or brown to buff or tan clay, tempered with crushed quartz and, rarely, other crushed hard rock or coarse sand. It has a compact, fine-grained texture, is hard and predominatly thin-walled. Vessels are of small to medium size with rounded bases and straight, everted or inverted rims. No decoration is present except rare lip nicking.

Type Description

Method of manufacture.—Same as Potomac Creek Cord Impressed.

Paste.—Same as Potomac Creek Cord Impressed.

Color.—Same as Potomac Creek Cord Impressed.

Firing.—Same as Potomac Creek Cord Impressed.

Surface treatment.—Exterior surfaces are smoothed over all areas, usually over previous cord roughening, but some sherds suggest no previous cord roughening (Pl. XVIII K, L, M).

Interior surfaces are evenly smoothed.

Vessel forms.—Same as Potomac Creek Cord Impressed except that everted rims are in the minority and straight or inverted rims and hemispherical bowls predominate (Figs. 25, 26).

Decorations.—None except for rarely nicked lips.

Other.—None.

Vessel size.—Medium to small. Diameters are usually 10 to 18 cm with depths only 1 to 2 cm greater. Vessels rarely range up to 25 cm in diameter.

Sample size.—164 rim sherds, and 6 reconstructed vessel sections. Body and basal sherds of both component types of the Potomac Creek ware are lumped together as they are indistinguishable.

Temporal position.—Late Woodland.

Moyaone Ware
(New ware name)

This ware is defined on the basis of 311 rim sherds, 710 body sherds, 78 basal sherds and 10 reconstructed vessel sections from the Accokeek Creek site, and on a description in the literature of a tentative type "Potomac Creek Sand Tempered" (Schmitt, n.d., pp. 26-7). The sherds here described fit well into the type that Schmitt suggested, but go beyond it. The sample is larger than was Schmitt's sample from the Patawomeke site and includes many more incised and plain examples. On this basis it seemed more reasonable to establish the pottery as a ware with three component types and to distinguish it by name from the Potomac Creek ware from which it differs markedly.

The Moyaone ware is a pottery group consisting of vessels manufactured by the coiling technique with paddle-malleated or smooth surfaces and composed of a gray, brown, buff, or reddish clay, tempered with extremely fine-grained micaceous sand often mixed with coarser sand and occasionally with crushed quartz. It has a compact, fine-grained texture but is always gritty, soft, and slightly friable. The extremely fine sand temper is the main distinctive characteristic. Vessels are small to medium small, with globular bodies, rounded bases, and flaring, straight or slightly inverted rims. Rims are usually constricted. Decoration, when present, is by cord impressing or incising.

The ware derives its name from the historic, seventeenth century name of the village then occupying the Accokeek Creek site.

Moyaone Cord Impressed
(New type name)

Summary Definition

The type Moyaone Cord Impressed is a coiled pottery with cord-wrapped paddle malleated surfaces often smoothed over, smoothed interior surfaces, and of a gray, brown, buff, or

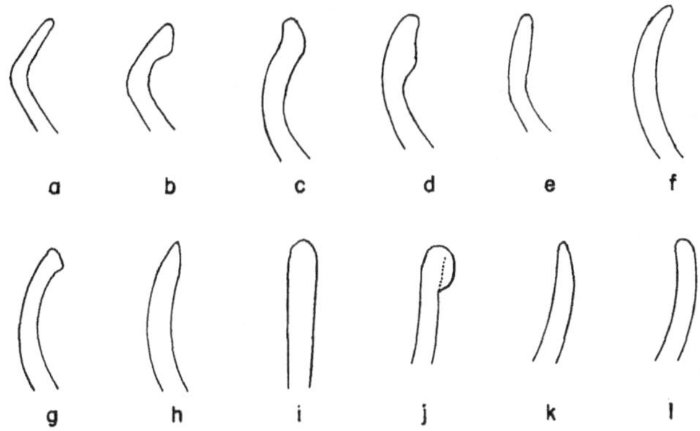

RIM PROFILES OF MOYAONE WARE
Interiors to left.

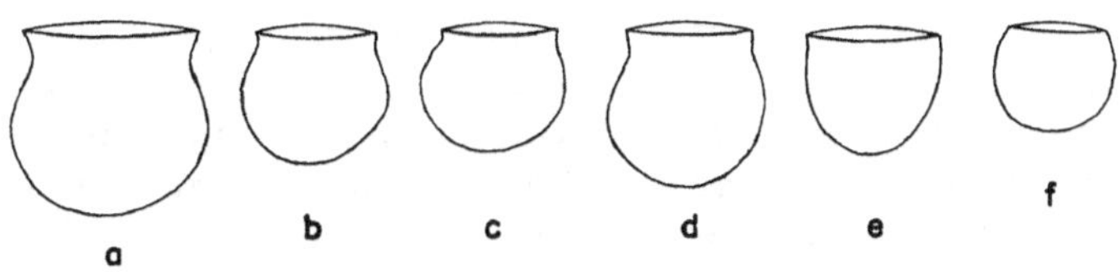

VESSEL PROFILES OF MOYAONE WARE

Fig. 27. Profiles of Moyaone ware.

reddish clay, tempered with extremely fine-grained sand often mixed with some coarser sand and occasionally with crushed quartz. It has a compact, fine-grained texture but is always gritty and slightly friable. Vessels are small, rarely ranging to medium small, with globular bodies, rounded bases, and flaring, straight, or slightly inverted, rims (Fig. 27). Decoration is confined to the rim area and consists of any of several variations of cord impressions. Rims are sometimes thickened by application of a strip of clay.

Type Description

Method of manufacture.—Coiled with paddle-malleated surfaces. Coil breaks are rare but present.

Paste.—Temper is predominantly fine and with minute flecks of mica. The sand gives the sherds a distinctive, gritty feel and the mica specks often produce a slight glitter. A minority of the sherds also contain small quantities of coarser sand or crushed quartz.

Plastic is a fine-grained, compact, well-mixed clay.

Hardness in Moh's scale is 2.0 to 2.5. Medium.

Texture is soft, smooth, and compact. The extreme fineness of the sand is quite distinctive and readily discernible to the feel, giving the sherds a texture like that of gritty powder.

Color.—Exteriors are predominantly light gray to gray-brown but range from almost black through brown, gray, and reddish-buff to tan.

Interiors are about the same as exteriors but sometimes a shade darker or a shade lighter.

Core color is usually the same as the surface but occasionally a little darker or lighter. A distinct core color is seldom perceptible.

Firing.—Moderate temperature, usually evenly fired in an oxidizing atmosphere with no smudging. Sometimes uneven fire-clouding or over-all smudging is apparent.

Surface treatment.—Exterior surfaces are predominantly malleated with a cord-wrapped paddle leaving cord marks usually vertical to the rim but sometimes horizontal, diagonal, or criss-crossed. A substantial minority of the surfaces are partly or completely smoothed after cord roughening (Pl. XIX, L-Q).

Interior surfaces are carefully smoothed. Rarely are fine tool striations, either vertical or horizontal, to be seen.

Vessel form (Fig. 27).—Lips are rounded but often flattened or wedge-shaped. Rarely do lips have cord markings along the top or diagonally along the outer edge.

Rims are usually flaring with a neck constriction. Sometimes they are only slightly everted, inverted or straight. Rarely a strip of clay has been added around the rim to thicken it. Rims are usually low, ranging from 10 to 35 mm in height or but 10 to 15 per cent of the vessel height.

Bodies are usually globular but rarely are hemispherical or cylindrical.

Bases are rounded.

Thickness of the vessel walls range from 5 to 10 mm but usually is 6 to 8 mm. Thickened rims range to 10 or 12 mm as do basal sherds. In proportion to the vessel size the sherds are moderately thick.

Lugs are absent.

Decoration.—Technique: decoration is confined to the rim area and lip and consists of horizontal, vertical, or diagonal cord impressions either stamped or rolled onto the vessel or applied as a single cord (Pl. XIX, L-Q).

Designs are usually simple, vertical cord impressions around the rim or 3 to 5 horizontal cord or cord-wrapped dowel impressions encircling the rim. Rarely are diagonal cord-wrapped dowel impressions found and complex designs are absent.

Other.—Mending perforations are rare but present.

Vessel size.—Predominantly small, ranging to medium. Maximum diameters are usually 8 to 12 cm rarely up to 20 cm. Depths are usually 10 to 15 cm rarely ranging up to 20 cm. Orifices are usually about the same as, or slightly smaller than, maximum diameters. Depths are slightly greater than diameters.

Sample size.—189 rim sherds, 710 body sherds, 78 basal sherds, and 6 reconstructed vessel sections. Body and basal sherds of all three types of the Moyaone ware are lumped together here as they are indistinguishable.

Temporal position.—Late Woodland.

Moyaone Incised
(New type name)

Summary Definition

The type Moyaone Incised is a coiled pottery with paddle-malleated and smoothed exterior surfaces, smoothed interior surfaces, and of a gray, brown, or buff clay, tempered with extremely fine sand. It has a compact, fine-grained texture but is always gritty to feel and slightly friable. Vessels are small with globular bodies, rounded bases, and flaring, straight, or slightly inverted rims, usually with constricted rim areas. Decoration by fine or heavy line incising is confined to the rim area or rarely on the upper portion of the body.

Type Description

Method of manufacture.—Same as Moyaone Cord Impressed.

Paste.—Same as Moyaone Cord Impressed.

Color.—Same as Moyaone Cord Impressed.

Firing.—Same as Moyaone Cord Impressed.

Surface treatment.—Same as Moyaone Cord Impressed but

fewer are cord marked and more are smoothed over the exterior surfaces.

Vessel form.—Same as Moyaone Cord Impressed.

Decoration.—Confined to the lip, rim, and upper body area. They consist of incised lines made with a sharp tool, or a wide, dull tool, or rarely with a curved tool such as a fingernail (Pl. XIX, A-K). Rarely the incising is applied over cord-wrapped dowel impressions. Designs are usually horizontal lines, chevrons, crosshatching, or random lines. A few designs are short, diagonal, parallel lines in a horizontal row about the rim. Fingernail impressions are in horizontal or vertical rows.

Other.—None.

Vessel size.—Same as Moyaone Cord Impressed.

Sample size.—74 rim sherds and 3 reconstructed vessel sections. Body and basal sherds are listed with the type Moyaone Cord Impressed as they are indistinguishable.

Temporal position.—Late Woodland.

Moyaone Plain
(New type name)

Summary Definition

The type Moyaone Plain is a coiled pottery with smoothed exterior and interior surfaces, of a gray, brown, or buff clay, tempered with extremely fine sand. It has a compact, fine-grained texture but is always gritty to feel and slightly friable. Vessels are small with globular bodies, rounded bases, and flaring, straight, or slightly inverted rims, and usually constricted rim areas. Decoration is entirely lacking.

Type Description

Method of manufacture.—Same as Moyaone Cord Impressed.

Paste.—Same as Moyaone Cord Impressed.

Color.—Same as Moyaone Cord Impressed.

Firing.—Same as Moyaone Cord Impressed.

Surface treatment.—Both interior and exterior surfaces are smoothed over paddle malleating but some appear to be smoothed without prior paddle malleating (Pl. XIX R).

Vessel form.—Same as Moyaone Cord Impressed but tend more to simple bowl forms rather than everted rim jars.

Decoration.—None.

Other.—None.

Vessel size.—Same as Moyaone Cord Impressed or slightly smaller.

Sample size.—48 rim sherds and one reconstructed vessel section. Body and basal sherds are counted with those of the type Moyaone Cord Impressed as they are indistinguishable.

Temporal position: Late Woodland.

Miscellaneous Pottery Groups

After formalizing the bulk of any large mass of pottery sherds into specific, named types there usually seems to be a residue of sherds that doesn't quite fit any of the types but that do not have enough attributes in common to form useful new types. The material from the Accokeek Creek site is no exception and there remains a residue of 1,008 sherds and 18 reconstructed vessel sections (less than 2 per cent of the total) that do not fit any of the established types described here or elsewhere in the literature. These sherds are described on the following pages as seven Miscellaneous pottery groups, each with a letter designation.

The specimens included within each group have certain attributes in common with the others of the group and may, or may not, bear resemblances to establish types. Such resemblances as exist are noted in the comments on the group.

Group A
(Related to the Popes' Creek ware)

The sherds of this group have attributes of paste, color, thickness, interior scoring, and probable vessel shape and size, typical of the pottery type Popes' Creek Net Impressed. The exterior surface treatment of cord-wrapped paddle roughening, however, eliminates them from that type and suggests that they represent a second component type within the Popes' Creek ware. This suggestion is supported by Holmes' material from the Popes' Creek Shell Mound as he mentions (Holmes, 1903, p.154) a small quantity of cord-marked sherds that otherwise resemble the net-impressed pottery from that site. The small quantity of cord-marked sherds from either site, though, is hardly sufficient material upon which to base a pottery type. It is suggested that these sherds be considered a variety of the Popes' Creek ware and if more material of this kind is eventually recovered from other sites, that a Popes' Creek Cord

Marked type may ultimately be established within that ware. It is an Early Woodland pottery.

Sample size.—10 rim sherds and 74 body sherds representing 7 to 10 vessels.

Group B
(Related to the Accokeek ware)

Sherds of this group possess many of the attributes of the type Accokeek Cord Marked but are crudely made, poorly fired, have heterogeneous temper, and thus do not fit into the type as described. Temper is predominantly coarse to fine sand but crushed quartz, other crushed rock, and rounded gravel is also present. Surface treatment, color, thickness, and apparent vessel size and shape are identical to those attributes of the type Accokeek Cord Marked. It may be that these sherds simply represent poorly made vessels of that type but the aberrant temper has been considered of sufficient significance to set them apart as a separate group. This is a Middle Woodland pottery.

Sample size.—21 body sherds, representing 5 to 6 vessels.

Group C
(Related to the Accokeek ware?)

A typical Accokeek ware paste is represented in these sherds but the exterior surface treatment is extremely distinctive. No attempt has been made to weld the coils together over any part of the exterior surface of the vessels (Pl. XX A). Interior surfaces are smooth and coils are carefully welded on the interior but on the exterior each coil retains its unaltered form. The sherds thus have the appearance, except for paste characteristics, of some of the Brown ware pottery (Haury, 1936; Hawley, 1936, p. 105) and the neck-banded culinary vessels of the early pit house periods of the American Southwest (Roberts, 1931, pl. 11 d; Wormington, 1947, fig. 24).

The identity of the paste, vessel form, and other attributes of these sherds, to the Accokeek ware removes any likelihood of these vessels being imports to the Accokeek Creek site but the presence of unwelded coils on obviously carefully finished pots is certainly unusual, if not unknown elsewhere in the eastern United States. This appears to be a Middle Woodland pottery.

Sample size.—4 rim sherds and 4 body sherds representing at least five vessels.

Group D
(A mica-tempered pottery)

The paste of this small group of sherds resembles that of extremely well-made Accokeek Ware in hardness, texture, and other attributes except that there is a high percentage of mica in the temper. The mica flakes are large and abundant giving the sherds a readily distinguishable glitter. Otherwise the sherds resemble the type Accokeek Cord Marked in having cord-wrapped paddle malleated exterior surfaces, smoothed interior surfaces, reddish-black to gray-black color and vessel size and shape appropriate for that type (Pl. XX B, C). This appears to be a Middle Woodland pottery.

Sample size.—4 rim sherds and 16 body sherds representing at least 8 vessels.

Group E
(Related to the Townsend ware)

This small group of sherds is of a shell-tempered pottery resembling the Townsend Ware in many attributes. Specifically the texture, form, color, thickness, and paste resemble the type Rappahannock Fabric Impressed. Exterior surfaces, though, are malleated with a cord-wrapped paddle rather than a fabric and the temper contains some small bits of crushed limestone along with the predominant shell. These sherds appear to be closely related to the Townsend Ware of the Chickahominy Series but on the basis of the small sample from the Accokeek Creek site cannot be considered as a part of either. Additional material from other sites will be needed to clarify their affiliations with certainty. It appears to be a Late Woodland pottery.

Sample size.—4 rim sherds, 15 body sherds, and 2 basal sherds, representing at least 6 vessels.

Group F
(Related to the Potomac Creek ware)

This is a group of miniature vessels of a paste resembling that of the Potomac Creek ware but with little tempering material in most sherds. Some of the vessels appear to be of coiled construction but most are modeled or pressed from small lumps of clay. Some have small amounts of sand or crushed quartz temper but most have no temper at all. Firing was careless and both oxidizing and reducing atmosphere and high

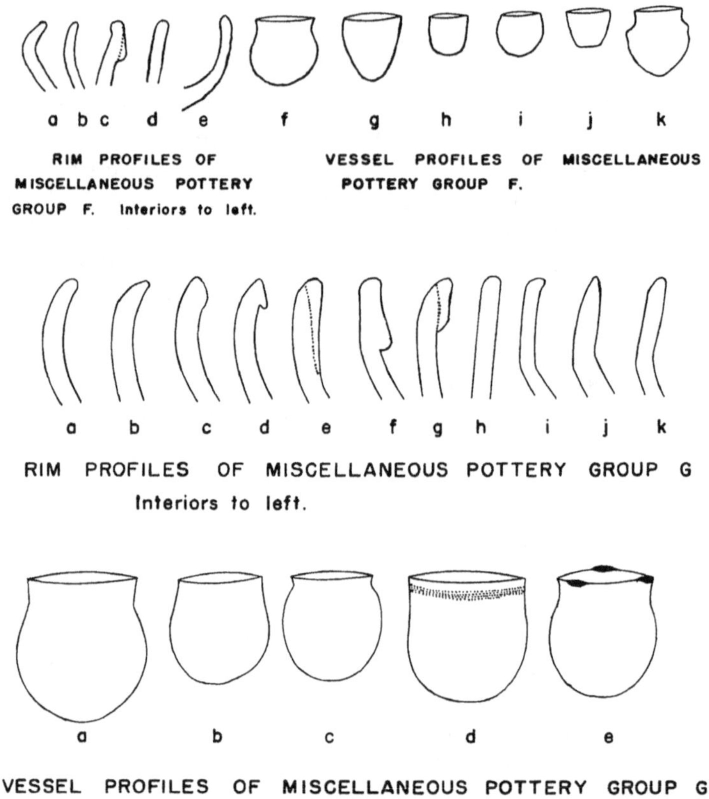

Fig. 28. Profiles of Miscellaneous groups F and G.

and low temperatures are apparent. Sherds range from soft to hard and of medium to fine texture, often tending to feel gritty or, in some cases, clayey. Exterior surfaces are usually poorly smoothed with tool or finger marks showing but some are malleated with a cord-wrapped paddle. Interiors are roughly smoothed. Colors range from tan and buff to brown, orange, or black. Vessels are usually tiny, hemispherical bowls with conical, rounded, or flat bases. A few vessels have everted rims (Fig. 28). The majority are undecorated but 32 per cent have various sorts of cord-impressed or incised decorations in simple patterns around the rim or rarely, over the whole surface (Pl. XX D-F). Vessels range from 20 to 105 mm in diameter and 35 to 105 mm deep.

These miniature vessels appear to have been the products of inexperienced potters, perhaps children, who were experimenting with the ceramic art. The small size, irregular shapes, and haphazard decorations are the kind of things one might expect from children who were trying to imitate the adult potters, as they watched pots being made. As growing children, learning to be participants in the adult culture, they would have been given lumps of clay and shown how to form vessels from them. They would have made just such small, misshapen vessels, gradually acquiring the skill of a mature potter. They also may well have used these experimental pots as playthings. The basic attributes of the vessels of this group are so similar to those of the Potomac Creek ware that there can be little doubt that the group is a part of the Late Woodland complex of Potomac Creek ware ceramics.

Sample size.—49 rim sherds, 107 body sherds, 7 basal sherds, and 14 reconstructed vessel sections representing 55 to 65 vessels.

Group G
(Related to the type Keyser Cord Marked)

This is the largest of the miscellaneous pottery groups and most nearly conforms to known types. These sherds possess attributes of both the types Keyser Cord Marked and Page Cord Marked (Manson, MacCord, and Griffin, 1944, p. 405; Schmitt, n.d., p. 28). Many sherds possess attributes of one or the other of these types and many others combine attributes of both types, while still others combine some of the attributes of those types with attributes of the types Potomac Creek Cord Impressed and Moyaone Cord Marked. None of the sherds can be placed in the latter two types, though, because of temper, but many might well be placed in one or the other of the former two types. They were not so placed, however, because of the generally aberrant nature of the group as a whole and the distinctive combinations of attributes of both types in this group of sherds. This is a Late Woodland pottery.

Description

A coiled pottery with cord-wrapped paddle malleated or smoothed surfaces.

Temper consists of: (*a*) Irregular bits of crushed limestone that are often difficult to distinguish from crushed shell except under microscopic examination. Particles range from tiny flecks to pieces 3 to 4 mm in diameter. (*b*) Large and small bits of crushed, unburned shell. These are sometimes flaky but more often are angular lumps

(Pl. XX G, H, K). (*c*) Combinations of shell and limestone with minor quantitites of crushed quartz or rounded quartz gravels. (*d*) Extremely fine sand as in the Moyaone Ware combined with crushed limestone is found in about 10 per cent of the sherds. In all varieties the temper constitutes but 10 to 25 per cent of the paste.

Plastic is a fine-grained, compact clay.

Hardness is 2.5 to 3.0 in Moh's scale. Medium.

Texture is compact, firm, and quite fine, often with a clayey rather than gritty feel.

Color of the exterior is dark gray to black ranging to light gray, buff, or reddish tan.

Firing temperature is medium to high with oxidizing or reducing atmosphere and smudging on some sherds.

Surface treatment of about half of the sherds is smoothing over cord-wrapped paddle malleating and the other half are cord roughened on the exterior (Pl. XX G-K). Interiors are smoothed.

Vessel form is globular with round bases, constricted necks and flaring rims on 65 per cent of the vessels. Others are cylindrical or hemispherical vessels with rounded or nearly flat bases and straight or slightly everted rims (Fig. 28). Added rim strips are rare but present. One vessel has three rudimentary lugs around the lip that appear as only "swellings" on the lip (Pl. XX J).

Decoration is absent on about 25 per cent of the vessels. Others have vertical or horizontal cord-wrapped dowel impressions about the rim. Several vessels have 2 to 5 horizontal rows of punctations about the rim (Pl. XX G, K). A few have deep heavy cord impressions on the lip.

Vessel size is medium with diameters ranging from 16 to 30 cm and depths of 15 to 25 cm.

The several kinds of temper in this group of sherds seldom correlate with the two kinds of surface treatment nor do these correlate with decorative style or vessel shape.

Sample size.—118 rim sherds, 526 body sherds, 47 basal sherds, and 4 reconstructed vessel sections representing at least 70 to 80 vessels.

TABLE II

TABULATION OF POTTERY BY WARE, TYPE, AND GROUP

Name	Rim Sherds		Body Sherds		Basal Sherds		Vessel Sections	
Marcey Creek ware.		39		186		49		3
Marcey Creek Plain.	39		186		49		3	
Popes' Creek ware.		179		2,078		87		3
Popes' Creek Net Impressed . .	179		2,078		87		3	
Accokeek ware.		1,093		8,223		398		12
Accokeek Cord Marked	1,093		8,223		398		12	
Albermarle ware.		39		685		14		..
Albemarle Cord Marked	28		474		14		..	
Albemarle Net Impressed. . . .	9		160		...		..	
Albemarle Fabric Impressed. . .	2		51		...		..	
Mockley ware		818		6,885		268		8
Mockley Cord Marked.	248		2,278		109		3	
Mockley Net Impressed	531		4,456		132		5	
Mockley Plain	39		151		27		..	
Townsend ware.		89		213		3		3
Rappahannock Fabric Impressed .	12		213		3		2	
Rappahannock Incised.	77		....		...		1	
Potomac Creek ware		4,836		28,904		997		51
Potomac Creek Cord Impressed .	4,672		28,904		997		45	
Potomac Creek Plain.	164		....		...		6	
Moyaone ware		311		710		78		10
Moyaone Cord Impressed	189		710		78		6	
Moyaone Incised	74		....		...		3	
Moyaone Plain	48		....		...		1	
Miscellaneous Groups.		189		763		56		18
A (related to Popes' Creek ware)	10		74		...		..	
B (related to Accokeek ware). . .	....		21		...		..	
C (related to Accokeek ware). . .	4		4		...		..	
D (related to Accokeek ware). . .	4		16		...		..	
E (related to Townsend ware). . .	4		15		2		..	
F (related to Potomac Creek ware)	49		107		7		14	
G (related to Keyser Cord Marked)	118		526		47		4	
Totals	7,593	7,593	48,647	48,647	1,950	1,950	108	108

Grand Total: 58,298 potsherds and 108 restored vessels and vessel sections

POTTERY TOBACCO PIPES

Accokeek Plain

Summary Definition

This is a thick, tubular, pottery pipe made of a paste resembling that from which the Accokeek ware pottery vessels were made. The over-all shape is that of an elongated cone with the bowl occupying the forward half of the cone. Exterior surfaces are uneven, poorly smoothed, and without decoration. Color is dark gray to orange-tan (Pl. XXI, X).

Type Description

Paste.—A coarse textured, compact clay, tempered with crushed quartz and some sand. Firing is poorly controlled and of low temperature. Specimens tend to crumble.

Color.—Exterior and interior colors are the same and range from dark gray-brown to tan and orange-tan.

Size.—Medium large. The only measurable specimen is 11.0 cm long with a maximum diameter of 3.6 cm. Fragments of others appear to have been about the same size.

Bit.—Rounded, thick and tapering, the bits often exhibit chewing marks. Bit diamters are 8 to 15 cm.

Stem.—Short and evenly expanding from bit to bowl. Maximum diameters are 2.1 to 2.9 cm. Lengths are 4.5 to 6.2 cm. Bores are 3 to 6 mm.

Elbow.—None.

Bowl.—The bowl is large and comprises about half the length of the pipe. It is conical with a rounded bottom on the interior and is but an extension of the stem on the exterior. Bowl diameter is 3.6 cm and depth is 5.2 cm.

Decoration.—None. Exterior surfaces are poorly smoothed and uneven.

Sample size.—10 fragmentary and 1 nearly complete specimens.

Variant

A single specimen of a variant of this type of pottery pipe resembles the Accokeek Plain specimens in all respects except that the stem is flattened to form an oval cross section (the bowl is missing) and the exterior surface is covered with large, punctate impressions made by a hollow tube such as a reed or a bird bone. The fragment is 5.1 cm long, 2.6 cm wide, and 1.8 cm thick. The bore is 6 mm in diameter (Pl. XXII, H).

Potomac Creek Cord Impressed

Summary Definition

This is an obtuse-angled, short-stemmed, pottery elbow pipe of fine-textured, untempered clay. The paste, except for apparent lack of temper, resembles that from which the Potomac Creek ware pottery vessels were made. The conical bowl expands evenly from its juncture with the stem and the elbow and forms an angle of large degree. The bit is round and contracting. Color is gray to orange-tan. The bowl and elbow are elaborately decorated with extremely fine, cord-wrapped tool impressions in zoned designs (Pl. XXI, A-U).

Type Description

Paste.—A fine-textured, compact clay plastic without temper but sometimes containing some very fine sand and minute flecks of mica that appear to be unintentional inclusions within the clay.

Color.—Exteriors range from dark gray through buff and tan to orange-buff. The interior is black and the core is usually the same as the exterior or slightly darker.

Size.—Over-all length ranges from 6 to 9 cm (Pl. XXI, C).

Bit.—The bit is smaller than the stem, rounded or square at the end and usually chewed from use. Bit diameters are 6 to 8 mm.

Stem.—The stem is usually round in cross section, but 17 per cent are flattened on the top, on the top and 2 sides, or on all 4 sides. The stem expands evenly from bit to elbow. Diameters at the midpoint of the stem are 9 to 15 mm. Stem lengths are 3.5 to 5.1 cm. Bore diameters are 4 to 5 mm.

Elbow.—The bowl forms an obtuse angle from the top of the stem, usually of 160 to 185 degrees. One specimen is but 125 degrees.

Bowl.—The bowl interior is usually conical with vertical striations on the walls. A few specimens have flat-bottomed bowl interiors. Exteriors expand evenly from the elbow to the rim, sometimes with a slight constriction at the rim. Two bowls have a slight, vertical, shoulder expansion at the base. Bowl lips are rounded or flattened. Bowl height is 2.1 to 3.1 cm. Maximum bowl diameters are 1.5 to 2.1 cm.

Decoration.—Designs are applied on the bowl and elbow areas of the pipes, sometimes extending part way down the stem (Pl. XXI, H). These are cord-wrapped tool impressions, very delicately and carefully applied (Pl. XXI, A-U). The designs are so delicately made that they are difficult to distinguish from incising or dentate stamping except with a microscope or use of plasticine impressions. Experiments with plasticine and various tools and materials have demonstrated that such designs could have been (and probably were) applied by tightly wrapping a fine fibrous thread (about 40 or 50 gauge) or a very fine, twisted sinew, about a sharp tool edge, such as a thin stone flake, or a mussel shell, and lightly impressing the sharp edge of this cord-wrapped tool into the plastic clay. No dowel or stick could be made that would be small enough to produce so fine a design.

Design elements consist principally of bands of diagonal impressions encircling the pipe and separated by smooth areas of equal size. There are also series of triangles and some spiral bands of diagonal or vertical impressions that encircle the pipe several times. The diagonal impressions are usually bordered by a single, vertical impression. Undecorated areas are carefully smoothed.

Sample size.—5 nearly whole pipes; 123 fragmentary sections of bowls, or bowls and stems, and 142 stem sections.

Variant A (Tubular)

A group of 3 specimens resemble the type Potomac Creek Cord Impressed in all respects except that they are tubular rather than elbow pipes and are decorated from bit to bowl lip. The decoration is a series of filled triangles made by fine, cord-wrapped tool impressions. The pipes expand evenly from bit to bowl lip; are 5.0 to 6.3 cm long; have bowl diameters of 1.8 to 1.9 cm; and bowl depths of 1.2 to 2.2 cm (Pl. XXII, I, K, L).

Variant B (Flattened, decorated bits)

Fragments of 8 pipe bits resemble the type Potomac Creek Cord Impressed in all respects except that the bits are flattened and decorated, and have oval or diamond-shaped cross sections. Decoration consists of triangles of parallel lines of fine, cord-wrapped tool impressions and one specimen combines circular punctations with this. Maximum bit widths are 14 to 28 mm and thicknesses are 7 to 14 mm (Pl. XXII, J).

Variant C (Punctated)

Stem and elbow sections of 2 pipes resemble the type Potomac Creek Cord Impressed in all respects except that the stems are unusually long and decoration is applied by punctation. In one, the stem is more than 8 cm long (it is broken and may have been 2 to 6 cm longer) and an encircling band of six rows of tiny, triangular punctations, spirals around the stem elbow and bowl. The stem is round in cross section and the elbow angle is 135 degrees (Pl. XXII, N). The second has a wide stem, round on the bottom with flattened top and planoconvex cross section. It is more than 9 cm long (broken), has an elbow angle of 155 degrees, and is decorated with diagonal lines of tiny triangular punctations around the bowl.

Variant D (Bird effigy)

This is a single specimen of a bird effigy pipe made from the same paste and decorated with the same technique as the pipes of the type Potomac Creek Cord Impressed (Pl. XXII, M). A part of the stem (the bird's tail) is broken. The bowl extends upward from the center of the bird's back and is 2.1 cm in diameter and 3.2 cm deep. The elbow is nearly a right angle (95 degrees). The bird's head extends forward of the bowl 3.2 cm. The sides of the bird's body, at the base of the bowl, extend latterally representing the position of the wings closed and the width of the pipe at this point is 3.7 cm. The head is decorated with an incised eye and mouth and is quite rounded with a short, stubby beak. Three bands of cord-wrapped tool impressions encircle the bowl with smoothed areas between. A similar band of decoration encircles the head and similar decoration covers the body of the bird. Total height of the specimen is 4.8 cm, and it is 3.7 cm wide and 6.4 cm long. The latter dimension includes 1.2 cm. of stem (the bird's broken tail) but may have originally been 2 or 3 cm longer.

Potomac Creek Plain

Summary Definition

This is an obtuse-angled, short-stemmed, pottery, elbow pipe of fine-textured, untempered clay. The conical bowl expands evenly from the stem and the elbow forms an angle of large degree. Color is gray to orange-tan and surfaces are smooth and undecorated (Pl. XXI, V-W).

Type Description

Paste.—Same as Potomac Creek Cord Impressed.
Color.—Same as Potomac Creek Cord Impressed.
Size.—Same as Potomac Creek Cord Impressed.
Bit.—Same as Potomac Creek Cord Impressed.
Stem.—Same as Potomac Creek Cord Impressed.
Elbow.—Same as Potomac Creek Cord Impressed, except for a single specimen with a "heel" at the external point of the angle of the elbow. This "heel" is 8 mm long, 8 mm in diameter, and rounded at the end.
Bowl.—Same as Potomac Creek Cord Impressed.
Decoration.—None. Smoothed on all surfaces.
Sample Size.—2 nearly complete specimens and 33 fragments.

Variant A (Tubular)

Three complete specimens and fragments of 2 others resemble the type Potomac Creek Plain in all respects except that they are tubular instead of elbow pipes. Four of the specimens are more crudely made than the usual Potomac Creek Plain pipes and have a slight "swelling" around the lips of the bowl. They are 5.5 to 7.9 cm long with maximum diameters of 2.0 to 2.7 cm. Bowl depths are 2.2 to 2.4 cm (Pl. XXII, D-G).

Variant B (Grooved)

A stem and two bowl specimens resemble the Potomac Creek Plain type except that wide, deep, incised, U-shaped grooves encircle all stem and bowl areas, over plain, smoothed surfaces. Bowl diameter is 2.0 cm and they are 2.8 cm deep. The bore is 5 mm in diameter but the elbow angle is unknown.

Variant C (Incised)

A bowl-elbow section and a section of stem resemble the Potomac Creek Plain type except that they are incised over a plain, smooth surface. The stem section is flattened on top and has 5 longitudinal incised lines on it. The bowl-elbow section has 2 figures incised on opposite sides of the bowl. Incising is by a fine, sharp instrument and the 2 figures are nearly identical, representing quadrupeds with long, erect necks.

Potomac Creek Broad Bit

Summary Definition

This is an obtuse-angled, short-stemmed, pottery elbow pipe of fine-textured, untempered clay. The conical bowl expands evenly from the stem and the elbow forms an angle of large degree. Color is gray to tan. The bowl, elbow, and usually the stem and bit, are elaborately decorated with extremely fine, cord-wrapped tool impressions in zoned designs. The bit is tabular, broad, and larger than the stem (Pl. XXI, Y-I').

Type Description

Paste.—Same as Potomac Creek Cord Impressed.
Color.—Same as Potomac Creek Cord Impressed.
Size.—Over-all length is 7 to 11 cm.
Bit.—Bits are tabular, flat expansions from the end of the stem with lenticular cross section and flat or convex end. Outline shape is trapezoidal 10 to 23 mm long, 7 to 16 mm wide, and 6 to 8 mm thick. The juncture of bit and stem forms square shoulders 2 to 3 mm greater in width than the stem. A few specimens are almost circular, rather than lenticular, in cross-section.
Stem.—Same as Potomac Creek Cord Impressed.
Elbow.—Same as Potomac Creek Cord Impressed.
Bowl.—Same as Potomac Creek Cord Impressed.
Decoration.—Same as Potomac Creek Cord Impressed except that they are frequently decorated over the full length of the stem and bit.
Sample size.—1 nearly complete and 41 fragmentary specimens.

Susquehannock Plain

Summary Definition

This is a right-angled, long-stemmed, pottery elbow pipe of fine-textured, untempered clay. The conical bowl expands evenly from the stem upon the upturned end of which it sits. The elbow is a long, even curve of 90 degrees, well back from the juncture of stem and bowl. The bit is round and of the same diameter as the stem. The bore is large. Color is gray to orange-buff. Surfaces are smoothed and undecorated (Pl. XXII, A-C).

Type Description

Paste.—Same as Potomac Creek Cord Impressed.
Color.—Same as Potomac Creek Cord Impressed.
Size.—Over-all length of the only complete specimen is 18.7 cm.
Bit.—An undifferentiated continuation of the stem with a square-cut end. Often chewed.
Stem.—The stem is cylindrical and of even diameter from bit to bowl, ranging from 12 to 16 mm in diameter and 10.6 cm long. The bore is 4 to 6 mm in diameter.
Elbow.—The elbow is a continuation of the stem in a smooth, even curve from the horizontal to the vertical forming a 90 degree angle. The stem thus enters the bowl at the bottom rather than at the side.
Bowl.—The bowl interior is conical and deep with the opening in the bottom. Bowl exteriors expand evenly from stem to lip or have a slight constriction at the juncture of bowl and stem. Rims are slightly constricted and lips are flat. Bowl height is 3.8 to 4.3 cm with diameters of 2.3 to 2.4 cm.
Decoration.—None. Smoothed over all surfaces.
Sample size.—1 complete specimen and 36 fragmentary specimens.

OTHER POTTERY OBJECTS

There are 27 miscellaneous objects of pottery in the collections from the Accokeek Creek Site. Four of these are semi-conical objects 2 to 4 cm long and 1 to 2 cm in diameter having rounded ends and no perforations. The large end of each is broken and, in one specimen, appears to be partly hollowed out. Perhaps these were legs for a "footed" vessel or fragments of figurines. More likely they were some sort of gaming pieces.

There are seven perforated beads in the collections. One is a spherical specimen 2 cm in diameter with two small perforations. Two are of similar size and shape but have only one perforation each. Two are tubular beads, 2.5 cm long and 0.6 cm in diameter with polished ends. One specimen appears to be a small, rectangular, perforated lug from a pottery vessel with a portion of the vessel rim remaining. The seventh specimen is a flat, circular object with two longitudinal perforations parallel to the flat sides. All are of untempered, fine-textured clay resembling the Moyaone ware.

A single, small lump of clay of Popes' Creek ware paste is

TABLE III

TABULATION OF POTTERY TOBACCO PIPES

Name	Whole or Nearly Whole	Bowl Frag- ments	Stem Frag- ments	Total
Accokeek Plain	1	10	. . .	11
Varient A (punctate)	. .	. . .	1	1
Potomac Creek Cord Impressed .	5	123	142	270
Variant A (tubular)	3	. . .	. . .	3
Variant B (flattened bits). . . .	. .	. . .	8	8
Variant C (punctate)	. .	. . .	2	2
Variant D (effigy)	1	. . .	. . .	1
Potomac Creek Plain.	2	20	13	35
Variant A (tubular)	3	2	. . .	5
Variant B (grooved)	. .	2	1	3
Variant C (incised)	. .	1	1	2
Potomac Creek Broad Bit	1	. . .	41	42
Susquehannock Plain	1	8	28	37
Totals	17	166	237	420

5.5 cm long and 3 cm in diameter, with what appear to be finger marks on its long axis. Apparently this was a piece of clay left over from pottery-making, squeezed in the fist and thrown into the fire.

Nine pieces of fine-textured, fired clay, buff in color and apparently representing irregular, assymetrical fragments of miniature vessels are present. They are quite thick, 6 to 11 mm, and of but 2 to 4 cm in length and breadth.

Two small "pinches" of clay suggest bits of pottery material that had been pinched between the fingers and discarded in the fire.

A single flat object, oval in outline with a notch in each end measures 1.8 cm wide, 0.7 cm thick and of unknown length, is of unknown use.

Two clay discs appear to be very small spindle-whorls. About one-third of each specimen is present. They are plano-convex in cross section, 2 to 3 cm in diameter and 8 to 11 mm thick. They are perforated with bores of 3 to 9 mm diameter.

These might be beads, but the larger one, at least, has characteristics of a spindle-whorl.

One object made of Accokeek ware paste may be an ornament, toy, or gaming device. It is biconical with a large, central ridge encircling the maximum diameter and a tiny pinhole perforation through the longitudinal dimension. It is 3.7 cm in length, and the central, encircling ridge is 1.7 cm in diameter and 0.6 cm wide. The object can be spun like a top when snapped between the thumb and fingers and may have served as a toy top or as a gaming device.

PROJECTILE POINTS

Steubenville Stemmed Point

Summary Definition

This is a typically large, wide, moderately thin projectile point with very rudimentary shoulders; a wide, straight stem; and straight or concave base. It is moderately well made, by percussion chipping, from dark gray argillite or slate. The blade has convex edges and is usually about three-fourths as wide as it is long. The stem is almost as wide as the blade (Pl. XXIII, P-V).

Type Description

Method of manufacture.—Moderately well made by percussion chipping on all surfaces. Basal thinning is usual but without fluting or edge grinding.

Material.—Dark gray argillite or gray slate is usual but occasional specimens are made from chert, flint, quartzite, or quartz.

Form.—(*a*) blade edges are usually convex from shoulder to tip but occasional ones are nearly parallel from shoulder to midpoint and taper evenly from midpoint to tip. The tip is usually blunt but a few are pointed; (*b*) the stem is nearly as wide as the blade, usually with parallel edges but some specimens have slightly concave edges or are slightly contracted toward the base. Shoulders are barely perceptible. The stem constitutes 30 to 40 per cent of the total length of the specimen; (*c*) The base is typically straight or slightly concave and is usually thinned.

Size.—Large and wide. Lengths range from 40 to 70 mm with

a mean of 58 mm. Widths range from 24 to 40 mm with a mean of 32 mm. Thicknesses range from 8 to 12 mm with a mean of 10 mm. Weights range from 10 to 26 grams with a mean of 17 grams.

Sample.--There are 88 whole, or nearly whole, specimens from the Accokeek Creek site.

Steubenville Lanceolate Point

Summary Definition

This is typically a large, wide, moderately thin projectile point of lanceolate form and straight or concave base. It is moderately well made, by percussion chipping, from dark gray argillite or slate. Edges are usually parallel from base to midpoint and taper evenly from midpoint to tip (Pl. XXIII, W-Z).

Type Description

Method of manufacture.—Same as for Steubenville Stemmed.

Material.—Same as for Steubenville Stemmed.

Form.—Lanceolate. Edges are usually parallel from base to midpoint and taper evenly from midpoint to tip, but in a few specimens the edges are slightly convex from base to tip. The tip is usually blunt but a few are pointed. The base is typically straight or slightly convex and is usually thinned. General form resembles the type Steubenville Stemmed but is narrower in relation to length and has no shoulders.

Size.--Large and wide. Lengths range from 50 to 80+ mm with a mean of 69 mm. Widths range from 22 to 30 mm with a mean of 28 mm. Thicknesses range from 7 to 13 mm with a mean of 9 mm. Weights range from 10 to 25 grams with a mean of 16 grams.

Sample.—There are 28 whole or nearly whole specimens from the Accokeek Creek site.

Bare Island Point

Summary Definition

This is typically a long, slender, thick, projectile point with rudimentary shoulders, parallel-sided or slightly contracting stem and rounded or straight base. It is moderately well made by percussion chipping, from quartzite or rarely quartz or shale (Pl. XXIII, G-O).

Type Description

Method of manufacture.—Moderately well made by percussion chipping.

Material.—Typically these are made from gray, red, or brown quartzite, rarely from opaque white quartz or black shale.

Form.—(*a*) The blade is typically an elongate triangle with straight or slightly convex edges, a sharp tip, and thick lenticular cross section. Slight beveling occurs on some blades. Abrupt, though slight, shoulders separate the blade and stem; (*b*) the stem is straight or slightly contracting, thinner than the blade and wider than it is long. The base comprises 10 to 15 per cent of the total length of the specimen; (*c*) the base is straight or slightly rounded but a few specimens have a slightly concave base.

Size.—Long and slender. Lengths range from 45 to 83 mm with a mean of 69 mm. Widths range from 16 to 30 mm with a mean of 21 mm. Thicknesses range from 8 to 15 mm with a mean of 12 mm. Weights range from 8 to 24 grams with a mean of 14 grams.

Sample.—There are 269 whole or nearly whole specimens from the Accokeek Creek site.

Clagett Point

Summary Definition

This is typically a long, slender, thick, projectile point with pronounced shoulders, constricted stem and expanded, straight, or concave base. It is well made by percussion chipping, from quartzite or rarely, quartz or argillite (Pl. XXIV, W-D').

Type Description

Method of manufacture.—Moderately well made by percussion chipping.

Material.—Typically, these are made from gray, red, or brown quartzite, but some specimens are made from argillite or opaque white quartz.

Form.—(*a*) the blade is typically an elongate triangle with straight or slightly convex edges, a sharp tip, and thick, lenticular cross section. Slight beveling occurs on some blades. Abrupt, prominent shoulders separate the blade from the stem; (*b*) the stem constricts sharply from the shoulders to the midpoint of the stem and expands sharply to a wide base. The stem is thinner than the blade but the "neck" constriction gives it an oval cross section. The stem is wider than it is long and comprises 15 to 20 per cent of the total length of the specimen; (*c*) the base is straight or slightly concave and a few are slightly convex.

Size.—Long and slender. Lengths range from 43 to 89 mm with a mean of 65 mm. Widths range from 15 to 29 mm with a mean of 22 mm. Thicknesses range from 6 to 13 mm with a mean of 10 mm. Weights range from 8 to 23 grams with a mean of 14 grams.

Sample.—There are 236 whole or nearly whole specimens from the Accokeek Creek site.

Calvert Point

Summary Definition

This is typically a short, thick, wide, projectile point with rudimentary shoulders, parallel-sided or contracting stem, and straight or slightly rounded base. It is moderately well made, by percussion chipping and pressure flaking, from white quartz (Pl. XXIV, K-V).

Type Description

Method of manufacture.—Moderately well made by percussion chipping with some pressure flaking around the edges and, rarely, over all surfaces.

Material.—Typically these are made from opaque white quartz but many are of clear or rose quartz. Some 10 per cent of the specimens are of brown, red, or gray quartzite and a few specimens are of gray shale, gray flint, or argillite.

Form.—(*a*) the blade is a short, thick, stubby triangle, with convex edges a sharp tip, and thick, irregular cross section. Abrupt, though slight, shoulders separate the blade and the stem; (*b*) the stem is straight or slightly contracting, thinner than the blade and usually wider than it is long though in some specimens width and length are about equal. The contracting stem specimens made up but 20 per cent of the specimens and these intergrade from moderately contracting to almost straight. The stem comprises 32 to 45 per cent of the total length of the specimen; (*c*) the base is usually straight, often convex, especially in the contracting stem examples.

Size.—Medium and stubby. Lengths range from 25 to 48 mm with a mean of 36 mm. Widths range from 18 to 27 mm with a mean of 22 mm. Thicknesses range from 8 to 13 mm with a mean of 10 mm. Weights range from 5 to 15 grams with a mean of 9 grams.

Sample.--There are 538 whole or nearly whole specimens from the Accokeek Creek site.

Vernon Point

Summary Definition

This is typically a short, thick, wide projectile point with pronounced shoulders, constricted stem, and expanded, straight base. It is crudely to moderately well made, by percussion chipping and pressure flaking, from white quartz and red, brown, or tan quartzite (Pl. XXIV, A-J).

Type Description

Method of manufacture.—Crudely to moderately well made by percussion chipping and usually finished by pressure flaking along the edges or occasionally over all surfaces.

Material.—Typically these are made of white quartz, though some 25 per cent are of red, brown, or tan quartzite and a few specimens are of gray or black shale, gray flint and black argillite.

Form.—(*a*) the blade is typically a short, thick, stubby triangle with convex edges, usually a sharp tip, and thick, irregular cross section. The base of the blade forms abrupt, prominent shoulders at the junction with the stem; (*b*) the stem constricts sharply from the shoulders to the midpoint of the stem and expands to a wide base. The stem is slightly thinner than the blade but the "neck" constriction gives it an oval cross section. The stem constitutes 30 to 40 per cent of the total length of the specimen; (*c*) the base is usually straight but some specimens have slightly convex or slightly concave bases.

Size.—Medium and stubby. Lengths range from 24-49 mm with a mean of 37 mm. Widths range from 16 to 30 mm with a mean of 23 mm. Thicknesses range from 6 to 13 mm with a mean of 10 mm. Weights range from 5 to 12 grams with a mean of 8 grams.

Sample.—There are 423 whole or nearly whole specimens.

Rossville Point

Summary Definition

This is typically a medium sized, thin, well-made projectile point with prominent shoulders, contracting stem and pointed or rounded base. It is made from quartzite or quartz by pressure flaking (Pl. XXIII, A-F).

Type Description

Method of manufacture.—Well made by pressure flaking on all surfaces.

Material.—Red or brown quartzite is typical but some 30 per cent of the specimens are of white quartz with occasional specimens of tan flint, black flint, shale, and chert.

Form.—(*a*) Blade edges are typically convex to straight with a sharp tip. The base of the blade forms sloping, prominent shoulders at the juncture with the stem and is 25 to 30 per cent wider than the stem. The blade has a lenticular cross-section; (*b*) the stem contracts toward the base with straight or convex edges; (*c*) the base is pointed or rounded.

Size.—Medium. Lengths range from 24 to 58 mm with a mean of 40 mm. Widths range from 17 to 30 mm with a mean of 21 mm. Thicknesses range from 6 to 9 mm with a mean of 7 mm. Weights range from 4 to 9 grams with a mean of 7 grams.

Sample.—There are 29 whole or nearly whole specimens from the Accokeek Creek site.

Potomac Point

Summary Definition

This is typically a small, thin, triangular projectile point without notches or stem. It is carefully made from white quartz by pressure flaking. The blade edges are usually straight and the base is either straight or concave (Pl. XXVI, L-W).

Type Description

Method of manufacture.—Very well made by pressure flaking on all surfaces.

Material.—Opaque or translucent, white quartz is typical but 9 per cent of the specimens are brown quartzite, brown flint, black slate, or argillite and are less well made than are the quartz specimens.

Form.—The blade is typically a nearly equilateral triangle with straight edges, sharp tip, and a thin, lenticular cross section. Edges of 12 per cent of the specimens are slightly concave or slightly convex and 21 per cent are longer than they are wide. There is no stem. The base of 50 per cent of the specimens is concave, often being extremely concave. The other 50 per cent of the specimens have straight bases.

Size.—Small. Equilateral specimens range from 16 to 26 mm in length and width and are 3 to 7 mm thick with a mean of 21 mm by 21 mm by 4 mm. Longer specimens are 20 to 36 mm long, 15 to 25 mm wide, and 5 to 8 mm thick with means of 24 mm by 17 mm by 4 mm. Weights range from 1 to 5 grams with a mean of 2 grams.

Sample.—There are 536 whole or nearly whole specimens from the Accokeek Creek site.

Piscataway Points

Summary Definition

This is typically a small, narrow, thick, projectile point with rudimentary shoulders, sharp tip, contracting stem, and pointed or rounded base. It is well made by pressure flaking from white quartz (Pl. XXVI, X-E').

Type Description

Method of manufacture.—Well made by pressure flaking on all surfaces.

Material.—Opaque or translucent white quartz is typical but rare specimens are made from brown quartzite or black ryolite.

Form.—(*a*) The blade is typically a long, slender, triangle, with straight or convex edges and thick, lenticular, cross section. In 18 per cent of the specimens the blade is beveled; (*b*) the stem is small and contracting with an almost imperceptible shoulder separating it from the blade. The stem is oval or triangular in outline, and oval in cross section, and constitutes 20 to 25 per cent of the total length of the specimen; (*c*) the base is rounded or pointed.

Size.—Small. Lengths range from 29 to 49 mm with a mean

of 37 mm. Widths range from 10 to 21 mm with a mean of 14 mm. Thicknesses range from 5 to 10 mm with a mean of 7 mm. Weights range from 2 to 5 grams with a mean of 3 grams.

Sample.—There are 301 whole or nearly whole specimens from the Accokeek Creek site.

Miscellaneous Projectile Point Groups

There are 401 projectile points in the collection that, for one reason or another, do not fit into the formalized types described above. These have been grouped as follows:

Group A.—Large, thin, lanceolate blades—19 specimens. These are all fragmentary, basal sections of large, thin blades without stems. The bases are straight or slightly concave. Blade edges are parallel or gently expanding from base to midpoint and then taper toward the tip. Cross sections are lenticular and very thin. No edge or basal grinding is present. Lengths can only be estimated as no specimen is whole, but probably range from 80 to 150 mm. Widths range from 30 to 70 mm with a mean of 41 mm. Thicknesses range from 7 to 12 mm with a mean of 9 mm. They are moderately well made by percussion chipping from argillite or slate, and one specimen is of chert (Pl. XXV, A-B).

These specimens resemble the type Stuebenville Lanceolate in outline form, material, and technique of manufacture but are thinner and several times as large. They probably served as lance or spear points or perhaps as knives.

Group B.—Large, contracting stem blades—56 specimens. These are broad, thin, long points with pronounced, sloping shoulders, contracting stem, and pointed or rounded base. Blade edges are straight or slightly convex. The cross section is lenticular. They are moderately well made from gray or brown quartzite, or, rarely, from tan chert or gray shale, by percussion chipping. Lengths range from 68 to 128 mm with a mean of 85 mm. Widths range from 30 to 60 mm with a mean of 45 mm. Thicknesses range from 6 to 15 mm with a mean of 10 mm. Weights range from 10 to 67 grams with a mean of 33 grams (Pl. XXV, C-G).

In outline form, material, and technique of manufacture they resemble the Rossville Point type but the specimens are several times as large. They probably served as lance or spear points though some of the smaller ones may have been dart points.

Group C.—Large, straight stem blades—53 specimens. These are long, thin, narrow blades with small, straight shoulders, parallel sided, rectangular stem, and concave base. The blade is two to three times as long as it is wide and has straight to convex edges and sharp tip. Cross section is lenticular. Specimens are moderately well made, by percussion chipping, from gray or brown quartzite or, rarely, chert. Lengths range from 71 to 142 mm with a mean of 96 mm. Widths range from 25 to 60 mm with a mean of 35 mm. Thicknesses range from 7 to 14 mm with a mean of 10 mm. Weights range from 19 to 45 grams with a mean of 25 grams (Pl. XXV, H-J).

This group resembles the Bare Island Point type in general outline, material, and technique of manufacture but specimens are several times larger and the consistently concave base is not typical of the Bare Island Point. They probably served as lance or spear points or possibly as knives, though some of the smaller examples might have been used on darts.

Group D.—Large, thick, lanceolate blades—9 specimens. These are stemless, narrow specimens, with straight or convex bases. The edges expand from the base to midpoint or less and then taper to a somewhat blunt point. Cross sections are diamond-shaped to thick lenticular. They are moderately well made by percussion chipping from red or brown quartzite. Lengths range from 67 to 97 mm. Widths range from 23 to 34 mm. Thicknesses range from 11 to 15 mm. Weights range from 21 to 36 grams (Pl. XXV, K). Except for being stemless, these bear no relationship in form or in material to the specimens of Group A. Instead they resemble in proportions, material, and general style the specimens of Group C, except for the lack of stems, and have the appearance of being a part of the series to which Group B, Group C, the Bare Island Point type, and the Clagett Point type all belong.

Group E.—Small, thick, lanceolate blades—58 specimens. These are identical, in all respects except size and material, to the larger specimens of Group D. They are made from opaque or translucent white quartz with but five specimens made from gray argillite or brown quartzite. Lengths range from 45 to 65 mm with a mean of 51 mm. Widths range from 21 to 27 mm with a mean of 24 mm. Thicknesses range from 8 to 12 mm with a mean of 10 mm. The largest specimens of this group are slightly smaller than the smallest of Group D (Pl. XXV, L).

Group F.—Large, triangular points—71 specimens. This is a group of large, thin, elongate, or equilateral triangular points with straight, slightly convex, or slightly concave edges, straight or concave base, sharp tip, and thin, lenticular cross section. They are well made by pressure flaking from opaque or translucent white quartz, but a small minority are made from black or brown chert, tan quartzite, or greenish-gray flint. Lengths range from 31 to 57 mm with a mean of 40 mm. Widths range from 23 to 43 mm with a mean of 32 mm. Thicknesses range from 5 to 11 mm with a mean of 8 mm. Weights range from 6 to 14 grams with a mean of 9 grams (Pl. XXV, M-O).

These specimens, except for size, are identical to the type Potomac Point, but there is no intergradation between the two. The largest of the latter are approximately half the size of the smallest of the Group F specimens.

Group G.—Small, elongate triangular points—28 specimens. In general, these specimens combine the elements of the triangular and the lanceolate categories. They have a straight, thinned base but the blade edges tend to be almost parallel for about one third the distance to the tip and then converge to a sharp tip. The general appearance, though, is more triangular than pentagonal. Most examples are very thin and well made and are approximately three times as long as they are wide. Four of the stubbier specimens, made from white quartz, however, are quite thick, and crudely made. The others are moderately well made, by percussion chipping and pressure flaking along the edges, from opaque or translucent quartz or, rarely, gray chert, tan quartzite, or black flint. Lengths range from 31 to 60 mm with a mean of 46 mm. Widths range from 16 to 23 mm with a mean of 20 mm. Thicknesses range from 5 to 12 mm with a mean of 7 mm (Pl. XXVI, A-C).

In general form, size, and material these resemble

the Potomac Point type but are slightly larger and much longer in proportion to width.

Group H.—Large, side-notched points—9 specimens. Moderately well made by percussion chipping from quartzite, chert, or flint, these specimens have thinned, straight or concave, broad bases. Stems have constricted edges giving a "fishtail" appearance. Shoulders are sloping but pronounced, and blades are broad, short, straight-sided triangles with sharp tips. Lengths range from 45 to 72 mm. Widths range from 27 to 38 mm. Thicknesses range from 8 to 12 mm. These specimens resemble no others in the site and are presumably of "outside" origin (Pl. XXVI, D).

Group I.—Notched base points—10 specimens. Thick, stubby, quartz points with triangular blades; knobby, small shoulders; straight or expanding stems, and deeply concave or notched bases; these are 32 to 43 mm long, 20 to 28 mm wide, and 7 to 11 mm thick (Pl. XXVI, E).

Group J.—Broad-based, side-notched points—11 specimens. Locally referred to as "periwinkle" points, these have serrated edges of varying degree along the blade; crude, side notches and pronounced lateral expansion of the base. They are crudely made of quartz or chert and are 32 to 44 mm long, 18 to 24 mm wide, and 5 to 11 mm thick (Pl. XXVI, F).

Group K.—Large, straight-stemmed points—14 specimens. These have broad blades with straight or convex edges, straight shoulders, rectangular stems and straight bases. They are moderately well made from opaque, white quartz, brown quartzite, or gray or black flint. They are 48 to 72 mm long, 28 to 40 mm wide, and 8 to 14 mm thick (Pl. XXVI, G).

Group L.—Broad, barbed points—5 specimens. Well made by percussion chipping from gray flint, white quartz, and brown quartzite, these are as wide as they are long, are thin with straight base, rectangular stem, and reversed shoulders that form pronounced barbs. The blades are short and broad. They are 36 to 41 mm long, 29 to 40 mm wide, and 7 to 9 mm thick (Pl. XXVI, H).

Group M.—Side-notched, serrated points—16 specimens. These are well-made, straight-based, broad-stemmed points of triangular form with the stem made by a deep, narrow side notch on each edge of the blade. Fine serrations occur along the entire blade edges. They are pressure

TABLE IV

TABLE OF PROJECTILE POINT WEIGHTS AND MEASURES

Type or Group	No.	Per cent	Length (In mm.)			Width (In mm.)			Thickness (In mm)			Weight (In grams)		
			Min.	Max.	Mean	Min.	Max.	Mean	Min.	Max.	Mean	Min.	Max.	Mean
Steubenville Lanceolate	28	1.0	50	80	69	22	30	28	7	13	9	10	25	16
Steubenville Stemmed	88	3.1	40	70	58	24	40	32	8	12	10	10	26	17
Clagett Point	236	8.2	43	39	65	15	29	22	6	13	10	8	23	14
Bare Island Point	269	9.4	45	83	69	16	30	21	8	15	12	8	24	14
Rossville Point	29	1.0	24	58	40	17	30	21	6	9	7	4	9	7
Calvert Point	538	19.0	25	48	36	18	27	22	8	13	10	5	15	9
Vernon Point	423	14.6	24	49	37	16	30	23	6	13	10	5	12	8
Potomac Point	536	19.0	16	26	21	15	25	21	3	8	4	1	5	2
Piscataway Point	301	10.6	29	49	37	10	21	14	5	10	7	2	6	3
Group A	19	0.6	80	150	?	30	70	41	7	12	9	?	?	?
Group B	56	2.0	68	128	85	30	60	45	6	15	10	10	67	33
Group C	53	1.8	71	142	96	25	60	35	7	14	10	19	45	25
Group D	9	0.3	67	97	..	23	24	..	11	15	..	21	36	..
Group E	58	2.0	45	65	51	21	27	24	8	12	10	..	..	..
Group F	71	2.5	31	57	40	23	43	32	5	11	8	6	14	9
Group G	27	1.0	31	60	46	16	23	20	5	12	7	..	..	..
Group H	9	0.3	45	72	..	27	38	..	8	12	..	..	..	..
Group I	10	0.3	32	43	..	20	28	..	7	11	..	..	..	..
Group J	11	0.4	32	44	..	18	24	..	5	11	..	..	..	..
Group K	14	0.5	48	72	..	28	40	..	8	14	..	..	..	..
Group L	5	0.2	36	41	..	29	40	..	7	9	..	..	..	..
Group M	16	0.6	34	49	..	19	24	..	6	9	..	..	..	..
Group N	10	0.3	45	55	..	21	30	..	6	10	..	..	..	..
Group O	32	1.1	22	40	..	13	21	..	5	10	..	..	..	..
Total	2,849	100.0												

flaked from brown or tan flint, various cherts, gray shale, tan quartzite, and quartz. They are 34 to 49 mm long, 19 to 24 mm wide, and 6 to 9 mm thick (Pl. XXVI, I).

Group N.—Broad-stemmed, corner-notched points, 10 specimens. Well made by pressure flaking, this heterogeneous group has rectangular stems, pronounced shoulders, or small barbs, deep corner notches and convex-edged blades. They are made from quartzite, flint, or chert and are 45 to 55 mm long, 21 to 30 mm wide, and 6 to 10 mm thick (Pl. XXVI, J).

Group O.—Small, stemmed quartz points—32 specimens. This group is a heterogeneous catch-all of small points, 22 to 40 mm long, 13 to 21 mm wide, 5 to 10 mm thick, and made from opaque white quartz. Bases are straight or convex, stems are broad, and shoulders are straight or slightly barbed (Pl. XXVI, K).

Projectile point fragments.—Fragments of broken tips, midsections, and other portions of projectile points that are not distinguishable as to type or group—1,289 specimens.

OTHER CHIPPED-STONE ARTIFACTS

Cores and Core Tools
(928 specimens)

These are large pebbles or small boulders of quartzite or quartz from which chips have been struck by percussion along one or more faces, leaving a generally oval, high-backed, round-edged tool. Sizes range from 16 by 8 by 4 cm to 5 by 3 by 2 cm. Weights range from 20 to 500 grams. In most instances one face of the specimen retains a part of the original surface of the stone suggesting that most, or all, of the large chips were struck off from one side only. There are 684 of these specimens that show no evidence of secondary usage as tools in themselves and represent only the cores from which chips were struck for use in making other artifacts. The remaining 244 specimens were themselves used as tools and show evidence of hammering along one or more edges or are slightly shaped with moderately sharp edges to form rough chopping or scraping tools.

Scrapers
(902 specimens)

Core scrapers (279 specimens).—Like the cores and core tools, these are pebbles of quartz, quartzite, chert, or ryolite from which large chips have been struck for fashioning of other tools. They differ, though, in that they have been further shaped into a fairly uniform style for use as scraping tools. Each has a moderately sharp point on one end and a rounded opposite end. The central portion is thick and both sides are convex, though one side is usually much more convex than the other. Rarely does one face retain a part of the original surface of the stone. The edges are laterally convex and thinned by percussion chipping with some secondary chipping on a few specimens. Sizes range from 9 by 6 by 4 cm to 4 by 3 by 2 cm. Weights range from 16 to 100 grams.

Ovate scrapers (175 specimens).—Cores of quartz, quartzite, chert, and ryolite, rather well shaped with one pointed end and one rounded end, moderately thin, and of uniform pattern, form a group of distinctive scraping tools. A few specimens exhibit secondary chipping along the edges making rather sharp and even cutting surfaces. One large specimen is 17 by 8 by 2 cm. Others range from 12 by 7 by 3 cm to 4 by 2 by 1 cm. Weights range from 7 to 65 grams except for the large specimen which weighs 175 grams. Over half of the specimens fall within the lower third of the size range and are made exclusively of quartz cores.

Lanceolate scrapers (148 specimens).—These specimens are long, narrow, thick tools, with rounded or straight base, parallel sides,and pointed tip, fashioned from a core of quartzite, quartz, or chert with irregular surfaces. Usually one surface is more convex than the other. Edges are asymmetrical suggesting that the tool was held in the hand or hafted on a short handle and used for cutting or scraping with one edge receiving the bulk of the usage. Sizes range from 11 by 3.5 by 2.5 cm to 6 by 2.5 by 1 cm and weights range from 16 to 55 grams.

Rectangular scrapers (58 specimens).—Distinctive specimens of tabular or rectangular form with rounded corners and parallel sides and ends are carefully made, and percussion chipped over all surfaces. Edges are sharp and length is usually about one- and one-half times the width. Materials are predominantly quartz but a few specimens are of quartzite, argillite, and ryolite. Sizes range from 7 by 3.5 by 1.5 cm to 3.5 by 2.5 by 0.8 cm. Weights range from 8 to 42 grams.

Flake scrapers (238 specimens).—Unshaped, thin flakes of quartz, quartzite, chert, or ryolite have been used as scraping and cutting tools without intentional alteration except that resulting from usage. They are thin and small and have one or more sharp edges which often show extensive usage chipping. A few specimens have a convex edge. Sizes range from 5 by 5 by 0.6 cm to 2 by 2 by 0.2 cm.

Other scrapers (4 specimens).—There are 2 circular, flat slabs of water-smoothed, fine-grained sandstone, split laterally so as to form sharp-edged tools. The edges have been altered by extensive chipping. One is 6 cm in circumference, 1.2 cm thick, and weighs 61 grams. The other is 7 cm in circumference, 0.6 cm thick and weighs 39 grams. A single plano-convex scraper is made of opaque, white quartz. It is triangular in outline with all chipping from the convex surface. It is 3.7 cm wide, 4.7 cm long, 1.8 cm thick and weighs 33 grams. One side scraper is made of a thin piece of slate that may have originally been a projectile point or knife that was broken and converted to a scraper. It is triangular with a rounded base and one sharp edge. In the opposite edge is a deep notch that suggests the original function of a projectile point. It is 6 by 4.2 by 0.8 cm in size and weighs 19 grams.

Perforators
(73 specimens)

Chipped-stone specimens that appear to have served as drills, awls, or other types of perforators may be grouped into 3 varieties and 3 unique specimens. The largest group (48 specimens) is composed of long, slender, poorly chipped, quartz, or quartzite objects resembling the Piscataway projectile point. A few are pointed at both ends but most have one rounded and one pointed end and all have sharp lateral edges with lenticular or diamond-shaped cross sections. Lengths range from 30 to 52 cm, widths from 11 to 18 cm, thickness from 6 to 14 cm. A second variety (10 specimens) is made from brown quartzite and black ryolite. They are long, slender, well-made tools with a lenticular cross section, one sharp point and the opposite end expanding into a T-shaped or rounded base with concave or convex basal edge. Lengths range from 45 to 55 cm, widths range from 11 to 13 cm, and thickness from 6 to 10 cm. The third group (12 specimens) consists of reworked projectile points with rounded or concave bases and broad stems, 10 to 20 mm long, with an abruptly constricted shank terminating in a sharp point. The shanks, or drilling portion, range from 10 to 40 mm in length and 9 to 16 mm in width. Thicknesses are 4 to 10 mm. A single specimen, in addition to these, has been chipped from a large triangular projectile point of white quartz. The perforating tip is 8 by 4 by 2 mm. Another single specimen is a perforating tip that has been chipped out of a large, brown quartzite projectile point of unknown type. The perforator is 7 by 5 by 3 mm. The final specimen is a very carefully fashioned white quartz perforator with a concave base and triangular stem with the apex of the triangle at the base of the shank of the perforator. The stem is 22 by 15 by 4 mm and the shank (broken) is more than 15 mm long, 6 mm wide and 4 mm thick.

Choppers
(6 specimens)

These are large, flat stones of quartzite and ryolite with a chipped notch on each lateral edge and large percussion chips struck off the bit edge. The poll is left unaltered as is most of the surface of each face. They are crudely made but probably served as chopping implements. The notches suggest that they were hafted. They range in size from 12 to 16 cm long, 10 to 12 cm wide, 3 to 4 cm thick, and weigh 400 to 500 grams.

Net Weights
(26 specimens)

Flat stream pebbles of various sizes and shapes, each with a pair of notches chipped from opposite edges appear to have been used as net weights. They average about 7 by 6 by 3 cm in size and weigh 20 to 45 grams.

GROUND- AND POLISHED-STONE ARTIFACTS

Grooved Axes and Mauls
(21 specimens)

Three-quarter grooved axes (4 specimens).—The highly polished grooves around these granitic axe heads are deep and wide on both sides and one edge but are absent on the other edge. The poll is rounded and ground smooth but shows abrasion marks resulting from hammering. The body of each specimen is convex on both sides and tapers to a sharp bit that is slightly convex, narrower than the body, and highly polished. They range in size from 15 to 18 cm long, 9 to 12 cm wide, 3 to 6 cm thick, and weigh 4 to 5 pounds each.

Full-grooved axes (15 specimens).—Only 1 of these is a well-made specimen of the caliber of workmanship seen on the three-quarter grooved axes. In fact, there is some question as to whether this specimen is a full-grooved or three-quarter grooved axe as it is broken in half with one side missing. The portion of the groove remaining, though, seems to suggest a full groove. This specimen has a highly polished, sharp edged, squared bit. The body is carefully shaped by allover pecking and grinding and is convex on all faces. The groove is pecked and not ground and the poll is pecked to a rough, rounded form with hammer abrasion on the top. It is 17.5 by 9.2 by 4.9 cm in size and weighs 4.5 pounds. Another specimen unusually wide and flat, has a broken bit that seems to have been polished and the body is partly pecked and ground to shape, leaving some natural surfaces of the stone. The edges and the deep groove are pecked to shape and the poll is rounded and badly battered from hammering. It is 21.4 by 13.4 by 4.3 cm in size and weighs 4 pounds.

The remaining 13 specimens are smaller, ranging from 12 by 6 by 3 cm to 17 by 10 by 4 cm and weighing 1.5 to 3 pounds. Each is formed by pecking over most of the surface but leaving some of the natural surface of the stone showing. Polishing and grinding occurs only on the bits which are rather dull and narrow, being, in each instance, chipped or broken, apparently from use. The grooves are pecked with but little grinding in a few specimens, but are fairly deep. Polls are partly pecked and rounded but battered from hammering. One of these specimens, the most crudely made of the lot, is distinguished by having 2 parallel, shallow grooves rather than the single one seen on the other specimens.

Full-grooved mauls (2 specimens).—These are double-headed mauls with a pecked groove encircling the central part of each. The body is smooth but is the natural surface of the granitic boulder. The polls are scarred by abrasion but not extensively and each has one poll broken, apparently from usage. They are 21 by 10.5 by 5.2 cm, and 7 by 8 by 5 cm in size and weigh 2 and 2.5 pounds respectively.

Celts
(20 specimens)

A wide variety of forms is present in these specimens. One green granite specimen is long, well-made, and highly polished with a sharp, convex bit, rounded poll and rounded body. It is 25.3 by 4.4 by 2.6 cm in size. Two smaller green granite specimens are equally well made by grinding, pecking, and polishing and otherwise resemble the long specimen except in size. They measure 9 by 3 by 2 cm. Four bit sections with sharp, square bits and convex bodies have nearly parallel sides suggesting that they are parts of long celts resembling the first one described above. Two examples are triangular in outline with sharp, square, highly polished bits, convex faces, and abrasion marks on the rounded poll. These average 10 by 6.5 by 2.6 cm in size. Four specimens are poll fragments. Each is well-made and shows abrasion marks on the end. These have almost parallel sides suggesting long celts such as the first one described above.

The remaining seven are of crude workmanship utilizing maturally shaped stones and fashioned by varying amounts of pecking and grinding. Two of these are crudely formed, thin, small specimens with dull, convex bits; thin, squared polls; and no apparent pecking, but shaped by grinding. Average size is 7.4 by 4.2 by 1.5 cm. One is a thick, poorly made celt with a chipped bit and a battered poll. It is unusual in that it has a suggestion of a rudimentary groove on one edge formed by a series of deep scratches. Most of the surfaces retain the natural form of the stone. It is 11 by 5 by 2.5 cm in size. Another specimen is large and oval in outline, shaped by allover pecking, has a sharp, convex, highly polished bit and the poll is slightly battered from hammering. It is 16.2 by 7.5 by 3.6 cm in size. The fifth celt in this group is small and has a sharp, convex, highly polished bit, but the body and squared poll are shaped by chipping. It is 7.7 by 3.6 by 0.7 cm in size. A rectàngular celt is included in the group. It is moderately well formed by pecking and grinding on all surfaces; has a sharp, squared bit that is highly polished and a squared, flat, battered poll. It is 6.4 by 4.2 by 1.6 cm in size. One crudely made, triangular example is shaped by pecking and grinding. It is 11.6 by 6.1 by 3.4 cm.

Mortars and Pestles
(17 specimens)

Six of these long, stone pestles are well made by allover pecking and grinding into a long, tapering, cylindrical form having one blunt, convex end and one semipointed end. They range from 30 to 45 cm in length and 5 to 8 cm in maximum diameter. The remaining 11 specimens are of essentially the same long, tapering form but are crudely made by partial pecking and grinding over most of the surfaces. The diameters are uneven, often being flat on one side, and natural surfaces of the stone remain at least partially unaltered on all of them. Each, though, has a blunt, battered, convex end and an opposite semipointed end. These range from 17 to 33 cm in length by 4 to 7 cm in diameter.

Insofar as no deep-bowl stone mortars are present in the materials from the site it is to be assumed that these long, stone pestles were used with wooden mortars or with steatite bowls.

Hammerstones
(48 specimens)

Twenty-one of these are elongate, cylindrical quartz or quartzite cobbles with no alteration of the body but having extreme battering on each convex end. They range from 10 to 25 cm in length and are 4 to 8 cm in diameter. The remaining 27 hammerstones are irregularly spherical cobbles with one or more flattened sides and battered edges and ends. Some of these are battered on all faces and show extreme usage while a few show but slight use along one edge or end. They range from 6 to 12 cm in average diameter.

Pitted Stones
(41 specimens)

In all of these specimens, a naturally shaped stone of irregularly spherical, or flat slab shape has had one or more shallow pits pecked into its surface. Sixteen examples are rough cobbles with battered edges and a shallow depression pecked into each of the roughly flat sides, probably used as hammerstones. These are 5 to 14 cm in average diameter with pits of 0.5 to 1.8 cm in depth and 1.5 to 3.0 cm in diameter. Twelve others are similar but with a pit in only one side. One unusual example is an irregular cube, batttered on all edges, and with a single pit pecked into each of the six flat surfaces. It is 7 to 8 cm in each dimension. Another is a large, loaf-shaped stone, battered on all edges with a single pit in the convex surface. It measures 32 by 12 by 14 cm. Eleven pitted stones are flat, unshaped slabs of limestone with pecked depressions in one or both the flat surfaces. They range from 20 to 40 by 18 to 30 by 3 to 7 cm in size. Two of these are slightly larger than the others and each of these has 15 pits pecked into one surface. The other 9 have but 2 or 3 pits each.

Grinding Slabs and Manos
(36 specimens)

Five grinding slabs are flat, unshaped sandstone fragments with a round or oval depression worn into one flat surface. The sixth is similar but with a depression on each flat surface. The depressions are 2.5 to 4 cm deep and range from 16 to 34 cm in diameter. The shape of the abrasions in these shallow depressions suggests that, in all instances, they were used by rubbing a small mano against them with a rotary motion.

The 29 small, crudely shaped, oval manos each have one or both wide surfaces ground to a convex shape. These manos resemble the hammerstones and pitted stones mentioned above except for the shaping of the working surfaces. One additional mano is quite distinctive as it is well shaped into a round-cornered rectangular loaf with both working surfaces worn smooth by a back-and-forth, rather than a rotary, motion. The manos range from 15 to 31 cm in length, 7 to 11 cm in width, and 3 to 6 cm in thickness.

Stone Tobacco Pipes
(7 specimens)

One complete and 6 fragmentary pipes made of stone are present in the collections. The complete one is a flat-stemmed, platform pipe of steatite (Pl. XXII, O-P). The platform is 14.5 cm long, 3.5 cm wide, and 1.1 cm thick. It is slightly convex on both sides and the edges contract slightly just forward of the midpoint to each squared end. The bowl is at the center of the platform and at an 88 degree angle to it. The bowl is 3.7 cm high, 4.2 cm deep and 4 mm thick at the rim. The interior of the bowl is conical. The stem bore is 4 mm in diameter and so off-center that it breaks out along the top of the platform and enters the bowl at an obtuse angle of 45 degrees. The interior of the bowl is vertically striated from manufacture. Obviously, with the exposed bore, the pipe was never smoked. This pipe is quite certainly of foreign manufacture, and one might speculate on the consternation of the purchaser of this pipe when he found it could not be smoked, especially if he had traded some rather valuable item for it.

One long, steatite tube in the collection may have been a pipe stem as one end is cut off square in the usual manner of pipe bits. It is 8.6 cm long, 1.5 cm in diameter and has a bore 5 mm in diameter. Another steatite tube is curved and may have been the elbow section of a stone pipe. It is 1.6 cm long and 1.4 cm in diameter. The bore has a 4 mm diameter at one end but expands abruptly at the other end to 8 mm as if this were the beginning of the pipe bowl. A third fragment is a curved elbow section of a fine-grained, granite pipe with a portion of the bottom of the bowl clearly to be seen. It is 17 mm in diameter at the elbow and the bowl is at a 90 degree angle to the stem. A fragment of steatite appears to be an unfinished pipe bowl. It is oval, roughly cut over all surfaces and has a drilled hole, 7 mm in diameter, at the base. It is 3.3 cm high, 4.1 cm in the long diameter, and 2.9 cm in the short diameter. The base is broken which may be the reason for its remaining unfinished. In addition to these, 2 small fragments of granite appear to be portions of a pipe bowl but are too fragmentary for positive identification.

Pendants
(53 specimens)

These are tabular, perforated, ground-stone artifacts that appear to have been suspended on a cord or thong and worn as ornaments. Of these, 8 have a single perforation; 19 have two or more perforations; and 26 are too fragmentary to determine the perforation pattern. The 8 pendants with single perforations vary considerably in style. One complete specimen of green granite is oval in outline with truncated ends. It is 12.5 cm long, 4.1 cm wide and 1.2 cm thick, and is highly polished on all surfaces. The perforation is near the narrower of the two ends and is drilled from one side only (Pl. XXVII, A). This end also has seven notches along its edge. Another specimen is a small, blue slate pendant measuring 3.2 by 1.4 by 0.3 cm, is scraped, scratched, and ground. It is oval in outline and perforated near one narrow end but the perforation is drilled from both sides (P. XXVII, H). A third specimen is very similar to this one but slightly larger. Three pendants of blue-gray schist are rectangular, flat, well-polished specimens with a perforation near one edge and drilled from both sides. They are of similar size and measure 4.5 by 4.7 by 0.9 cm. Two others are small, oval quartzite stream pebbles, smoothly polished and with a perforation drilled from one side near the small end (Pl. XXVII, I). They are of similar size and measure 4.5 by 2.4 by 1.3 cm.

The 19 pendants, with two or more perforations each, are oval or rectangular in outline with perforations near each end or with two perforations near the center (Pl. XXVII, G, J, S). Seven are drilled from both sides and the remaining 12 are drilled from one side only. Two are of steatite (Pl. XXVII, R), and 3 of schist (Pl. XXVII, O), 9 of blue-gray slate (Pl. XXVII, N), and 5 are of green granite. Two are shaped and ground smooth but obviously were broken during the drilling of the perforation as in each case one perforation is incomplete and the specimen is broken across that perforation (Pl. XXVII, C, F). Nine of these are large, measuring 12 by 5 by 0.5 cm; 6 are smaller, averaging 7 by 3.5 by 0.7 cm. The other 4 are too fragmentary to indicate their size but appear to be nearer the smaller group.

The remaining 26 are fragments of tabular, ground, and polished pendants with one or more perforations and are apparently within the size ranges of those mentioned above (Pl. XXVIII, D). Six are of schist, 1 of steatite, 11 of blue-gray slate, and 8 are of green granite. One of the larger fragments has a small longitudinal groove across the face of one side.

Bannerstones and Boatstones
(8 specimens)

A single butterfly-type bannerstone made of black schist is present in the collections. One lateral half of the specimen is present including half of the central, hafting perforation (Pl. XXVII, P). This central perforation is evenly drilled from both edges and is 8 mm in diameter. A second, smaller perforation is present including half of the central, hafting performation (Pl. XXVII, P). This central performation is evenly drilled from both edges and is 8 mm in diameter. A second, smaller perforation is lateral ridge on one surface.

Of the seven boatstones or atlatl weights, one is of steatite, has a small perforation drilled near one end and is oval in outline with one convex and one concave surface. The concavity is 3 mm deep. The specimen is broken almost exactly in half and the half that is present measures 6.7 cm long (13.4 cm whole) by 3.2 cm wide by 0.9 cm thick (Pl. XXVII, K). A second fragmentary specimen appears to be nearly identical to the first but is made of green schist. A third specimen is of green granite, has a perforation near each of two opposite edges, is rectangular in outline, with one convex and one concave surface. The concavity is 4 mm deep. About half the specimen is missing and the remaining part is 5.4 cm long by 2.5 cm wide (5.0 cm whole) by 0.8 cm thick (Pl. XXVII, L). Another specimen is of very fine-grained quartzite, unperforated, oval in outline, and has a convex and a concave surface. The concavity is 7 mm deep and the specimen measures 9.8 by 3.9 by 0.7 cm. Three specimens are thick, triangular in outline, with a wide groove in the base of the triangle and a notch at the apex. The groove is 1.1 cm in diameter, the notch is 3 mm deep, and over-all measurements average 4.6 by 3.1 by 2.2 cm. One is of steatite, the other 2 are of quartzite.

Miscellaneous Stone Objects
(188 specimens)

Five ornamental discs are roughly circular in outline, thin, and have notches around all edges. Two of these are elaborately incised on all surfaces with fine crosshatching (Pl. XXVII, E). The others have plain, unpolished surfaces (P. XXVII, B). Thicknesses are 2 to 3 mm and diameters are 3.5 to 4 cm. Two are of blue-gray slate and 3 of green granite.

One polished disc bead is made of a flat, quartz stream pebble 18 mm in diameter and 7 mm thick. The central perforation is 7 mm in diameter. Seven tubular beads measure 2 to 3 cm in length, 7 to 10 mm in diameter and have bores of 4 to 5 mm diameter.

One large, spherical quartzite object has a pecked and ground notch in each of two opposite sides. It is 5 cm in diameter.

Seven small, flat, unshaped fragments of sandstone have excessive scratching and grinding on one surface and appear to have been abrading stones (Pl. XXVII, M).

Twenty tabular fragments of various sorts of stone are roughly shaped into flat rectangles and suggest usage as blanks from which pendants were to be fashioned.

Sixty-eight pieces of hematite and 40 pieces of limonite have scratching and grinding marks on them suggesting use as pigment in making mineral paints.

Thirty-nine other random stone fragments exhibit scratches and cut marks probably representing waste pieces from the manufacture of various artifacts.

SHELL ARTIFACTS
(5,336 specimens)

Artifacts fashioned from the shells of various species of mollusks are represented abundantly in the collections. Mussel shell tools are the most numerous and may be separated into three kinds of artifacts. According to Mrs. Ferguson's field notes there were more than 1,500 of these recovered during the excavations. They were so numerous that only samples of the various kinds were saved as they were usually quite fragile and difficult to preserve. Unworked mussel shells found in the site numbered many thousands and no doubt the flesh of these animals served as one of the staples of diet.

There are 226 mussel shell specimens in the sample collection that have serrated edges. In these, a series of small notches extends around the lip from the hinge. In some cases these notches extend entirely around the lip but more often only about half way. Notches are 1 to 2 mm deep and 1 to 3 mm apart. Such notched shells may have served as scrapers in removing the hair from hides or as cutting tools or otherwise in the preparation of meat and vegetables for food.

Seven of the notched mussel shells and 24 without notches had a small, drilled hole near the hinge. The perforations range from 3 to 5 mm in diameter and are usually drilled from both sides, although three specimens are drilled from the inside only. These probably served as ornaments suspended on a thong.

Another group of these mussel shells exhibit extreme wear and some accidental chipping along the edge of the lip. These may have served as fleshers in rubbing down hides preparatory to making leather or may have been small digging implements. There are 54 specimens of this sort.

Shell beads, made from sections of conch shell columella, are abundant and most of them were found associated with Ossuaries Numbers 2, 3, and 4. There are three varieties. One variety is a large, thick, barrel-shaped, tubular bead, cut and ground smooth at both ends, and drilled from both ends. They are 13 to 43 mm long and 8 to 17 mm in diameter, with perforations 3 to 7 mm in diameter. There are 1,542 of these beads. A second variety is a smaller, spherical bead, ground on all surfaces, and perforated from both ends. The perforated ends are usually flattened. These beads are 8 to 15 mm in diameter with perforations of 3 to 5 mm diameter. There are 373 of this variety. The third group consists of small, tubular beads of even circumference, cut square at each end and perforated from both ends. They are 5 to 9 mm in diameter and 11 to 22 mm long with perforations of 1 to 4 mm in diameter. There are 204 of these. The three varieties of conch columella beads occur together in each instance where provenience is known.

Other shell beads include 186 small, tubular specimens 4 to 6 mm long and 2 to 5 mm in diameter, probably also made of conch shell; 368 perforated, spherical, fresh-water pearls; 986

tiny disc beads 2 mm in diameter and 1 mm thick, made from mussel shell; and two long cylindrical beads of conch shell with lateral perforations. There are 1,365 oliva shell beads from Ossuary Number 4, with one edge of the large end ground flat, exposing the interior and forming an opening for stringing.

Shell artifacts of other kinds are rare. One clam shell with ground lip edges, a few abrasion chips and scratches is present as is a single oyster shell with similar usage evidence. Two other oyster shells have drilled holes near the center of the shell and probably served as pendants. Both clam and oyster shells were abundant in the site but no others showed evidence of usage. There are two whole and one unfinished flat mussel shell discs with central perforations. They are 23 mm in diameter and 1 mm thick, with perforations 3 mm in diameter. One limpet shell is ground and polished on all surfaces and perforated near the hinge.

ANTLER ARTIFACTS
(198 specimens)

There are 15 antler tine projectile points made from the tips of the tine, sharpened to a fine point and the proximal end cut off smoothly. The cancelous center of the tine has been drilled out for insertion of the shaft. They are 2.8 to 5.7 cm long and 0.9 to 1.3 cm in diameter, are well-made, and slightly polished. There are 39 antler tine flakers with blunted and scratched tips and broken or cut proximal ends which were presumably used in pressure flaking of stone tools. In 4 other antler tine specimens the cancelous material has been drilled out of the center and a drilled perforation extends from one side to the hollowed interior. One of these is 27.1 cm long and 4.2 cm in diameter, and appears to have been a handle for a knife or scraper blade that would be inserted into the hollowed interior and fastened by use of the lateral perforation. The other 3 are smaller but may have served the same purpose. Four solid antler tine cylinders are present, with blunt ends and shaped to a uniform diameter. They are 4 to 8 cm long and 1.4 to 1.7 cm in diameter. These may be gaming pieces.

Partly worked antler objects include 87 central sections of antler tines with the tips cut off by encircling grooves and the basal part either cut or broken off. Some of these appear to have been partly cut and scraped into semicylindrical objects and a few have partly cut encircling grooves around them, as if to cut off short lengths of the antler. Short cylindrical beads of antler, with the interiors drilled out number 14 and are 1.5 to 3 cm long by 1.1 to 2.7 cm in diameter. Eighteen midsections of antler have broken rather than cut ends and have been worked on all surfaces by scraping and smoothing. Seventeen antler basal sections with scratched and smoothed sides, and cut proximal ends, have parts of the cranium still attached on the broken distal ends. Besides these worked antler tools, there are 386 fragments of antler with some cutting or scratching visible, but none appear to have been used as implements. All of the antler material that has any indication of having been worked appears to be deer antler, although in the identified unworked specimens, 4 fragments of elk antler are represented.

BONE ARTIFACTS
(499 specimens)

Splinter awls made from split fragments of the long bones of deer number 225 (Pl. XXVIII, L-Q, T). The pointed end of each has been sharpened, by scraping, to a needle-fine point and is worn smooth, often to a high polish, by usage. The remainder of the bone is unaltered except by breakage and in only 1 specimen is even a part of the joint retained (Pl. XXVIII, S). Polishing on the pointed end extends over 15 to 25 per cent of the specimen. These splinter awls are 4 to 12 cm long. Other splinter awls of the split bird bone, turkey in all identifiable instances, are made in the same manner as the deer bone awls and are of approximately the same length. There are 51 of these. Twelve awls made from whole bird bones with the distal end cut diagonally in the manner of an old-fashioned quill pen point, have sharp points with high polish from usage over all surfaces. Lengths of these awls are 7 to 14 cm.

Other types of awls include 39 specimens made from short pieces of small, whole bone with no alteration other than sharpening of the tip and breaking off of the joint end. These are small, 3 to 6 cm long, but 8 are of heavy bone and 7 to 11 cm long. Two awls are made from splinters of deer leg bones and have spatulate ends rather than sharp points. Ten awls are made from deer ulnae with sharpened points and intact proximal joints (Pl. XXVIII, U, V). Four similar specimens are made from fox ulnae (Pl. XXVIII, R). Ten awls are made of deer leg bone with the proximal joint remaining intact and with but slight sharpening of the tip.

Bone flaking tools are rare in this site but 6 fragmentary specimens of splintered deer leg bone with blunted and battered tips are identifiable (Pl. XXVIII, K).

Bodkins are well-made, smoothly polished specimens with spatulate tip and rounded butt, made from split bird bones (Pl. XXVIII, D-H). A single hole has been drilled near the butt end of each. They range from 5 to 22 cm long and all are thin and fragile. There are 18 of these.

Otter penis bones are ground and polished smooth and have a single lateral perforation drilled across the distal end. Three have spatulate proximal ends, 4 have rounded proximal ends and the other 4 are broken at the proximal end (Pl. XXVIII, A-C).

Eighteen small, cylindrical sections of garfish jaw with the dental channel scraped out and the rest of the bone scraped and ground to an even, cylindrical form with smoothly rounded ends are present. One has a single groove encircling one end.

Nine large bone beamers were found. Each is made from a deer (1 may be elk) long bone. All have cut, ground, and polished central sections with the long, oval channel usual for this type of tool.

Associated with the burial in Feature 159 were 23 tiny bone pins. These are double pointed, 33 mm long, 2 mm in diameter, and appear to be made from fishbone but the identification is uncertain.

Bone beads are rare, but one polished disc bead is 10 mm in diameter, 2 mm thick, and has a perforation drilled from one side only. Two tubular beads are short sections of bird bone with square cut ends. A single canine tooth of a dog has been altered by an encircling groove around the tip of the root.

A long, spatulate bone object with bifurcated tip and expanded, notched opposite end was found. Along the flat surface, between the bifurcated point and the expanded area, is a series of scratched triangles pendant to each edge with their points meeting at the center of the specimen. The object is 11.1 cm long, 2.2 cm wide, and 0.3 cm thick.

A large number of fragmentary and whole turtle carapaces were recovered, 29 of which had been fashioned into ornaments. The entire carapace was used in each case. The exterior surfaces were left unaltered and the interior surfaces and edges were ground smooth. Two holes were drilled near the anterior end of the carapace, one on each side. Notches were cut in 4 specimens in the anterior edge between the two perforations. These specimens may have been suspended from the neck or tied around the arms or legs of the wearer but none indicate use as rattles as they were not closed containers.

Miscellaneous pieces of cut or scratched bone numbered 37 specimens including 23 deer hoof bones with the pointed tips sharpened.

TABLE V

TABULATION OF NONCERAMIC ARTIFACTS

Artifact	Count	Subtotal	Artifact	Count	Subtotal
Projectile points		2,849	Shell artifacts		5,336
Projectile point fragments		1,289	Mussel, serrated	226	
Other chipped-stone artifacts		1,935	Mussel, drilled	24	
Cores	684		Mussel, ground	54	
Core tools	244		Conch beads, barreled	542	
Core scrapers	279		Conch beads, spherical	373	
Ovate scrapers	175		Conch beads, tubular	204	
Lanceolate scrapers	148		Conch beads, small	186	
Rectangular scrapers	58		Mussel, disc beads	986	
Flake scrapers	238		Pearl beads	368	
Misc. scrapers	4		Oliva beads	1,365	
Perforators	73		Miscellaneous	8	
Choppers	6		Antler artifacts		198
Net weights	26		Projectile points	15	
Ground-stone artifacts		439	Flakers	39	
Three-quarter grooved axes	4		Handles	4	
Full-grooved axes	15		Cylinders	4	
Full-grooved mauls	2		Beads	14	
Celts	20		Midsections, cut	87	
Pestles	17		Midsections, broken	18	
Hammerstones	48		Basal sections	17	
Pitted stones	41		Bone artifacts		499
Grinding slabs	6		Awls, split	288	
Manos	30		Awls, short, whole	39	
Tobacco pipes	7		Awls, spatulate	2	
Pendants	53		Awls, ulna	14	
Bannerstone	1		Flakers	6	
Boatstones	7		Bodkins	18	
Ornamental discs	5		Otter penis, worked	11	
Disc bead	1		Cylinders, gar jaw	18	
Tubular beads	7		Beamers	9	
Sphere	1		Pins	23	
Abraders	7		Beads	4	
Tabular blanks	20		Bifurcate spatula	1	
Hematite	68		Carapaces	29	
Limonite	40		Miscellaneous	37	
Miscellaneous	39		Grand Total		12,545

COLONIAL ARTIFACTS

The objects of non-Indian origin and those of Indian origin that were made of materials of Caucasian provenience have not been fully analyzed. Objects of metal, glass, crockery, china, and other non-native materials relating to the seventeenth and eighteenth centuries, or later, are not numerous in the collections from the Accokeek Creek site but those that were recovered, including a collection of fragments of white clay tobacco pipes will be analyzed at a later date. It will be sufficient to say here that such materials as were recovered from the site are too few to demonstrate, with any conclusiveness, the nature and origins of the European contact with the Indians at this site during the seventeenth century.

V

CULTURAL RECONSTRUCTION AND CHRONOLOGY

BACKGROUND

The Middle Atlantic states have not, for one reason or another, received a great deal of archaeological attention over the years. Ethnological commentaries have been numerous since the beginning of exploration and colonization by Europeans, and hints of the prehistoric remains are to be found in many of these. The concern with archaeological remains, though, as a subject for systematic study itself was neglected until nearly the end of the eighteenth century. Nor was it given much attention until the last two decades of the nineteenth century. During the period from about 1880 until about 1905 much work was done in the region and again it was neglected until the 1930's. Since 1930 a great deal of work has been accomplished, particularly in the way of individual site excavations and reports. Only two major syntheses of the prehistory of the area have, even yet, appeared (Holmes, 1903; Schmitt, 1952).

This is still an area of many cultural unknowns. There are several reasons for this. Archaeology, as a separate study, did not develop in North America to any appreciable extent until the middle of the nineteenth century. When it did begin to develop, the more obvious, above-ground mounds and earthworks received the earliest attention. Simple village sites without elaborate features and artifacts were by-passed for the more spectacular. Even in the early decades of the twentieth century such fields as the American Southwest claimed the attention of the handful of archaeologists working in the United States. Meanwhile metropolitan and agricultural developments along the Atlantic coast were taking their toll on the antiquities and rendering them even less conspicuous and enticing than they had been in their native condition.

The archaeological impetus provided by, among other things, the Federal Works Projects of the 1930's and the increase in available, trained archaeologists has materially changed the situation during the past quarter century (Guthe, 1952; Johnson, 1961). An awareness of the archaeological potentialities of all regions of North America has developed. Concern with the less conspicuous manifestations of prehistoric cultural entities has accelerated. The Middle Atlantic states have thus come into some prominence as a field of study. A great deal of work remains to be done, but no less than two dozen students have made their contributions to the understanding of the prehistory of this region since 1930.

The cultural reconstructions and chronology of the Accokeek Creek site are based in part on these antecedents and it is appropriate here to review some of the highlights of archaeological activity in this area. The following review is not exhaustive but covers most of the previous work in which the present report has had its roots.

The earliest record of a systematic treatment of the antiquities of this area is that of Thomas Jefferson. He listed some of the more obvious prehistoric villages but was principally concerned with mounds and other more elaborate monuments. His conclusion was that the prehistoric Indians of this area had never produced anything worthy of being called an Indian monument (Jefferson, 1787, pp. 152-57). His cultural reconstructions consisted of little more than a listing of the antiquities known to him and a description of some of the excavated materials. Yet this was a start, and more than half a century prior to any general interest in North American antiquities.

It was nearly a century after Jefferson's report appeared before this area was again approached with a view to systematizing the archaeological remains. In the final three decades of the nineteenth century members of the staff of the Smithsonian Institution became active in the region. William Henry Holmes and his associates at that time examined collections of antiquities and investigated sites in Virginia, Maryland, Delaware, Pennsylvania, and New Jersey as a part of their studies of the general antiquities of the eastern United States. Gerard Fowke (1894) published some of his results as did Cyrus Thomas (1891), Otis T. Mason (1877), Frank H. Cushing (1894), and others. Fowke's report dealt specifically with the area of concern here but the others were principally reports of the general area of the eastern United States with but small sections dealing with the Middle Atlantic states.

Holmes, too, dealt with the general eastern United States but he gave a prominent place to the area of his special interest and field work, the Middle Atlantic Seaboard. His main work in the area, begun about 1880, gave rise to four significant reports that, together, form the earliest systematic cultural reconstruction of the prehistory of the area (Holmes, 1889; 1897 *a;* 1897 *b;* 1903). In his report of 1897, he systematized the stone implements and delineated a "Potomac-Chesapeake Tidewater Province" (Holmes, 1897*a;* pp. 13-18, Pl. I). In his report of 1903, he systematically defined the pottery groups and delineated a "Middle Atlantic Province" (Holmes, 1903, pp. 145-58). The pottery and stone implement groupings that he made, and the Middle Atlantic Province that he described are still useful concepts over a half century later.

The next few decades provided little in the way of general reconstructions of the prehistory of the area as a whole. Many sites were excavated and reported. In many of these reports allusions were made to the archaeological sequences of the area, generally, but over-all cultural syntheses were lacking. Many of these were very good reports and contributed greatly to the accumulating store of data concerning the area. Christopher Wren (1914) reported on excavations in the Wyoming Valley, Lock Haven, and elsewhere in eastern Pennsylvania. E. W. Hawkes and Ralph Linton (1916) reported on the Koens-Crispin site in New Jersey. Leslie Spier (1918) reported on the Trenton Argillite Culture in New Jersey. The decade of the 1920's passed without much attention to the Middle Atlantic states. In the 1930's Robert W. Jones (1931) reported on the Clemson Island site in south central Pennsylvania. Carl Clausen (1932) reported on the Wolve's Den Shelter in eastern Pennsylvania. Donald A. Cadzow (1933; 1936) reported on Pennsylvania materials. Frederic A. Godcharles (1934) reported on sites in Pennsylvania. David I. Bushnell (1935; 1937) reported on sites in Virginia. William J. Graham (1935) reported on the Port Tobacco site in Maryland. T. Dale Stewart and Waldo R. Wedel (1937) reported on the Anacostia site in Maryland. Mary Butler (1939) reported on the Mononghela sites of western Pennsylvania. T. Dale Stewart (1939; 1940 *a*) reported on the Patawomeke site in Virginia. In the 1940's, Richard E. Stearns (1940) reported on the Hughes site in Maryland. James L. Swauger (1940) reported on the McKees Rock Mound in eastern Pennsylvania. T. Dale Stewart (1940*b*) reported on a site on the York River in Virginia. Dorothy Cross (1941) reported on a great number of sites investigated by the Federal Works projects in New Jersey. C. A. Weslager (1942) reported on sites near Cambridge, Maryland. Carl Manson, Howard A. MacCord, and James B. Griffin (1944) reported on the Kayser Farm site in Virginia. Gates Slattery (1946) reported on the Selden Island site in Maryland. Carl Manson (1948) reported on the Marcey Creek site in Maryland. Other sites were excavated and reported on during these decades and many more were located, tested, or excavated without reports. Karl Schmitt and Gates Slattery excavated the Sheppard site in Maryland and prepared a manuscript on the work (Schmitt and Slattery, ms., n.d.). This has since been published (MacCord, Slattery, and Schmitt, 1957). Karl Schmitt prepared a manuscript on the work at the Patawomeke site in Virginia (Schmitt, ms., n.d.). Margaret C. Blaker (1950) described the pottery from the Townsend site in Delaware. John Witthoft investigated many sites in Pennsylvania. William J. Mayer-Oakes investigated sites in western Pennsylvania. Amateur archaeologists have been making collections from many sites throughout the area. Alice L. L. Ferguson's work has already been mentioned. The list of sites reported, tested, and excavated is, indeed, a long one and each has added its bit to the accumulated information.

In 1947, Karl Schmitt attempted the first synthetic summary of the archaeological chronology of the Middle Atlantic states since the work of Holmes. This was his doctoral thesis at the University of Chicago and later appeared as a chapter in *Archeology of the Eastern United States,* edited by James B. Griffin (Schmitt, 1952). Here Schmitt, in essence, used Holmes' Middle Atlantic Province as an areal entity but included all of western Pennsylvania and western Virginia which Holmes did not, and set the southern limits at the Virginia-North Carolina line, while Holmes continued the province on to the south. Schmitt utilized the temporal periods of Archaic, Early Woodland, Middle Woodland, and Late Woodland. He listed components, and in some cases foci, within these periods and described some of their principal traits. This was an excellent contribution to the understanding of the archaeological sequences and prehistoric cultures of the area.

The latest addition to the information on the Middle Atlantic states is the work of Clifford Evans on the ceramic analysis of Virginia material (Evans, 1955). Evans' study covers only a part of the area—Virginia—and deals only with the pottery, but is a useful clarification of the ceramic sequences in that area. He has included, also, in the same publication, an appendix on the projectile points and large blades by C. G. Holland. In both the report and the appendix seriation is the basic analytical technique.

CULTURAL SEQUENCE AT THE ACCOKEEK CREEK SITE

This site, on the lower Potomac River in Prince George's County, Maryland, has provided an unusually large quantity of archaeological material in comparison to other sites in the Middle Atlantic states. It was an unusually large site, was occupied over a long time span by several cultural groups, and was excavated more extensively than any other site in this region. The resulting archaeological data, described in the preceding sections, provide a basis for certain cultural reconstructions. Some portions of these reconstructions rest upon fully substantiated evidence. Other portions are less certain but seem to be supported by the data. In general, though, the reconstructions are supported by enough data to warrant consideration as a general framework for the prehistory of the site. New material from other sites in the area will fill the gaps further in the framework or will alter portions of its structure.

The culture patterns represented at the Accokeek Creek site may conveniently be ordered within the broad framework that Schmitt has suggested (Schmitt, 1952, p. 59). The periods involved may readily be accommodated in the terms Archaic, Early Woodland, Middle Woodland, Late Woodland, and Colonial (Fig. 29). The cultural manifestations within these periods, likewise, may be accommodated by the framework Schmitt proposed. He has used the concepts of component and focus as set forth in the Midwestern Taxonomic System (McKern, 1939) and some of the foci that he has suggested are applicable to the Accokeek Creek site material. Some of the components that Schmitt listed without focus designation may now be grouped into foci on the basis of the data from this site. Still others of his proposed components and foci are not applicable here.

The culture periods and the foci within the culture periods that are represented by the material from the Accokeek Creek site are as follows:

The Archaic Period (before 500 B.C.)
Several undifferentiated, intermittent occupations.

The Early Woodland Period (500 B.C. - A.D. 300)
Accokeek Creek Component of the Marcey Creek Focus
Accokeek Creek Component of the Pope's Creek Focus

The Middle Woodland Period (A.D. 300 - A.D. 1200)
Accokeek Creek Component of the Accokeek Focus
Accokeek Creek Component of the Mockley Focus

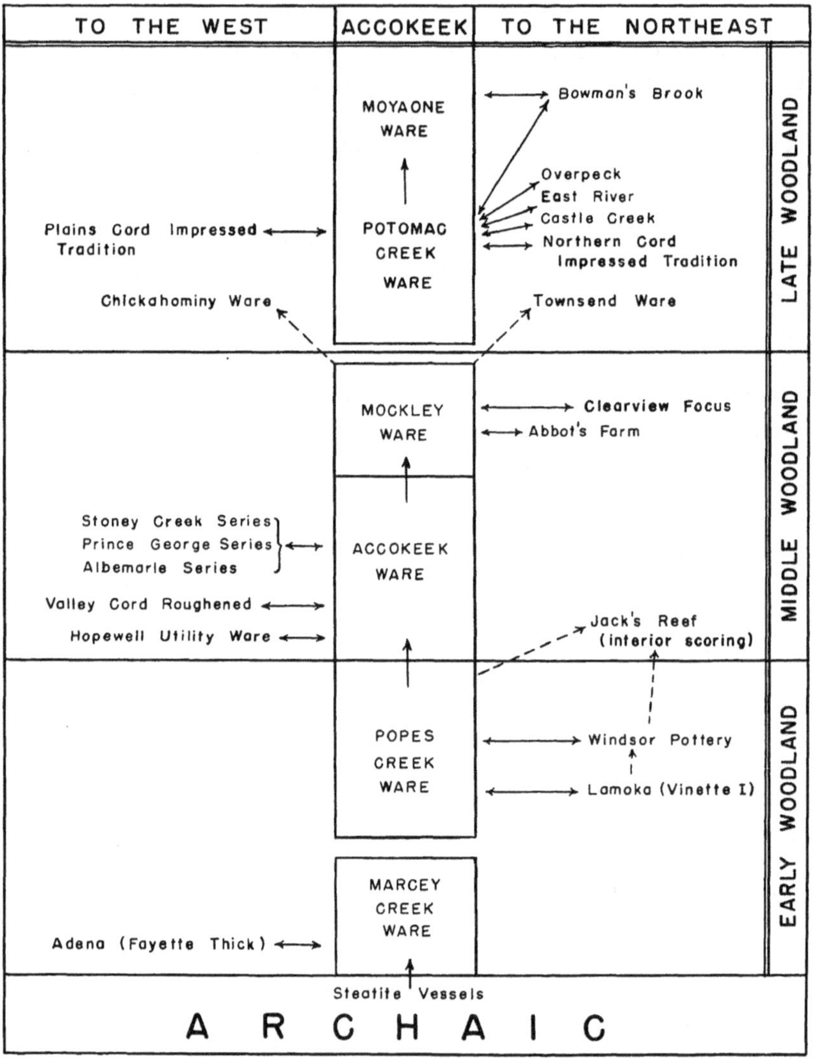

Fig. 29. Chronological placement and relationships of the pottery ware at the Accokeek Creek site.

The Late Woodland Period (A.D. 1200 - A. D. 1700)
Accokeek Creek Component of the Potomac Creek Focus
The Susquehannock occupation

The Historic Period (after A.D. 1700)
Several undifferentiated white occupations.

THE ARCHAIC PERIOD

The earliest occupation of the Accokeek Creek site is indicated by a small number of specific culture traits that are distinctive of the generalized eastern Archaic period of the prehistory of North America (Griffin, 1952*a*, pp. 355-56). These traits, while nowhere abundant in the site, were found in each of the occupied areas with more concentration in the Mockley Point area than in either of the others. Certain other, nondistinctive traits of such generalized form and function that they may be attributable to this period as well as to subsequent periods, may supplement the list of materials representative of the Archaic period. The small total quantity of those early materials, and their scattering over so much of the site without any major concentrations at any one place, suggests brief, intermittent occupations at irregular, and perhaps long, intervals throughout most of the Archaic period from early to late.

Among the specific traits of this period are steatite bowls of which some 30 or 40 individual specimens are represented by the fragments recovered (Pl. IV). Holmes has discussed steatite vessels from this area (Holmes, 1897*a*, pp. 106-34) and later writers have consistently attributed them to the Archaic period. (Griffin 1952*a*, pp. 355-56; Schmitt, 1952 pp. 59-60). They are a part of the early components at the Koens-Crispin, Red Valley, and Abbotts' Farm sites in New Jersey; the Poplar Island site and the Chickis Rock Shelter in Pennsylvania; and the Zekiah Swamp, Marcey Creek, Pope's Creek, Selden Island and other early sites in Maryland. In such of these sites as stratigraphy is indicated, the steatite vessel sherds are beneath, or but slightly mixed with, the earliest forms of pottery.

Another major trait of the Archaic at this site is the series of large projectile point forms made from nonquartzitic materials, largely ryolite, argillite, and slate. It is especially significant that, in this site, the projectile point forms that can be attributed to the early cultural manifestations are made almost entirely from these nonquartzitic stones while those attributable to the late horizons are made almost entirely of quartz. Forms attributable to the middle periods are made predominantly of quarzite or quartz but a strong minority are of nonquarzitic stone. This sequence of the uses of the various stone materials in different time periods was pointed out by Holmes (1897*a*, pp. 134-50) and was used as a basic criterion in discussions of the Trenton Argillite Culture (Volk, 1911; Cross, 1941, pp. 1-3, and 207-8). Among the large, nonquartzitic projectile points from the Accokeek Creek site are those of the types Steubenville Lanceolate, Steubenville Stemmed, Bare Island, and Clagett and the specimens of Miscellaneous groups A and D (Pls. XXIII, XXVI).

Mayer-Oakes(1955) discussed the two Steubenville types at length, though he did not fully describe them. He consistently referred to them as time-markers for the Panhandle Archaic period in the upper Ohio Valley. He also mentioned (p. 207) their specific similarities "to a largely hypothetical Late Paleo-Indian (Krieger, 1950) period." The Accokeek Creek site specimens substantially support Mayer-Oakes' usage of these specimens as types. They are distinctive, both in published illustrations (Mayer-Oakes, 1955, pp. 138-9) and in the Accokeek Creek site examples. The differences between the two types are a bit difficult to discern, as the shoulders of the stemmed type are often rudimentary, yet the distinction between most of the examples can be made readily. Perhaps the two could be combined into a single type of "Steubenville Point." In view of the fact that both names are in the literature (Ritchie, 1961, pp. 50-51) and that distinctions can be made in most cases, the two names have been retained here.

Further reference should be made to the similarities and differences between these points and those of the eastern version of the Paleo-Indian period. The Steubenville points have no basal or edge grinding, no fluting, and are made predominantly of argillite or other slatey stone, thus differing from the earlier, Paleo-Indian points, particularly as exemplified by the materials from the Shoop site (Witthoft, 1952) and elsewhere. Specific similarities, however, are seen in outline form, style and quality of workmanship, size, and general proportions of length, breadth, and thickness. This comparison does not imply relationship between the Enterline Complex of the Shoop site and the Steubenville points but the similarities should be noted.

Mayer-Oakes demonstrated, at site after site in the upper Ohio valley, an early Archaic context for these points. Ritchie illustrates examples from random sites in New York State (Ritchie, 1944, pp. 311, 313), relating them to the Abbott Farm material in New Jersey. He also suggests a possible early ceramic context for some of the New York specimens of this type (Ritchie, 1961, pp. 50-51). Dragoo suggests a late Archaic context for the upper Ohio valley specimens (Dragoo, 1959, pp. 202-6, 210-13). Cross illustrates them from the Abbotts' Farm material (Cross, 1956, pl. 20*a*). They are not among the specimens that Holland describes from Virginia (Holland 1955). Obviously without concrete stratigraphic evidence the specimens from the Accokeek Creek site cannot be tied to any one part of the Archaic period there. It seems reasonably certain that they are, though, a part of the Archaic complex and were in use for a good portion of the period—perhaps even throughout the period.

Projectile points of Miscellaneous Group A are large lanceolate blades of argillite that appear to relate to the type Steubenville Lanceolate.

The Bare Island Point and the Clagett Point types are closely related (Pl. XXIII, G-O; XXIV, W-D'), the essential differences between them being that the former is longer relative to the width and has a straight stem rather than a constricted, or "fishtail" stem, Kinsey (1959, pp. 114-5, pl. 4-5) has discussed two projectile point types from the Kent-Halley site on Bare Island in the lower Susquehanna River in Pennsylvania that are nearly identical to these points. He described a "straight-stemmed" group that he now calls the Bare Island Point (Ritchie, 1961, pp. 14-15), which is identical to the specimens from the Accokeek Creek site that have here been grouped under this name. Kinsey also described a "large, corner-notched" group that is similar, if not identical, to the specimens here included under the name Clagett Point. The two types at the Kent-Hally site have been demonstrated to occur in an Archaic context and nothing in the Accokeek Creek site material would deny this temporal placement. Holland (1955) has described a group of points from Virginia that resemble the Clagett Point, but none comparable to the Bare Island Point type. Holland's "Type I" specimens are wider relative to the length, thinner, and with longer stems than the Clagett Point type at the Accokeek Creek site. The similarity, though, should be noted. The differences may reflect only local variation of the tradition. Similarly it may be noted that both Holland's "Type I" and the Clagett Point resemble the type Orient Fishtail discussed by Ritchie (1961, p. 39).

Points of Miscellaneous Group D are large, thick, blades that resemble the Bare Island Point and are probably related to that type.

Other Accokeek Creek site culture traits that are generally attributable to the Archaic period in the eastern United States include the "butterfly" form of bannerstone (Schmitt, 1952, Fig. 21), boatstones, large choppers, celts, three-quarter-grooved axes, full-grooved axes (Griffin, 1955, pp. 31-43), and polished stone pendants (Pl. XXVII). Some of the other traits of the Accokeek Creek site inventory may possibly relate to the Archaic period, too, but may even more probably belong to the later occupations. Such generalized artifacts as the various bone and shell tools, the chipped-stone scrapers, core tools and others are of such nondiagnostic form that they may be attributed to any of the occupations of the site but to no specific one exclusively. Likewise, some of the nonartifact traits such as a few of the individual burial pits and fire hearths may belong to the Archaic occupation but nothing specific nor diagnostic is in evidence upon which to demonstrate this placement.

These data suggest that the Accokeek Creek site was first occupied at sometime during the Archaic period, probably early in the period, and that there followed a series of brief, intermittent occupations throughout the remainder of the period. Data are not sufficient to distinguish between the various occupations within the Archaic here and no names can be assigned to components or foci at this site. Rather, there is suggested, a series of undifferentiated components that may represent several foci. The principal location of the Archaic camps within the larger area of the site itself was in the low knoll at Mockley Point but camps were also made from time to time in the other portions of the site.

The culture pattern of these people was that of marginal hunting and gathering groups living in small bands of perhaps little more than an extended family and moving about frequently in search of the game upon which their economic welfare depended (Steward, 1938, pp. 258-60; 1946, p. 4). Camps may have been but for a night or two or perhaps as much as several weeks duration in any one place. Within a series of generations the pattern of camp locations may have been in a regular sequence with the group returning to this site at regular intervals. Over the centuries, though, there were intervals of various lengths when the site may have known no human inhabitants—perhaps intervals as long as several centuries. Simple brush shelters, or none at all, would have been in use and no structural evidence remained for the archeologist to recover. Economic subsistence was upon wild products of the hunt, both game animals and vegetable products, as well as perhaps both fresh and salt water fish and shellfish. Burial of the dead was in single, flexed interments in oval pits with little burial accompaniment. While none of the many burials at the Accokeek Creek site can be positively identified with the occupations of the Archaic period, burials of this type were found and conform to burial practices at Archaic sites elsewhere.

Material possessions were few and utensils, tools, and implements apparently consisted of carved stone bowls, long stone pestles, full-grooved stone axes, three-quarter-grooved stone axes, possibly celts, and large chipped-stone choppers. Though evidence is, of course, lacking these people also probably used skin and wood containers, made basketry and mats, and wore untailored skin clothing when they wore any at all. Weapons included the atlatl and dart, probably spears, and large projectile points, percussion-chipped from nonquartzitic stone. Hides were prepared with rough stone flakes but slightly shaped or not shaped at all. Ornaments included polished stone pendants, bannerstones, boatstones for attachment to the atlatls, and probably shell beads. Dogs were probably a part of the family circle.

This was a simple culture complex that, over all of the eastern United States, has a certain homogeneity, though by no means a consistent uniformity. On this level of simplicity there is more uniformity over broad areas than there is on later levels. The basis of the culture is derived from outside the area of the Middle Atlantic Seaboard and the whole complex was a participant in a larger culture pattern. The similarity of the Archaic materials at the Accokeek Creek site to the cultures as far away as Grassy Island in Massachusetts (Johnson and Raup, 1947) Stallings Island I in Georgia (Claflin, 1931) and Indian Knoll in Kentucky (Webb, 1946) is indicative of this continuity.

On the basis of these resemblances to other materials mentioned above, a date range may be suggested for this Archaic occupation of the Accokeek Creek site. Such a range in terms of Griffin's chronological placements (1952 *a*, Fig. 205) would be within the bracket of 3000 B.C. to 500 B.C.

THE EARLY WOODLAND PERIOD

The general culture pattern of the Archaic period appears to have continued in much the same form into the next period but with some significant changes that mark the beginning of the Early Woodland period. Principal of these is the introduction of pottery into the cultural inventory. With the manufacture of fired clay vessels by people of this simple, rudimentary culture, certain other changes were brought about. A fragile item, manufactured in some quantity, was added to the kit of material possessions of the group and this made constant moving about from camp to camp a little more difficult. Also the manufacture of fragile pottery required the group to remain in one place for at least long enough to gather and prepare the clay, form it into vessels, let it dry, and fire it. This process did not take a great deal of time, but it did add somewhat to the tendency toward longer occupations of fewer camping places. The trend toward permanent villages had begun.

It may be, too, that at this time some of the first experiments with the planting of seeds and harvesting of the resulting crops took place. There is basis in logic for this assumption and in fact there is some suggestion in the data from other sites that incipient crop growing began in this period. It must be pointed out, though, that there is no incontrovertible evidence for it and especially at the Accokeek Creek site there is not one shred of evidence for agriculture during this period. Any implications in this regard must therefore rest entirely upon speculation.

Some of the projectile point styles from the Accokeek Creek site can be assigned to this period on the basis of similarity to projectile points from Early Woodland sites elsewhere and there is some associational evidence for these projectile point style changes at this site.

Basically, though, the pottery is the main trait, and indeed the only absolutely certain trait in this site upon which the Early Woodland occupations can be securely based. The pottery attributable to this period is of such quantity and diversity of style that not only can an Early Woodland occupation be established but two separate and distinct components within the period may be suggested. These are the Marcey Creek component and the Pope's Creek component in that order of temporal sequence. A date range for the period, including both components may be based on the chronological placements suggested by Griffin (1952*a*, Fig. 205) and would place these occupations of the Accokeek Creek site between 500 B.C. and A.D. 300.

The Marcey Creek Component

The earliest pottery at the Accokeek Creek site is the Marcey Creek ware (Pl. V). The vessel form, temper, lugs, and lack of decorative adornment suggest that this ware is a ceramic development, combining the basic pottery concept with the form and function of steatite vessels of the earlier, Archaic Period. Whether this is a local, independent development in the Middle Atlantic area, or an importation from elsewhere is not known. The two types of the ware—Marcey Creek Plain and Selden Island Cord Marked—suggest local development within the area. At this site the latter type is absent but elsewhere in the area is present in association with Marcey Creek Plain pottery (Manson 1948, pp. 225-26; Evans, 1955, pp. 54-5). Both types seem to be restricted to the area and technological relationships to ceramics of other areas seem somewhat tenuous. This is a thick, coiled pottery of a simple form and on the basis of "--body shape, heel, and temper proportions--" relationship to the type Fayette Thick of Kentucky and Ohio have been suggested (Manson, 1948, p. 225). Griffin's discussion of the latter type (Griffin, 1945, pp. 220-46) certainly presents evidence of typological similarities.

On the other hand, paste, temper, texture and surface characteristics differ markedly between the two. Still more tenuous relationships to the type Vinette I (Ritchie and McNeish, 1949, pp. 100, 119-23) of New York and to the type Marion Thick of Indiana (Helman, n. d.), (Griffin, 1952*b*, p. 97) may be suggested. Connections between the latter two types and Marcey Creek ware, however, appear to be little more than the fact that they are all thick, crude pottery. Sears and Griffin discuss the matter of stimulous diffusion with respect to the three types of fiber-tempered pottery in the southeast (Sears and Griffin, 1950). They comment on the Vinette, Baumer, and Marcey Creek pottery also, as being a ceramic addition to a common, Archaic stage culture complex, varying in content in the several localized areas.

This suggests then, that all of these early potteries are localized expressions of a widespread diffusion of the baked clay pottery concept. This would seem to be a sounder explanation of the otherwise tenuous connections between these several early ceramic developments than to try to explain them on typological similarities alone. Whether they are directly related or not, the Marcey Creek ware is certainly of the same general temporal position as the others.

Geographic range of the ware extends over Maryland and northeastern Virginia (Slattery, 1946; Manson, 1948; Schmitt, 1952; Evans, 1955). It is also present in New Jersey at Goose Island, Salisbury, and Koens-Crispin (Cross, 1941, pp. 52-66, 81-90; Hawkes and Linton, 1916, p. 77; Schmitt, 1952, p. 60). Probable extension of the range is throughout Delaware and New Jersey, and into eastern Pennsylvania and Coastal New York.

Differentiation of the nonceramic artifacts of the Marcy Creek component from those of the Archaic occupations at the Accokeek Creek site is difficult. Unfortunately the intrusive pits containing artifacts in the site are not very helpful in this respect, but four refuse pits may cast some light on the matter. Feature 2 (Fig. 6), is a group of four overlapping pits, designated (*a*), (*b*), (*c*) and (*d*). Pit (*a*) contained mixed materials of several occupations. Pits (*c*) and (*d*) contained sherds of Marcey

Creek Plain and two steatite sherds but no other pottery. In pits (*c*) and (*d*) the only projectile points found were of Bare Island and Vernon types. In pit (*b*), sherds of steatite but not pottery were found, and in association with projectile points of Miscellaneous Group A and the Steubenville Stemmed type, only. Pits (*c*) and (*d*) were unquestionably intrusive into pit (*b*). This single instance of superposition is but slim evidence, yet it does suggest a real separation between the Archaic occupations and a Marcey Creek occupation. Apparently steatite vessels carried over, to some extent, into Marcey Creek times as did the Bare Island Point type. The Vernon Point type (Pl. XXIV, A-J) was an addition to the Marcey Creek inventory. Points of Miscellaneous Group A and the Steubenville points did not last into Marcey Creek times. The relationship between the types Vernon Point and Calvert Point is marked, both in form and material and can be assigned to the same cultural context. Both are generally similar to those described by Holland as "type M-Side Notched" and "Type H-Stubby Barbed," that he attributes to a generally Early Woodland context (Holland, 1955). Manson (1948) reported projectile points from the Marcey Creek Site that resemble Calvert Point as did Slattery (1946) from the Selden Island site. Elsewhere along the Middle Atlantic Seaboard, projectile points similar to the Calvert and Vernon types are abundant and are attributed to early culture complexes, though more specific designations are not apparent (Holmes, 1897; Cross, 1941; Bushnell, 1937; Mayer-Oakes, 1955; Schmitt, 1952; Hawkes and Linton, 1916).

There is little valid means of distinguishing between the other Archaic and Early Woodland materials at the Accokeek Creek site.

A Marcey Creek component may be postulated for the early occupation of the Accokeek Creek site within the Early Woodland period. The definition of the component rests largely upon the identification of one of the earliest forms of pottery in the Middle Atlantic area—The Marcey Creek ware—and includes the Calvert and Vernon projectile point forms. The trait inventory includes many items that were included in the Archaic complex of earlier times but that are not now possible to sort by period with the data at hand.

This was a series of intermittent occupations by small bands of hunting, fishing, and gathering people, of somewhat less transitory habits than their predecessors but still not settled in villages of even semipermanent nature. They made pottery vessels of clay mixed with crushed steatite, used atlatls and darts and probably spears for hunting, and may have begun to cultivate some plants to supplement the wild food subsistence. They probably built movable huts but the remains of these are so inextricably mixed with the later house remains that we cannot be certain. Their camps were predominantly along the western edge of the Moyaone area of the site and on the knoll at Mockley Point but they also left some camp refuse in the other parts of the site. Clothing was still of untailored skins but substantial, twisted cordage was made and used for many purposes. Some polished stone ornaments were apparently in use but most of the stone tools were rather rough, rudimentary chipped implements, although polished stone axes and celts were still in use. The chronological position of this component is certainly within the early part of the Early Woodland period and it is suggested that it may have occupied the first four or five centuries of the period, from 500 B.C. to somewhere around 100 B.C.

The Pope's Creek Component

Another very early, but quite different, pottery at the Accokeek Creek site is the Pope's Creek ware (Pl. VI), including the type Pope's Creek Net Impressed and the sherds of Miscellaneous Group A. Direct evidence of the priority or subsequence of this pottery to the Marcey Creek ware is lacking, but it is so distinctively different from the latter ware as to suggest its manufacture by an entirely separate cultural group. Indirect evidence of time relationship to the Marcey Creek pottery, such as lack of association with steatite vessels either in technological features or in physical association suggests that the Pope's Creek pottery is later than the Marcy Creek pottery. The technological distinctions between the two also suggest an origin somewhere outside the local area and a disassociation with the Marcey Creek component. The vessel form, paste, temper, texture, and surface treatment of this thick, coiled pottery of conical form distinguish the two. Mention has been made above that the Marcey Creek ware bore certain resemblances to the type Fayette Thick of Kentucky and Ohio but only the vaguest similarities to the types Vinette I of New York and Marion Thick of Indiana. The reverse is true of the Pope's Creek ware. Vessel form, thickness, and surface treatment are reminiscent of those characteristics of the Vinette I and Marion Thick pottery but only vaguely so of Fayette Thick. Yet temper, texture, and some features of the surface treatment differ markedly from any of them.

The closest relationship to the Pope's Creek ware is to be

found in a group of sherds from Long Island. Carlyle Smith (1950, pp. 193-96) has described these within the Windsor Ceramic Tradition as the types North Beach Brushed, Windsor Cord Marked, Windsor Brushed, and Windsor Fabric Marked. These types are similar in form, decoration, and paste to the Pope's Creek ware, though the extreme sandiness and friability of the latter is lacking. The most notable similarity is the distinctive interior scoring (or brushing) that is almost identical to that of the Pope's Creek ware. Of the type Windsor Brushed, Smith says, "It is typical of the Windsor Aspect—The type is closely related to, and probably derived from, North Beach Brushed and the interior grooved pottery from the Vinette component of the Point Penninsula focus, the pottery also resembles that of the Chesapeake-Potomac Group from Pope's Creek Maryland." Of the type North Beach Brushed, Smith states that it is a trait of "The North Beach focus of the Windsor aspect. It appears to be one of the oldest definable pottery types in the region." The Windsor pottery, thus seems to be a close relative of the Pope's Creek ware, both perhaps developing out of an early Point Penninsula tradition. The Windsor style seems to have carried on into later times in Long Island and perhaps is ancestral to the interior scored pottery of central New York, such as the Jack's Reef pottery (Ritchie and McNeish, 1949, pp. 101-2). In the Potomac valley the Pope's Creek ware carried on to develop into the Accokeek ware of the Middle Woodland period.

Holmes (1903, pp. 153-55; 1907, pp. 126-28) discussed the Pope's Creek pottery at length and considered it to be very early in the Middle Atlantic Province. Other references to it are scanty. Perhaps it is a geographically limited ceramic style. Southern Maryland, Delaware, and the Virginia shore of the Potomac may be the extent of the range as described (Schmitt, n.d. pp. 28-29; Graham, 1935, pp. 11-15; Ferguson, 1937 *b*, p. 263; Bushnell, 1937, pp. 21-25; Slattery, 1946, pp. 262-66). It is, though a part of the widespread, early northeastern ceramic tradition.

Other culture traits of the Pope's Creek component are not separable from traits of the Marcy Creek Focus on the basis of the data at hand, but a few hints are given. The Calvert (Pl. XXIV, K-V) and Vernon projectile point types may belong to either or both and Holmes' collections from the Pope's Creek site include both forms as well as the Bare Island and Clagett types. Points of the Rossville type (Pl. XXIII, A-F) almost certainly are a part of the Pope's Creek component if that component can be derived from the New York area. Ritchie in personal communication has indicated that in the New York area, this point type is associated with thick, early pottery and Smith associates it with the Windsor pottery. This does not eliminate it from the Marcy Creek or late Archaic inventories, however, as the generalized form of the Rossville Point is widespread on the Late Archaic—Early ceramic levels throughout the southeast with types that range up to the size of the Miscellaneous Group B specimens from the Accokeek Creek site.

The way of life of the people of the Pope's Creek component here was probably not very different from that of their predecessors the Marcey Creek people. Yet the two must have had different origins, the one, in the Late Archaic of the immediate vicinity, the other in the Archaic of the New York area. However, they were both basically extensions of an Archaic culture pattern. The Pope's Creek people seem to have had somewhat larger social and economic grouping and occupied specific localities for longer periods than did the earlier people. Such is indicated by their more intensive occupation of the Accokeek Creek site where Pope's Creek ware was found in great quantities along the southwest portion of the Moyaone area and also in some quantity in all sections of the site. We can be certain that these people made excellent, twisted cordage and were skilled in knotting this cord into several kinds of open-mesh nets as indicated by the net marks on the surfaces of their pottery vessels. These nets may also have been used for fishing or snaring game, for bags and other containers and may even have developed into fabrics for clothing and other usages. Economic dependence must still have been on hunting, gathering, and fishing, but still no positive evidence is at hand in regard to agriculture. With the increasing stability of the community, though, the implications of crop raising continue to increase. Almost certainly some substantial form of shelter was in use but the specific data are lacking. The chronological position of the Pope's Creek component may be suggested as sometime during the period of around 100 B.C. to A.D. 300, if certain of the suppositions suggested above are correct.

THE MIDDLE WOODLAND PERIOD

The Middle Woodland remains recovered from the Accokeek Creek site are abundant but pottery stands almost alone as a basis for the reconstruction of culture patterns. There is some suggestion of distinctive projectile point styles that may be associated with the distinctive pottery styles but these are tenuous and other artifact types from this site are so generalized in form as to be almost useless as cultural diagnostics. Stone, bone, shell, and antler artifacts are not lacking but are of simple styles that, for the most part, could be assigned to any of the periods at the site. It is, in fact, of considerable significance that there is so little elaboration of the material objects of these culture complexes. This site, from early to late, was not a participant in any of the elaborate ways of life that were taking place elsewhere in the eastern United States. Yet the ceramics are of such differing styles as to clearly indicate the changing culture patterns and to suggest that these were not poor and backward cultures but rather that they were hyperconservative.

There are two distinctively different ceramic styles here that can be assigned to the Middle Woodland period and each forms the basis for a separate component during this period. The earlier style, the Accokeek ware, is considered to be a development out of the Pope's Creek ware and upon this pottery style is based the Accokeek component. The later style, the Mockley ware, is considered to be a further development out of the Accokeek ware, with some new characteristics added, and forms the basis for a Mockley component. In line with dates suggested for the other periods of this sequence a time span of approximately A.D. 300 to A.D. 1200 is suggested for this period.

The Accokeek Component

The pottery from the Accokeek Creek site that forms the main ceramic development within the Accokeek component is the Accokeek ware with its single component type, Accokeek Cord Marked (Pl. VII). The sherds that have been grouped together as Miscellaneous Pottery groups B and C, appear to be a part of this general ware but data are not sufficient upon which to distinguish these as valid types. A minority ware within the focus is the Albermarle ware with three component types; Albermarle Cord Marked, Albermarle Net Impressed, and Albemarle Fabric Impressed. The scarcity of this minority ware at the Accokeek Creek site and its predominance in some of the sites of the coastal area of Virginia (Evans, 1955, pp. 39-44,89-94) suggests that it is trade ware here. The similarities between the two wares, however, are such as to imply a similar developmental background and ceramic tradition for both.

The Accokeek ware, as defined here, is new to the literature.

It has been referred to simply as an early, cord-marked pottery (Slattery, 1946, pp. 262-66; Cross, 1941, pp. 117-27; Schmitt, 1952, pp. 60-62), or has been discussed in connection with the Marcey Creek ware (Manson, 1948, pp. 225-26)[1] and the Pope's Creek ware (Holmes, 1903, pp. 153-54; Ferguson, 1937*b*, Fig. 4). The material from the Accokeek Creek site is a large sample and the provenience analysis strongly supports a separation of the Accokeek ware from both the Marcey Creek and the Pope's Creek wares. Likewise the typological analysis demands a separation in terms of the criteria upon which wares and types are established here.

There are almost no attributes in common between this ware and Marcey Creek ware but there are certain similarities to the Pope's Creek ware. Accokeek ware attributes such as friability, hardness, temper, vessel shape, decoration, and color are but refinements of these attributes of the Pope's Creek ware. This strongly suggests that it is a local development out of the Pope's Creek ware and is based upon a widespread ceramic tradition with generalized affiliations over a large portion of the northern United States. Such affiliations are apparent in the similarity of many of the attributes of this ware to those of the Stoney Creek, Albemarle, and Prince George series of Virginia (Evans, 1955, pp. 39, 60, 69, 126) to which it is most closely related. Other related ceramics include the cord-marked utility wares of Hopewell (Griffin, 1952*b*, pp. 101-4, 121-22), some of the Point Peninsula and North Beach Focus materials of New York (Ritchie and McNeish, 1949, pp. 100, 102; Smith, 1950, pp. 135, 195) and comparable pottery from New Jersey (Cross, 1941, pp. 52-66, 117-27; Schmitt, 1952, pp. 60-2) and eastern Pennsylvania (Witthoft, 1948, p. 18; Schmitt, 1952, pp. 61-2).

There is some variety of style within the type Accokeek Cord Marked and the lumping of all of the sherds of this ware into a single type may require some justification. Several varieties were at first distinguished on the basis of attribute clusters. When compared, attribute by attribute, the varieties dissolved into a continuous gradation from coarse, soft, poorly made examples approaching the Pope's Creek ware characteristics, to fine, hard, well-made examples resembling the Albemarle Series pottery of Virginia. This wide range of technological variation, combined with abundance of the specimens, suggests

[1]The type Marcey Creek Cord Marked described by Manson is identical to the type Accokeek Cord Marked (Manson, personal communication).

a considerable time span for the ware in this site. Perhaps this span could include most of the Middle Woodland period.

Miscellaneous Pottery Group B is composed of crudely made specimens that have many of the attributes of the Accokeek ware. They are too aberrant, though, to justify inclusion within the types.

Sherds of Miscellaneous Group C are of the same paste as the finer varieties of the Accokeek ware but the unobliterated exterior coils eliminate them from the type (Pl. 20*a*). Nor, can these sherds be related to other material in the eastern United States on the basis of present data.

The Albermarle ware sherds recovered from the Accokeek Creek site are very few and in all respects fit the "Series" and type descriptions that Evans discusses for the Virginia material (Evans, 1955, pp. 39-44). These appear to have been trade vessels at the Accokeek Creek site.

Pipe smoking appears to have made its earliest appearance here during Accokeek times. The pottery pipes of the type Accokeek Plain are clearly made from the same paste as are the Accokeek ware pottery vessels. The single, stone pipe of platform type is of a form typical of the Hopewell complex to the west (Neumann and Fowler, 1952, Pl. 66) and therefore can be assigned to the time period of the Accokeek component as another trade item.

Projectile point forms appear to have continued from Early Woodland times through this period and may include such types as Vernon, Calvert, and Miscellaneous Groups E, H, and O (Pl. XXV, i; XXV, L).

The Accokeek component thus appears to have been a semi-sedentary people living in moderate sized groups in various parts of the site over a long period of time beginning with the early stages of the Middle Woodland period. Their distinctive pottery was found in all occupied sections of the site, with no particular concentration in any one area. They traded with people from Virginia and were at least in contact with Hopewell people to the west. Village form or structures have left no positive evidence nor has their agriculture, all of which were probably rather distinctive and the latter may have included tobacco to be smoked in tubular and other forms of pipes.

The Accokeek component, developing out of the Early Woodland Pope's Creek component would occupy a temporal position at the beginning of the Middle Woodland period and probably extend through a major portion of the period. In Griffin's correlations this would perhaps be from somewhere around A.D. 300 to A.D. 900.

The Mockley Component

A second occupation of the Accokeek Creek site within Middle Woodland times is represented by the Mockley ware with its three component types, Mockley Cord Marked (Pl. VIII), Mockley Net Impressed (Pl. IX), and Mockley Plain (Pl. X). The temporal position of this ware in the latter part of the Middle Woodland period is indicated by the provenience analysis of the sherds from this site, in which it tends to be more closely associated with sherds of the Accokeek ware than with any other pottery. Also the typological relationships are in this direction. Attributes of vessel shape, surface treatment, thickness, color, and decoration of the Mockley ware are strongly reminiscent of those attributes in the Accokeek ware. The net impressed type is even suggestive of the surface treatment of the earlier Pope's Creek ware. A divergent development out of the Accokeek ware is thus indicated. The semiconical bases tending toward round, rather than the conical bases suggests a little later temporal position than that of the Accokeek ware.

One attribute of major significance in this ware is the unburned, crushed shell temper. Shell temper is usually a part of the pottery of the late periods in the eastern United States. In the Mockley ware, though, the shell is unburned and otherwise unprepared for use except by being crushed, differing from the later, Mississippian shell temper which is burned and specially prepared before being mixed with the clay. This simple process of only crushing the shell would seem to be but a variation of the technique of crushing other materials to make grit temper and not a new technological process. The shell temper of the Mockley ware, therefore, cannot be considered as a part of the later shell temper tradition but only a variation of the grit temper tradition.

There are instances of the use of unburned shell temper elsewhere in sites of the Middle Woodland period. The Clearview pottery of coastal New York (Smith, 1950, pp. 134-35) is shell tempered and bears unquestionable resemblance to the Mockley ware (Smith, personal communication). An even closer similarity is seen in the pottery with leached shell temper at the Abbott's Farm site in New Jersey. This pottery is identical to the Mockley ware and constitutes 32.2 per cent of the total pottery analyzed from the site. It was found "predominantly in the third humus layer" and continuing on "into the second humus layer." The third humus layer represents a Middle Woodland component (Cross, personal communication). Both cord-marked and net-impressed types are present in this material. Other quite similar shell-tempered pottery is present in the collections from other sites in New Jersey at the New Jersey State Museum in Trenton, as well as in the collections in the Pennsylvania Museum at Harrisburg, from a few sites in southeastern Pennsylvania.

The Mockley ware does, though, have relationships in the later periods such as with the Chickahominy Series of Virginia (Evans, 1955, pp. 44-49, 126) and the Townsend ware of Delaware (Blaker, 1950, p. 11; Schmitt, n.d. p. 27). Evans, Blaker, and Schmitt considered these two potteries to be Late Woodland. The vessel shape and color of these resemble Mockley ware but thickness, surface treatment and color differ markedly. Shell temper is the main attribute of significance common to all three and in all three the shell is unburned. On the basis of the early position of the Mockley ware at the Abbott's Farm site and the late position of the Townsend ware at the Townsend site it seems obvious that the Mockley ware is the earlier and probably ancestral to the Townsend and Chickahominy pottery.

The major concentrations of Mockley ware at the Accokeek Creek site are in the Mockley Point and the Clagett's Cove areas with sporadic occurrences in the Moyaone area. A dating of A.D. 900 to A.D. 1200 is suggested for this component.

THE LATE WOODLAND PERIOD

The archaeological remains of the Late Woodland period occupation at the Accokeek Creek site are the most abundant and the most clearly identifiable of the remains of any of the culture periods. Pottery, tobacco pipes, projectile points, and archaeological features of this period are, for the most part, readily separable from those of earlier periods. Hence a fuller and sounder cultural reconstruction can be formulated for the Late Woodland period than for any of the others. Pottery, though, remains the basic criterion upon which the cultural reconstruction is made.

The site has provided two indigenous pottery wares and one trade ware of this period as well as sherds of three of the Miscellaneous groups. The indigenous wares are so closely related as to leave no doubt of their contemporaneity and association within the same culture context. The trade ware is of the same time period and can be presumed to represent contact with other nearby culture complexes. Other items that can clearly be identified with this period are pottery tobacco pipes, projectile points, a distinguishable village pattern, stockades, refuse pits, storage pits, ossuary burials, and dog burials. These traits combine readily into a single component of the Late Woodland period and date from somewhere around A.D. 1200 to the end of Indian occupation of the site about A.D. 1700.

A brief historic occupation of the site by Indians of the Susquehannock tribe is also a part of this period but was of such short duration, and such a specialized character, that little may be said of it archaeologically. The historic record of this brief occupation, substantially supported by the archaeological data, though, provides a clear picture of the site at the time of its transition to white ownership.

The Potomac Creek Component

The principal ceramic development of the Late Woodland period of this site is the Potomac Creek ware with its two component types, Potomac Creek Cord Impressed and Potomac Creek Plain (Pls. XIII-XVIII). The sherds that are included in Miscellaneous Pottery Group F are also a part of this ware (Pl. XX, D-F). Closely related to this pottery is the Moyaone Ware with its three component types, Moyaone Cord Impressed, Moyaone Incised, and Moyaone Plain (Pl. XIX). A trade pottery in this occupation is the Townsend ware with its two component types Rappahannock Fabric Impressed (Pl. XI) and Rappahannock Incised (Pl. XII). The sherds of the Miscellaneous Pottery Group E also appear to be a part of the Townsend ware. Sherds of Miscellaneous Pottery Group G resemble the Potomac Creek ware (Pl. XX, G-K), but appear to be more closely related to the pottery types Page Cord Marked, and Keyser Cord Marked, which are not a part of the Accokeek Creek site assemblage.

The Potomac Creek ware is clearly of the Late Woodland period (Manson, MacCord, and Griffin, 1944, pp. 406-9; Schmitt, n.d., p. 26) and references to it are abundant in the literature (Holmes, 1903; Bushnell, 1935; Stewart, 1939; 1940; Ferguson, 1937*b*; Schmitt, 1952). At the Piscataway Ossuary there is no question of its contemporaneity with historic trade materials (Ferguson and Stewart, 1940, pp. 4-13). How much time depth may be assigned to it in the Accokeek Creek site is uncertain but it apparently belongs to the entire period of the stockaded villages and thus represents several centuries.

Geographical range of the ware appears to center about the lower Potomac River at the sites of Patawomeke and Accokeek Creek (Stewart, 1939; 1940; Schmitt, n.d.; 1952; Ferguson 1937*a*; Holmes, 1903). Griffin has discussed the special relationships of this ware at length, suggesting that its southern boundary is in the vicinity of the Rappahannock River Valley and its northern boundary but slightly north of the Susquehanna River (Manson, MacCord, and Griffin, 1944, pp. 410-13). The ware extends westward as far as the Keyser Farm site in the Shenandoah River Valley. In view of the temporal position of the ware in the Potomac River Valley and the chronological placement of the Keyser Farm site (1550-1650) it is suggested that the appearance of the Potomac Creek ware that far west is related to the increased interchange of coastal and inland cultural materials and traditions resulting from early White contact in the early seventeenth century.

Less specific relationships of this pottery may be seen to the pottery of comparable temporal position throughout the northeastern United States and even out into the central part of the continent. As Griffin points out "The ceramic connections are rather to the north along the coastal plain and the drainage systems flowing into the Atlantic, until in the New York area there is a westward spread of cord-and pseudo-cord-impressed decoration which carries across southern Canada north of the lakes and across Michigan and Wisconsin into Minnesota" (Manson, MacCord, and Griffin, 1944, p. 412). In eastern Pennsylvania (Cadzow, 1936), New Jersey (Cross, 1941), New York (Ritchie, 1934; 1936; Smith, 1950), New England (Willoughby, 1935), and Nova Scotia (Smith and Wintemberg, 1929), the tradition is at once apparent. Likewise, in Michigan (Greenman, 1937), Wisconsin and Minnesota (Wilford, 1941; 1955), and on into the central and northern Plains (Kivett, 1952; Lehmer, 1954; Hurt, 1954; Strong, 1935; 1940; Wedel, 1940), relationships to the Late Woodland, cord-impressed pottery are seen. Cord-impressed rim decoration, rim and lip form, vessel shape and size, surface treatment and many paste characteristics of the pottery are clearly similar, and often nearly identical, to the Potomac Creek ware. Much of the late pottery such as that of the Upper Republican and Nebraska cultures (Aksarben, if you wish) of Nebraska, and many of the wares of the Middle Missouri from Over Focus to Stanley Focus times (Stephenson, 1954) is clearly a part of this cord-impressed, Late Woodland ceramic tradition. At the laboratory of the River Basin Surveys in Lincoln, Nebraska, specimens of Potomac Creek Cord Impressed pottery from the Accokeek Creek site were compared with pottery from sites in Kansas, Nebraska, and the Dakotas. The similarities were strikingly obvious.

The scarcity of such related pottery in Illinois, Indiana, and Ohio seems puzzling but may be explained by the dominance, in that area, of the strong Mississippian cultural tradition. Even there, though, some occurrences of the same cord-impressed tradition are to be seen in such material as the Oliver component in Marion County, Indiana (Griffin, 1943, Pl. 156), and in the Maples Mills components in the central and upper Illinois River Valley (Baker, and others, 1941, Pls. 23,24).

This is not to say that a single pottery extends over this vast area nor that all of the cultural areas mentioned possess a specific unity. It is to say that a close similarity of a number of ceramic attributes is present in the pottery of the several cultural entities of this broad area and that such similarity is more than just coincidence. There are, of course, variations from one cultural unit to another. Owasco pottery, for example, is thicker, softer, and less sandy than the Potomac Creek ware. A person familiar with either would not confuse them. This in no way denies the basic unity of a ceramic tradition over northern North America from the central plains to the Potomac Valley on a specific, late prehistoric, time horizon.

Two types have been established within the Potomac Creek ware, and this calls for some justification. As with the Accokeek ware, these sherds were separated into a number of varieties based upon various attribute clusters. When compared, attribute by attribute, the varieties dissolved into a continuous gradation of the pottery within which no clear lines of distinction could be drawn. The one exception was the completely plain, undecorated specimens. These were therefore separated as a type. They fulfilled the qualifications of a separate type in that surface treatment (smooth, without cord marking) and complete lack of decoration distinguished them from the other specimens of the ware. Numerically the Potomac Creek Plain type is very minor in the site collections. The incised and punctated sherds of this ware could have been separated into two additional types. They were not because they appeared to represent cord-marked and cord-impressed Potomac Creek pottery. The additional decorative techniques of incising and punctating were applied over the cord impressions, or in imitation, of the cord impressions.

Another distinction within the Potomac Creek pottery was considered as a basis for sorting out another type. It was assumed that cord impressions that appeared to be the imprint of a single, pliable cord were technologically distinct from those that appeared to have been made by impressing a rigid, cord-wrapped, stick into the plastic clay. This was the usual distinction between "single cord-impressed" and "cord-wrapped dowel impressed." Experiments with lumps of plasticene, however, gave ample evidence that both sorts of markings could have been made by the same technique, the use of a cord-wrapped dowel. In one experiment a large dowel was wrapped with cord, the wraps being 2-6 mm apart. The dowel was then held vertical to the vessel lip and rolled around the entire rim. This resulted in a decoration identical to those presumed to have been made by "single cord impressions." By varying the angle at which the dowel was held or the spacing of the cords as they were wrapped around the dowel any of the "single cord-impressed" decorations could be duplicated in the plasticene vessel model. In the second experiment a smaller dowel was wrapped tightly with cord and impressed (not rolled) along the rim of the vessel. This resulted in equally accurate duplication of the "cord-wrapped dowel impressions." Variations were accomplished by varying the size of the dowel and the tightness of the cord wrapping. The third experiment consisted of merely impressing single cords in the vessel rim and produced decorations similar to, but not as uniform, as those on the Potomac Creek pottery. The latter technique was difficult and clumsy to do and the result was sloppy, due to the difficulty of pressing a long string uniformly around the soft, pliable, thin surface of a vessel rim. Which technique was actually used by the Potomac Creek people is, of course, not known. The use of the dowel is possible for both styles. It is even highly probable because it is quicker and more easily applied and takes less practice to achieve a neat, symmetrical design.

The sherds of Miscellaneous Pottery Group F appear to be simply miniature vessels of Potomac Creek ware. Their probable origin as playthings or the products of children has been discussed above.

The second pottery ware of the Potomac Creek component is the Moyaone ware. Schmitt (n.d. pp. 26,27) has commented on this kind of pottery at the Patawomeke site but it seems to have escaped notice elsewhere. It is rather abundant at the Accokeek Creek site. A few sherds of the ware may be seen in the collections at the Rochester Public Museum and Carlyle Smith collected some from coastal New York that he classified as Bowman's Brook (Smith, 1950; pp. 122-23) and are very similar to the Moyaone ware sherds. The relationships of this ware are to the Late Woodland, Potomac Creek ware.

Relationships of the sherds of Miscellaneous Pottery Group G are in the direction of the Keyser Farm site in the Shenandoah Valley of Virginia. The group contains sherds similar in many respects to the types Keyser Cord Marked and Page Cord

Marked. Other sherds in the group combine attributes of both types with attributes that are a part of neither.

A significant cultural process may be indicated by this heterogeneous group of "foreign" sherds. It is suggested that these sherds indicate contact with the contemporary villages of the Shenandoah Valley; experimentation with the "foreign" techniques of pottery-making observed there, and ultimate rejection of those techniques by an ultraconservative people at the Accokeek Creek site. At the Keyser Farm site, Potomac Creek Cord Impressed and Keyser Cord Marked are the dominant pottery types and Page Cord Marked is a minor type. At the Accokeek Creek site, on the same time level, Potomac Creek Cord Impressed is predominant with only a few sherds present to suggest the other two types. Thus in the presumed contact between the two peoples, a one-way ceramic trade is indicated. It thus appears that the Group G sherds at the Accokeek Creek site represent a few "foreign" pots brought home from the western villages. These people then experimented with the "foreign" techniques represented in these pots by making them at home. They tried several combinations of these styles and mixed their own styles and techniques into the experiments. Traditional conservatism seems to have won out as but few such vessels were made. Sherds indicate that less than thirty vessels are represented with no two being even nearly alike. On the other hand the Keyser Farm people accepted the style and techniques of the Potomac Creek pottery and made great quantities of it. This hypothesis is but one explanation of the Group G sherds but as such it does account for the facts and is in harmony with the long tradition of conservatism and cultural stability at the Accokeek Creek site.

Projectile points that may be assigned to this time period include the Potomac Point (Pl. XXVI, L-W) and the Piscataway Point (Pl. XXVI, X-E'). The former is made predominantly of white quartz and is almost identical to projectile points from Late Woodland sites over most of the northeastern United States. Nearly all of the sites mentioned above in the discussion of the Potomac Creek ware pottery have produced projectile points of this type in association. Probably this is the same type as Ritchie (1961, pp. 31-2, 86-7) has recently described as Revanna Points. The only substantial difference between the two is that the latter appear to be made predominantly of the flinty rocks while the Potomac Point is 91 per cent quartz, in the Accokeek Creek site collections. This may be only local variation and combining the two named types under Ritchie's term should cause no trouble.

The Piscataway Point is quite another matter and does not appear in the literature. Ritchie was not familiar with it in the New York area. Holland does not mention anything like it for Virginia. It is a very narrow, thick, small point with a tiny, contracting stem and consistently made of white quartz. It is abundant at the Accokeek Creek site and associated with the Potomac Points and with Potomac Creek Cord Impressed pottery. It resembles, in outline, the Rossville Point and may be a typological relative of it but if so it is far removed in time and style.

Projectile points of Miscellaneous Group F are a part of the Potomac Point tradition but are larger, averaging almost twice the size of the latter (Pl. XXV, M-O). In the specimens studied there was no gradation between them, but, instead, a sharp break between the two size categories. Specimens of Miscellaneous Group G, also are of this same tradition differing from the Potomac Point only in proportion of length to width (Pl. XXVI,A-C). Group G specimens are two to three times as long as they are wide and no gradation is to be noted between these and the Potomac Points.

Nearly all of the pottery tobacco pipes recovered from this site belong with the Potomac Creek component as they are made from a pottery paste that is closely related to the paste of the pottery vessels of that component (Pl. XXI,XXII). The most numerous type is the Potomac Creek Cord Impressed with its four variant styles. Minor types are the Potomac Creek Plain and the Potomac Creek Broad Bit. All of these are common to other sites in the Middle Atlantic Seaboard area. Schmitt discusses them at some length as a part of the Patawomeke site material (Schmitt, n.d., pp. 32-3) and Mayer-Oakes (1955, pp. 107-15, Pls. 54,55) illustrates and discusses identical pipes from the Monongahela complex of western Pennsylvania.

Most of the recognizable, archaeological features, of this site are attributed to the Potomac Creek component. These include the stockades with their gates, and screens, refuse pits formed from borrow pits adjacent to the stockades, dog burials, large ossuaries with but few burial accompaniments, storage pits, and individual post molds that represent drying racks, scaffolds, house walls, trophy poles, hanging poles, etc. These features are associated in the site with Potomac Creek ware pottery. There is also substantial ethnohistorical evidence for the occurrence of these features in early, White contact sites of this immediate area (Lorant, 1946, pp. 155-285).

The reconstruction of the Potomac Creek component can be

more complete than that of any of the other occupations of the Accokeek Creek site. This was a permanent village of large population and long duration. It was surrounded by a stockade of vertical posts set close together. The village plan was a large, oval enclosure situated close to the bank of the river. From time to time, as the river bank was slowly washed away, or the population increased, the stockade was expanded toward the landward side in a series of concentric arcs. Gates in the stockade were overlapping sections with a protected entry between them. Houses within the compound were of vertical pole construction and covered with mats. Shapes of the houses are not certain but probably were rectangular, though some may have been circular. Repeated repair and reconstruction of the houses left a confused pattern of postholes that made it impossible for the archaeologist to delineate individual structures. Between and around the houses were drying racks, scaffolds, and individual poles upon which to hang things. Cooking fires were built as often outdoors as indoors and racks of small poles were often used over the cooking fires. Village refuse was partially disposed of in large pits along the inside of the stockade.

Burial of the dead took place with considerable ceremony and large ossuaries were filled with several hundred individuals. These were the accumulated dead of a specified length of time. Three of these ossuaries were within the village compound and a fourth was outside. Some who died were buried in small single or multiple interment graves within the compound. Grave goods were rare and apparently only incidental except for conch shell beads which were included with many of the infant, and a few adult, burials. The ossuary burial consisted of a few whole individuals placed in the bottom of a large shallow pit. Above these were placed bundled skeletal elements of the rest of the accumulated dead. Skulls were grouped separately, in the pit, from the other elements. Some cremation of a few individuals took place on the top of the ossuary pit, though this was rare. The whole pit was then covered with dirt and in two of the ossuaries a large fire was built after the final earth had been piled upon it. The single interments were either flexed or extended. Dogs were numerous in the village and some of them were buried in the manner of the single individual human burials.

Agriculture was practiced and corn, beans, squash, pumpkins, melons, gourds, tobacco, and other crops were probably grown. Products of hunting, fishing, and gatherings, though, were equally as important as the garden products. Deer, fish, and shellfish were supplemented with berries, roots, nuts and seeds.

Weapons for hunting and for defense included the bow and arrow and probably lances. The arrows were tipped with small, triangular, quartz points. Pottery was made in abundance and used as cooking vessels, storage jars and other containers of related purpose. Smoking pipes were made of pottery and were obtuse-angle, elbow pipes of varying form and decorative embellishment.

The people wove excellent matting and probably baskets and textiles. Clothing was semitailored and both tanned skins and textiles were probably used. Cordage and twisted fiber string were abundant and bone bodkins and bone awls were used to sew the hides and textiles into whatever article was needed. The main ornaments were conch shell beads, and pendants made of both marine and fresh water shell. Body and facial painting appears to have been practiced also.

These were a conservative people who did not readily accept innovation and did not elaborate the simple, utilitarian way of their life. They must have had a rather pleasant life and lived it rather prosaically for a dozen or so generations in this one village. They eventually came to know the white European and his encroachment on their land, and, of course, ultimately fell victim to this encroachment. The Potomac Creek people were the last Indians to occupy this area, except for the brief episode of the Susquehannocks there in 1675. Although they remained in the vicinity under the name of the Piscataway Indians until the end of the 17th century, their occupation of the Accokeek Creek site ended in the 1630's.

THE COLONIAL PERIOD

The Colonial period is difficult to define here and even more difficult to isolate in terms of the archaeological remains. Colonial occupation of this part of North America began with the Jamestown Colony, in 1607. Its direct influence reached the area of the Accokeek Creek site by the following year. A charter for colonizing the area that is now Maryland, however, was not granted until 1632, and settlement was not begun for yet another two years. Yet during this early half of the seventeenth century, and probably before, objects of European manufacture were being traded to the people at the Accokeek Creek site. By the mid 1630's, the Indians had left the immediate area of the site and white colonial settlement dominated the region. It is this time that can be identified, then, as the beginning of the Colonial period.

The preceding section on Historical Setting has provided some of the documentary details of this period. Now the few archaeological details may be discussed. There aren't many. Mrs. Ferguson has mentioned that the upper ten inches of the site were so thoroughly churned by plowing during the past two and a half centuries that objects found in this zone were of no clear provenience to her and were discarded. It is of interest to note that in all of the extensive excavation within the Moyaone and Mockley Point areas not a single object of white provenience is recorded. It is only in the Clagett's Cove area around the Susquehannock Fort that European objects are recorded and even here they are not abundant. The palisade of the Fort itself is the clearest evidence of white occupation. This was a large, rectangular palisade of vertical posts, set close together and measuring some two hundred feet on a side. Rectangular bastions protruded from at least two of the corners and may have existed on the other two also as the east side had been eroded away by the Piscataway Creek in Clagett's Cove. Within the Fort, several refuse pits, a storage pit, and one small ossuary provided remains of the Susquehannock defenders of the Fort during the siege of 1675. The historical records leave little doubt of this tribal identity and the general culture pattern of these people has been discussed by Cadzow (1936). The principal identifying feature is the small ossuary in which were found forty-two burials, artifacts of white provenience such as Jew's harps, copper bells, iron brackets, an iron hoe, a copper finger ring set with glass, a snuff box, and a musket ball. At the bottom of the ossuary were two pottery tobacco pipes of the type Susquehannock Plain, and other fragments of this pipe type were found in the general excavations in this area. This distinctive pipe type is virtually a "Trademark" of the Susquehannocks of the seventeenth century (John Whitthoft, personal communication).

This was the last of the Indian occupations of the Accokeek Creek site. The remnants of the Piscataways of the Potomac Creek component continued to live within a few miles of the site for some years but by the end of the seventeenth century even they had left Maryland to the white colonists.

At some time within the eighteenth century a colonial house of "noggen" construction was built between the Moyaone and Mockley Point areas. Another house of similar construction was built, during that century, near Ossuary No. IV in the southern part of the Moyaone area. The precise dates, sequence, or other details of these buildings are not known. Yet another cultural feature that relates to the eighteenth century is a brick lime kiln located along the southeastern edge of the present marsh adjacent to Accokeek Creek but again details of this feature are only to be guessed.

VI

THE MIDDLE ATLANTIC SEABOARD CULTURE PROVINCE

The archaeological sequence at the Accokeek Creek site, located on the eastern margin of a large continent, reflects but little of the cultural development that took place nearer the geographical centers of the large ecological areas elsewhere on that continent. The cultural entities at this site remained almost entirely unaffected by the great cultural developments of the Ohio and Mississippi valleys. Nor were they affected by those of the southeastern United States. Throughout the times when such spectacular developments as Adena, Hopewell, and Middle Mississippi were taking place but a few hundred miles to the west and Stallings Island, Swift Creek, and Macon cultures were reaching their peak only a few hundred miles to the south, the cultural manifestations here remained stable and consistently simple. Their roots were in the traditions of the northeastern United States, yet they were not full participants in the culture patterns of that area either. Instead, they, along with their geographically near neighbors, seem to have developed a culture pattern of their own at an early time, and maintained basically that same pattern through many centuries.

The Archaic occupations of the Accokeek Creek site resembled those of the same general time and culture periods elsewhere in the eastern United States to a greater extent than did any of the later occupations. Perhaps this can be attributed to the nature of the Archaic culture pattern over the whole of the eastern United States. It was based on a relatively simple hunting and gathering economy rather than an agricultural economy and had fewer potentialities for cultural elaboration and differentiation. The Eastern Archaic, of course, was no uniform complex. Each area had its own distinctive developments, but the broad similarities between these areas during the Archaic period were much greater than in later periods.

With a culture pattern once established on an Archaic level, and apparently stabilized to some degree, the later cultures of the area appear to have retained that stability and to have deliberately resisted elaborate change. With the development of ceramics and agriculture, simplicity of tradition seems to have continued to prevail. Traits that lend themselves to elaboration such as pottery decoration, complex burial practices involving large earthworks, carved shell ornaments and others, were practiced in only their simplest form. Geographic isolation may account for this stability to some degree, but not entirely. A few trade items such as the platform pipe and the potsherds of Miscellaneous Group G provide clear evidence of contact with other areas. This stability and resistance to change may be accounted for more by a stable economic environment, based in part on agriculture and in part on small game, shellfish, fish, and wild vegetal products. Such an economy providing a stable source of supply of a great variety of products may indeed have been the main factor limiting the tendency toward cultural elaboration.

There is some suggestion at the Accokeek Creek site of a cause and effect relationship between the agricultural potential and the level to which the culture developed. In terms of Meggers' four types of environment, the area here is to type three--an area of increasable, or improvable, agricultural potential (Meggers, 1954, pp. 803-4). The soil is sandy, in part swampy. In the early periods of occupation the area available for agriculture was smaller than in the later periods. At best it was not large. It was, though, improvable. With swamp drainage, fertilizers, and steel plows the agricultural potential has been greatly increased. In aboriginal times, though, the potential was limited and so was the degree of cultural elaboration. This correlation suggests support for the hypothesis set forth by Meggers, that the level to which a culture can develop is dependent upon the agricultural potential of the environment it occupies (Meggers, 1954, p. 822).

The cultural stability and continuity reflected in the materials from the Accokeek Creek site are not unique there. This same general pattern is clearly represented at other sites within a considerable geographic range. These several cultural entities, represented at the Accokeek Creek site as the Archaic, Marcey Creek, Pope's Creek, Accokeek, Mockley, and Potomac Creek components, may readily be projected into a broader interpretation of this area as a whole. Such a projection fits well within the concept that Holmes sets forth as a single culture province (Holmes, 1903, p. 145). With only slight adaptation of his term and of the boundaries of the area he covered by the term, a Middle Atlantic Seaboard Culture Province is at once reasonable. Both Schmitt

(1952, p. 59) and Evans (1955, pp. 141-45) imply their agreement with the concept of such a province as was proposed by Holmes. Schmitt arbitrarily sets his boundaries for this province in accordance with present state political boundaries. Evans established a series of ceramic areas within one state of the province and one of his ceramic areas has boundaries approximating those of the Virginia section of Holmes' province. This is Evans' coastal area (Evans 1955, Fig. 14). Neither of these writers, though, made fully explicit their interpretations of the boundaries of the province. Griffin has discussed the spacial relationships of one of the late manifestations in this area in terms that suggest partial boundaries (Manson, MacCord, and Griffin, 1944, pp. 410-13).

On the basis of the Accokeek Creek site material and of the implications derived from the above writers, it seems justifiable now to propose a Middle Atlantic Seaboard Culture Province as a distinct conceptual unit and to fix rather specific boundaries to that province. On the south the province is bounded by the Rappahannock River Valley. The western boundary is formed by the foothills of the Blue Ridge Mountains. To the north the boundary is along a line extending through the foothills from Harrisburg, Pennsylvania, to the Palisades of the Hudson River. The province thus includes the northern coast of tidewater Virginia, all of Maryland south and east of Frederick, all of Delaware, the southeastern corner of Pennsylvania, all of New Jersey except the northwestern quarter of the state and the coastal portions of New York, including Long Island (Fig. 30). Fuller justification for setting these boundaries so specifically may be suggested by the definitions of several foci within the area, based upon the Accokeek Creek site components.

It has been mentioned above that the components of the Archaic occupation at this site were not adequately represented nor isolated clearly enough to distinguish individual units within that time period. The earliest recognizable culture entity, then, that can be combined with other similar entities elsewhere, is the Marcey Creek component. This component, identified primarily on the basis of the Marcy Creek ware pottery but including the other traits of the complex as described above, is suggested as the basis for a Marcey Creek Focus. If such a focus is valid it should also include similar components at the Marcey Creek site (Manson, 1948), the Selden Island site (Slattery, 1946), the Goose Island and Salisbury sites (Cross, 1941), the Koens-Crispin site (Hawkes and Linton, 1916), and similar components at any other sites where the Marcey Creek ware is found in context.

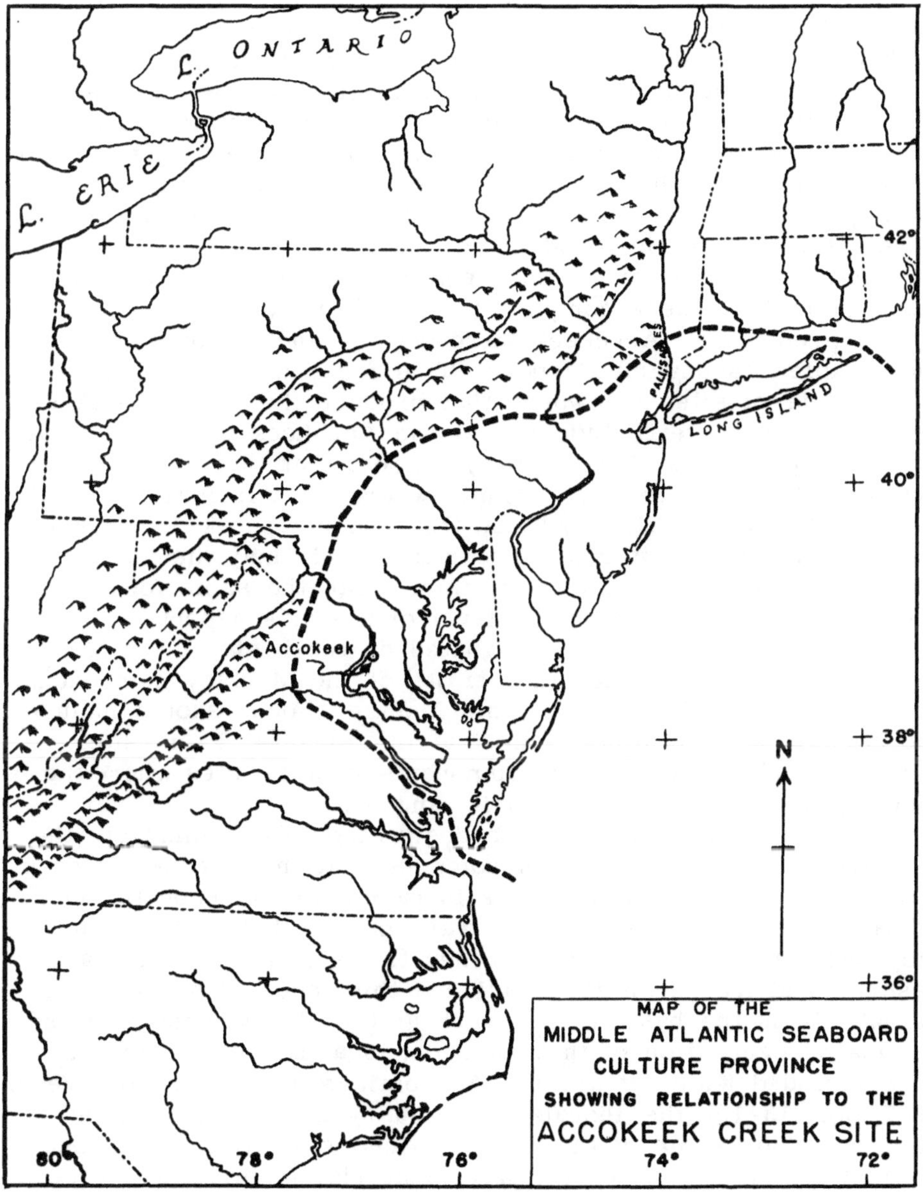
L. ONTARIO
L. ERIE
PALISADES
LONG ISLAND
Accokeek
N
42°
40°
38°
36°
80°
78°
76°
74°
72°
MAP OF THE
MIDDLE ATLANTIC SEABOARD
CULTURE PROVINCE
SHOWING RELATIONSHIP TO THE
ACCOKEEK CREEK SITE

Figure 30.

A Pope's Creek Focus can likewise be designated to accommodate the data from the Pope's Creek component at the Accokeek Creek site, and based primarily on the Pope's Creek ware pottery but including the other traits of the complex as described above. Other components that may be included within the focus are those of similar content from the Pope's Creek site (Holmes, 1903, pp. 153-55; 1907, pp. 126-28), the Patawomeke site (Schmitt, n.d., pp. 28-29) and similar components at other sites where the Pope's Creek ware is found in context.

The designation of an Accokeek Focus can be made on the basis of the Accokeek component here. It is identified primarily by the presence of Accokeek ware pottery and the other traits of the complex as described above. This focus would also include components of sites elsewhere that produce the pottery of Accokeek ware in context. Evidence at the Accokeek Creek site and at sites in Virginia (Evans, 1955) suggest that this focus is intimately related to sites in Virginia where the Albemarle ware is found and probably also to those that produce the Prince George and Stoney Creek potteries. The relationship may, indeed, be so close that these could all be combined into the same focus. Certainly, they are related on the level of a single aspect.

A fourth focus can be designated on the basis of the Mockley ware pottery and the other traits of the Mockley component at the Accokeek Creek site. This Mockley Focus should include the component of similar content at the Abbotts' Farm site (Cross, 1956) and any other components at other sites where the Mockley ware pottery is found in context.

Finally a fifth focus can be designated to accommodate the data from the Potomac Creek component at the Accokeek Creek site. The definition of the focus is based largely upon the identification of the Potomac Creek ware pottery but includes the Moyaone ware pottery and the other traits of the complex as described above. Schmitt established this focus (Schmitt, 1952, pp. 62-63) on the basis of his work at the Patawomeke site and the major occupation of that site, too, is a part of the focus. Also included within it are the Anacostia site (Stewart and Wedel, 1937, pp. 213-19), the Piscataway Ossuary site (Ferguson, and Stewart, 1940), some of the Port Tobacco sites (just which ones Judge Graham recovered the later material from is not certain. Graham, 1935), and any others where the Potomac Creek ware is found in context. The focus is contemporaneous, and in contact, with the Monongahela culture and components in Delaware, Maryland, and Virginia that produce the Townsend and Chickahominy pottery. It is also related to the Gala, Montgomery, and Luray Foci as proposed by Schmitt (1952, pp. 62-63).

Thus a series of five foci can be established that have components at the Accokeek site as well as at sites within the area delimited by the bounds of the Middle Atlantic Seaboard Culture Province, but not beyond. Within the bounds of the Province there are many other foci but it is not within the scope of the present paper to discuss these. Many of these foci will ultimately lend themselves to combinations into aspects within the general framework of the Midwestern Taxanomic System, but it would be premature to suggest these combinations at the present time. Various students are now at work on the many kinds of studies within this area that will ultimately lead to a clarification of all the culture complexes involved, of which there is yet a shred of evidence remaining. The effort toward an understanding of the cultural history of this small, but significant, section of the eastern United States over a period of 5,000 or more years has but begun.

REFERENCES CITED

Alexander, William H.

1911 The Climate of Prince George's County. Maryland Geological Survey, Prince George's County. Baltimore: The Johns Hopkins Press. Pp. 185-206.

Andrews, Charles M. (editor)

1915 Narratives of the Insurrections, 1675-1690. *In* Original Narratives of Early American History. New York.

Baker, Frank C., James B. Griffin, Richard G. Morgan, Georg K. Neumann,

1941 and Jay L. B. Taylor. Contributions to the Archaeology of the Illinois River Valley. Transactions of the American Philosophical Society, N. S., Vol. 32, Pt. 1, Philadelphia.

Besley, F. W.

1911 The Forests of Prince George's County. Maryland Geological Survey, Prince George's County. Baltimore: The Johns Hopkins Press. Pp. 219-46.

Blaker, Margaret C.

1950 Pottery Types from the Townsend Site, Lewes, Delaware. Eastern States Archaeological Federation Bulletin, No. 9, July.

Bozman, John Leeds

1837 History of Maryland. Vol. I. Baltimore.

Brown, Alexander

1890 The Genesis of the United States. Vol. 2, New York.

Burrage, Henry S. (editor)

1930 Early English and French Voyages (chiefly from Hakluyt), 1534-1608. *In* Original Narratives of Early American History. New York.

Bushnell, David I.

1935 The Manahoac Tribes in Virginia, 1608. Smithsonian Miscellaneous Collections, Vol. 94, No. 8, The Smithsonian Institution, Washington, D.C.

1937 Indian Sites Below the Falls of the Rappahannock, Virginia. Smithsonian Miscellaneous Collections, Vol. 96, No. 4, The Smithsonian Institution, Washington, D.C.

Butler, Mary

1939 Three Archaeological Sites in Somerset County, Pennsylvania. Bulletin of the Pennsylvania Historical Commission, No. 753, Harrisburg.

Cadzow, Donald A.
1933 Mr. George Fisher's Discoveries in Western Pennsylvania. The Pennsylvania Archaeologist, Vol. 3, No. 3. pp. 3-5. Harrisburg.

1936 Safe Harbor Report No. 2, Archaeological Section. Publications of Pennsylvania Historical Commission, Vol. 3. Harrisburg.

Claflin, William H., Jr.
1931 The Stalling's Island Mound, Columbia County, Georgia. Papers of the Peabody Museum of American Archaeology and Ethnology, Harvard University, Vol. 14, No. 1. Cambridge.

Clausen, Carl
1932 The Wolves' Den Shelter. The Pennsylvania Archaeologist, Vol. 3, No. 2, pp. 7-9, 19. Harrisburg.

Cross, Dorothy
1941 Archaeology of New Jersey. Vol. 1. Published by the Archaeological Society of New Jersey and the New Jersey State Museum. Trenton.

1956 Archaeology of New Jersey, Vol. 2. The Abbott Farm Site. *Ibid.*

Cushing, Frank H
1894 The Germ of Shoreland Pottery. Memoirs of the International Congress of Anthropology. Chicago.

deBrébeuf, Jean
1636 Relation de ce qué sést passé aux Hurons, en l'aunés. Paris.

Dragoo, Don W.
1959 Archaic Hunters of the Upper Ohio Valley. Carnegie Museum Anthropological Series, No. 3. Pittsburgh.

Evans, Clifford
1955 A Ceramic Study of Virginia Archeology. Bureau of American Ethnology Bulletin 160, The Smithsonian Institution, Washington, D.C.

Fenenga, Franklin
1953 The Weights of Chipped Stone Points: A Clue to Their Functions. Southwestern Journal of Anthropology, Vol. 9, No. 3, pp. 309-23.

Ferguson, Alice L. L.
1937*a* Moyaone and the Piscataway Indians. Washington, D.C. [Privately printed.]

1937*b* Burial Area in Moyaone. Journal of the Washington Academy of Sciences, Vol. 27, No. 6, pp. 261-67. Washington, D.C.

1941 The Susquehannock Fort on Piscataway Creek. Maryland Historical Mag., Vol. 36, No. 1, pp. 1-9.

n.d. Moyaone. Unpublished manuscript on file in the Ceramics Repository, Museum of Anthropology, The University of Michigan. [Prepared in 1948.]

Ferguson, Alice L. L., and Henry G. Ferguson
1960 The Piscataway Indians of Southern Maryland. Alice Ferguson Foundation, Accokeek, Maryland.

Ferguson, Alice L. L. and T. Dale Stewart
1940 An Ossuary Near Piscataway Creek. American Antiquity, Vol. 6, No. 1, pp. 4-18. Menasha.

Ferguson, Henry G.
n.d. Topography. Section in the unpublished manuscript by Alice L. L. Ferguson, entitled Moyaone. Prepared in 1948, pp. 23-33.

Ford, Worthington Chauncey.
1924 Captain John Smith's Map of Virginia. Geographical Review, Vol. 14, p. 433. New York.

Fowke, Gerard
1855 Archaeologic Investigations in James and Potomac Valleys. Bureau of American Ethnology, Bulletin 23, The Smithsonian Institution, Washington, D.C.

Godcharles, Frederic A.
1934 Rich Variety of Andaste Indian Material Yielded by Excavating Long House Sites in Clinton County, Pennsylvania. Pennsylvania Archaeologist, Vol. 4, No. 3, pp. 13-15. Milton.

Graham, William J.
1935 The Indians of Port Tobacco River, Maryland, and Their Burial Places. Washington, D.C.

Greenman, Emerson F.
1937 The Younge Site. Occasional Contributions from the Museum of Anthropology, The University of Michigan, No. 6.

Griffin, James B.
1938 The Ceramic Remains from Norris Basin, Tennessee. An Archaeological Survey of the Norris Basin in Eastern Tennessee, Bureau of American Ethnology, Bulletin 118. The Smithsonian Institution, Washington, D.C.

1943 The Fort Ancient Aspect, Its Cultural and Chronological Position in Mississippi Valley Archaeology. Ann Arbor: University of Michigan Press.

1945 The Ceramic Affiliations of the Ohio Valley Adena Culture. *In* The Adena People by W. S. Webb and C. E. Snow, University of Kentucky Reports in Anthropology and Archeology, Vol. 6, pp. 220-46. Lexington.

1952*a* Culture Periods in Eastern United States Archeology. Archeology of the Eastern United States, James B. Griffin, editor. Chicago: University of Chicago Press.

1952*b* Some Early and Middle Woodland Pottery Types in Illinois. Hopewellian Communities in Illinois. Thorne Dewel, editor, Scientific Papers, Vol. 5, No. 3. Springfield: Illinois State Museum.

1955 Observations on the Grooved Axe in North America. Pennsylvania Archaeologist, Bulletin, Vol. 25, No. 1. Milton.

Guthe, Carl E.
1952 Twenty-five Years of Archeology in the Eastern United States. *In* Archeology of the Eastern United States, James B. Griffin, editor. Chicago: University of Chicago Press, pp. 1-12.

Hack, John T.
1955 Geology of the Brandywine Area and Origin of the Upland of Southern Maryland. Geological Survey Professional Paper 267-A. Washington, D.C.: United States Government Printing Office.

Hall, Clayton H. (editor)
1925 Narratives of Early Maryland, 1633-1684. In Original Narratives of Early American History. New York.

Haury, Emil W.
1936 Some Southwestern Pottery Types, Series IV. Medallion Papers, No. 19. Globe, Ariz.

Hawkes, E. W., and Ralph Linton
1916 A Pre-Lenape Site in New Jersey. Anthropological Publications, University of Pennsylvania, Vol. 6, No. 3. Philadelphia.

Hawley, Florence M.
1936 Field Manual of Prehistoric Southwestern Pottery Types. University of New Mexico Bulletin, Whole No. 291. Albuquerque.

Helman, Vernon
n.d. The Cultural Affiliations and Relationships of The Oliver Farm Site, Marion County, Indiana. Unpublished manuscript on file at the Museum of Anthropology, The University of Michigan.

Hodge, Frederick Webb (ed.)
1919 Handbook of American Indians North of Mexico. Bureau of American Ethnology. Bulletin No. 30. The Smithsonian Institution, Washington, D.C.

Holland, C. G.
1955 An Analysis of Projectile Points and Large Blades. Appendix to A Ceramic Study of Virginia Archeology by Clifford Evans. Bureau of American Ethnology, Bulletin 160, The Smithsonian Institution, Washington, D.C.

Holmes, William H.
1884 Prehistoric Textile Fabrics of the United States Derived from Impressions on Pottery. Third Annual Report of the Bureau of American Ethnology, The Smithsonian Institution, pp. 397-425. Washington, D.C.

1889 Pottery of the Potomac Tidewater Region. The Aborigines of the District of Columbia and the Lower Potomac, A Symposium. Directed by Otis T. Mason. American Anthropologist, O. S. Vol. 2, pp. 246-52. Lancaster, Pa.

1897*a* Stone Implements of the Potomac-Chesapeake Tidewater Province. Fifteenth Annual Report of the Bureau of American Ethnology, Smithsonian Institution, Washington, D.C. Pp. 3-152.

1897*b* Primitive Man in the Delaware Valley. Science, N. S. Vol. 6, pp. 824-29. Washington, D.C.: American Association for the Advancement of Science.

1903 Aboriginal Pottery of the Eastern United States. Twentieth Annual Report of the Bureau of American Ethnology. The Smithsonian Institution, Washington, D.C. Pp. 1-237.

1907 Aboriginal Shell Heaps of the Middle Atlantic Tidewater Region. American Anthropologist, N. S., Vol. 9, pp. 113-28.

Hrdlicka, Ales
1937 Early Man in America: What Have the Bones to Say? *In* Early Man, George Grant MacCurdy, editor. Philadelphia and New York: J. B. Lippincott Co.

Hurt, Wesley R., Jr.
1954 Pottery Types of the Over Focus, South Dakota. Prehistoric Pottery of the Eastern United States, Museum of Anthropology, The University of Michigan. Ann Arbor.

Jefferson, Thomas
1787 Notes on the State of Virginia. London.

Johnson, Frederick
1961 A Quarter Century of Growth in American Archaeology. American Antiquity, Vol. 27, No. 1, pp. 1-6. Salt Lake City.

Johnson, Frederick, and Hugh M. Raup
1947 Grassy Island. Papers of the Robert S. Peabody Foundation for Archaeology, Vol. 1, No. 2. Andover, Mass.: Phillips Academy.

Jones, Robert W.
1931 The Clemson Mound. Annual Report of the Pennsylvania Historical Commission, No. 5, pp. 89-111.

Kinsey, W. Fred, III.
1959 Recent Excavations on Bare Island in Pennsylvania: The Kent-Halley Site. Pennsylvania Archaeologist, Vol. 29, Nos. 3,4. Gettysburg.

Kivett, Marvin F.
1952 Woodland Sites in Nebraska. Nebraska State Historical Society Publications in Anthropology, No. 1. Lincoln.

Lalemant, Jerome
1642 Lettre—escrite des Hurons...Paris. (Reprinted Quebec, 1858, and other dates).

Lehmer, Donald J.
1954 Archeological Investigations in the Oahe Dam Area, South Dakota, 1950-51. Bureau of American Ethnology Bulletin 158, River Basin Surveys Papers, No. 7, The Smithsonian Institution, Washington, D.C.

Lewis, Clifford M., S.J., and Albert J. Loomie, S.J.
1953 The Spanish Jesuit Mission in Virginia 1570-1572. Published for the Virginia Historical Society by the University of North Carolina Press, Chapel Hill.

Lorant, Stefan (editor)
1946 The New World. Duell, Sloan & Pearce, Inc. New York.

McGuire, Joseph D.
1899 Pipes and Smoking Customs of the American Aborigines, Based on Material in the United States National Museum. Annual Report of the Board of Regents of the Smithsonian Institution for the year ending June 30, 1897, pp. 351-646. Washington, D.C.

McKern, W. C.
1939 The Midwestern Taxonomic Method as an Aid to Archaeological Culture Study. American Antiquity, Vol. 4, No. 4, pp. 301-13, Menasha, Wisc.

MacCord, Howard A., Richard Gates Slattery, and Karl Schmitt, Jr.
1957 The Shepard Site Study. Archaeological Society of Maryland, Bulletin No. 1, July.

Manson, Carl
1948 Marcey Creek Site: An Early Manifestation in the Potomac Valley. American Antiquity, Vol. 13, No. 3, pp. 223-26. Salt Lake City.

Manson, Carl, Howard A. MacCord, and James B. Griffin
1944 The Culture of the Keyser Farm Site. Papers of the Michigan Academy of Science, Arts, and Letters, Vol. 29, Pt. 4, pp. 375-418.

Marye, William B.
1935*a* "Patowmeck Above Ye Inhabitants." (a comentary on an old map). Maryland Historical Magazine, Vol. 30, No. 1, pp. 1-11.

1935*b* Piscataway. *Ibid.* Vol. 30, No. 3, pp. 183-239.

Mason, Otis T.
1877 Anthropological News. American Naturalist, Vol. 11, pp. 624-27. Boston, Mass.

1901 The Technic of Aboriginal American Basketry. American Anthropologist, N. S., Vol. 3, No. 1, pp. 109-28.

Mayer-Oakes, William J.
1955 Prehistory of the Upper Ohio Valley. Anthropological Series, No. 2, Annals of Carnegie Museum, Pittsburg, Pa., Vol. 34.

Meggers, Betty J.
1954 Environmental Limitation on the Development of Culture. American Anthropologist, N. S., Vol. 56, No. 5, Pt. 1, pp. 801-24.

Miner, Horace
1936 The Importance of Textiles in the Archaeology of the Eastern United States. American Antiquity, Vol. 1, No. 3, pp. 181-92.

Mooney, James
1889 Indian Tribes of the District of Columbia. American Anthropologist, O. S., Vol. 2, No. 3, pp. 259-65.

Neill, Edward D.
1876 Founders of Maryland. Albany. As cited in Ferguson, Alice L. L., Moyaone and the Piscataway Indians. 1937.

Neumann, Georg K., and Melvin L. Fowler
1952 Hopewellian Sites in the Wabash Valley. Hopewellian Communities in Illinois. Thorne Dewel, editor. Scientific Papers of the Illinois State Museum, Vol. 5. Springfield.

Paulin, Charles O., and John K. Wright
1932 Atlas of the Historical Geography of the United States. Published jointly by the Carnegie Institution of Washington and the American Geographical Society of New York.

Powell, J. W.
1892 Indian Linguistic Families of America North of Mexico. Seventh Annual Report of the Bureau of American Ethnology, Smithsonian Institution, pp. 1-142, map.

Raisz, Erwin
1939 Map of the Landforms of the United States. To accompany Atwood's Physiographic Provinces of North America. Prepared at the Institute of Geographical Exploration, Harvard University, Cambridge, Mass.

Ritchie, William A.
1934 An Algonkin-Iroquois Contact Site on Castle Creek, Broom County, New York. Research Records of The Rochester Museum of Arts and Sciences, No. 2. Rochester, N.Y.

1936 A Prehistoric Fortified Village Site at Canandaigua, Ontario County, New York. Research Records of The Rochester Museum of Arts and Sciences, No. 3, Rochester, N.Y.

1940 Two Prehistoric Village Sites at Brewerton, New York. Research Records of the Rochester Museum of Arts and Sciences, No. 5. Rochester, N.Y.

1944 The Pre-Iroquoian Occupations of New York State. Rochester Museum of Arts and Sciences, Rochester, N.Y.

1961 A Typology and Nomenclature of New York Projectile Points. New York State Museum and Science Service. Bull. No. 384. Albany.

Ritchie, William A., and Richard S. MacNeish
1949 The Pre-Iroquoian Pottery of New York. American Antiquity, Vol. 15, No. 2, pp. 97-123. Salt Lake City.

Roberts, Frank H. H., Jr.
1931 The Ruins of Kiatuthlanna, Eastern Arizona. Bureau of American Ethnology, Bulletin 100, The Smithsonian Institution, Washington, D.C.

Schmitt, Karl, Jr.
1952 Archaeological Chronology of the Middle Atlantic States. *In* Archeology of the Eastern United States, James B. Gifffin, editor. Chicago: The University of Chicago Press.

n.d. Patawomeke: An Historic Algonkian Site. Unpublished manuscript of Doctoral thesis at the University of Chicago. On file in the Museum of Anthropology, The University of Michigan. Prepared March, 1942.

Schmitt, Karl, Jr., and Richard O. Slattery.
n.d. The Shepard Site, Montgomery County, Maryland. [Unpublished manuscript.]

Scully, Edward G.
1951 Some Central Mississippi Valley Projectile Point Types. Mimeographed report from the Museum of Anthropology, The University of Michigan, October.

Sears, William H., and James B. Griffin
1950 Fiber Tempered Pottery of the Southeast. Prehistoric Pottery of the Eastern United States. Museum of Anthropology, The University of Michigan.

Semmes, Raphael
1937 Captains and Mariners of Early Maryland. Baltimore.

Skinner, Alanson
1919 Exploration of Aboriginal Sites at Throgs Neck and Clasons Point, New York City. Contributions from the Museum of the American Indian, Heye Foundation, New York.

Slattery, Richard Gates
1946 A Prehistoric Indian Site on Selden Island, Montgomery County, Maryland. Journal of the Washington Academy of Sciences, Vol. 36, No. 8, pp. 262-66. Washington, D.C.

Smith, Carlyle S.
1950 The Archaeology of Coastal New York. Anthropological Papers of the American Museum of Natural History, Vol. 42, Pt. 2, New York.

Smith, John
1910 Voyages and Discoveries. Arber Edition, Edinburgh. As cited in Ferguson, Alice L. L., Moyaone and the Piscataway Indians. 1937.

Smith, Harlan I., and William J. Wintemberg
1929 Some Shell Heaps in Nova Scotia. National Museum of Canada, Bulletin No. 47, Anthropological Series, No. 9, Ottawa.

Spier, Leslie
1918 The Trenton Argillite Culture. Anthropological Papers of the American Museum of Natural History, Vol. 22, Pt. 4, New York.

Stearns, Richard E.
1940 The Hughes Site. Proceedings of the Natural History Society of Maryland, No. 6, Baltimore.

1949 Some Indian Village Sites of the Lower Patapsco River. Proceedings of the Natural History Society of Maryland, No. 10, Baltimore.

Stephenson, Robert L.
1954 Taxonomy and Chronology in the Central Plains--Middle Missouri River Area. The Plains Anthropologist, No. 1, Lincoln, Neb.

1959 The Prehistoric People of Accokeek Creek. Alice Ferguson Foundation, Accokeek, Maryland.

n.d. Some Problems Involved in the Typology of North American Projectile Points. Unpublished manuscript of thesis for Master of Arts Degree in the University of Oregon. Submitted May, 1942.

Steward, Julian N.
1938 Basin-Plateau Aboriginal Sociopolitical Groups. Bureau of American Ethnology, Bulletin 120, The Smithsonian Institution, Washington, D.C.

1946 Handbook of South American Indians. Bureau of American Ethnology, Bulletin 143, Vol. 1, The Smithsonian Institution, Washington, D.C.

Stewart, T. Dale

1939 Excavating the Indian Village of Patawomeke (Potomac). Explorations and Field Work of the Smithsonian Institution in 1938. The Smithsonian Institution, Washington, D.C. Pp. 87-90.

1940*a* Further Excavations at the Indian Village Site of Patawomeke (Potomac). Explorations and Field Work of the Smithsonian Institution in 1939, The Smithsonian Institution, Washington, D.C. Pp. 79-82.

1940*b* The Finding of an Indian Ossuary on the York River in Virginia. Journal of the Washington Academy of Sciences, Vol. 30, No. 8, pp. 356-64. Menasha.

1941 An Ossuary at the Indian Village Site of Patawomeke (Potomac). Explorations and Field Work of the Smithsonian Institution in 1940. The Smithsonian Institution, Washington, D.C. Pp. 67-70.

n.d. Report on the Skeletal Remains from Ossuary No. 1, Ferguson Site, Accokeek, Md. Report on Skulls from Mockley Point. Sections in the unpublished manuscript by Alice L. L. Ferguson, entitled Moyaone. Prepared in 1948, pp. 102-7,118-20.

Stewart, T. Dale, and Waldo R. Wedel

1937 The Finding of Two Ossuaries on the Site of the Indian Village of Nacotchtanke (Anacostia). Journal of the Washington Academy of Sciences, Vol. 27, No. 5, pp. 213-19. Menasha.

Strachey, William

1849 The Historie of Travaile in Virginia Britannia. Hakluyt Society Publication, Vol. 6. London.

Strong, Wm. Duncan

1935 An Introduction to Nebraska Archaeology. Smithsonian Miscellaneous Collections, Vol. 93, No. 10. The Smithsonian Institution, Washington, D.C.

1940 From History to Prehistory in the Northern Great Plains. Essays in Historical Anthropology of North America, Smithsonian Miscellaneous Collections, Vol. 100. The Smithsonian Institution, Washington, D.C.

Swauger, James L.

1940 A Review of F. H. Cerrodette's Notes on the Excavation of the McKees Rock Mound. The Pennsylvania Archaeologist, Vol. 10, No. 1, pp. 8-10. Milton.

Thomas, Cyrus

1891 Catalogue of Prehistoric Works East of the Rocky Mountains. Bureau of American Ethnology Edition, Bulletin 12, The Smithsonian Institution, Washington, D.C.

1894 Report on the Mound Explorations of the Bureau of American Ethnology. Twelfth Annual Report of the Bureau of American Ethnology, 1890-1891. The Smithsonian Institution, Washington, D.C.

Volk, Ernest
1911 The Archeology of the Delaware Valley. Papers of the Peabody Museum of American Archaeology and Ethnology, Harvard University.

Washburn, Wilcomb E.
1957 The Governor and the Rebel. Chapel Hill: University of North Carolina Press.

Webb, William S.
1946 Indian Knoll. The University of Kentucky Reports in Anthropology and Archaeology, Vol. 4, No. 3, Pt. 1. Lexington: The University of Kentucky.

Wedel, Waldo R.
1940 Culture Sequences in the Central Great Plains. Essays in Historical Anthropology of North America, The Smithsonian Institution Miscellaneous Collections, Vol. 100. The Smithsonian Institution, Washington, D.C.

Wertenbaker, Thomas Jefferson
1940 Torchbearer of the Revolution: The Story of Bacon's Rebellion and its Leader. Princeton, N.J.: Princeton University Press.

Weslager, C. A.
1942 Ossuaries on the Delmarva Peninsula and Exotic Influences in the Coastal Aspect of the Woodland Period. American Antiquity, Vol. 8, No. 2, pp. 141-51. Menasha.

Wilford, Lloyd A.
1941 A Tentative Classification of the Prehistoric Cultures of Minnesota. *Ibid.*, Vol. 6, No. 3, pp. 231-50.

1955 A Revised Classification of the Prehistoric Cultures of Minnesota. *Ibid.*, Vol. 21, No. 2, pp. 130-42.

Willoughby, Charles C.
1935 Antiquities of the New England Indians. Peabody Museum of American Archaeology and Ethnology, Cambridge, Massachusetts.

Witthoft, John
1948 Ceramic Sequences in Eastern Pennsylvania. Eastern States Archeological Federation, Bulletin No. 7.

1952 A Paleo-Indian Site in Eastern Pennsylvania: An Early Hunting Culture. Proceedings of the American Philosophical Society, Vol. 96, No. 4, pp. 464-95.

Wormington, H. Marie
1947 Prehistoric Indians of the Southwest. Colorado Museum of Natural History, Popular Series, No. 7. Denver.

Wren, Christopher
1914 A Study of North Appalachian Indian Pottery. Proceedings and Collections of the Wyoming Historical and Geological Society, Vol. 13, pp. 131-222, Wilkes-Barre, Pa.

PLATES

PLATE I

Air photograph of the early stage of excavation in the Moyaone area, 1936. The excavated area shown includes the two outer stockade lines.

PLATE II

A. Row of exposed post moulds in stockade line B.
B. Row of exposed post moulds in stockade line I.
C. Row of cross-sectioned post moulds in stockade line J.
D. Stone pile No. 58.
E. Firepit No. 57.
F. Profile of storage pit No. 39.

PLATE III

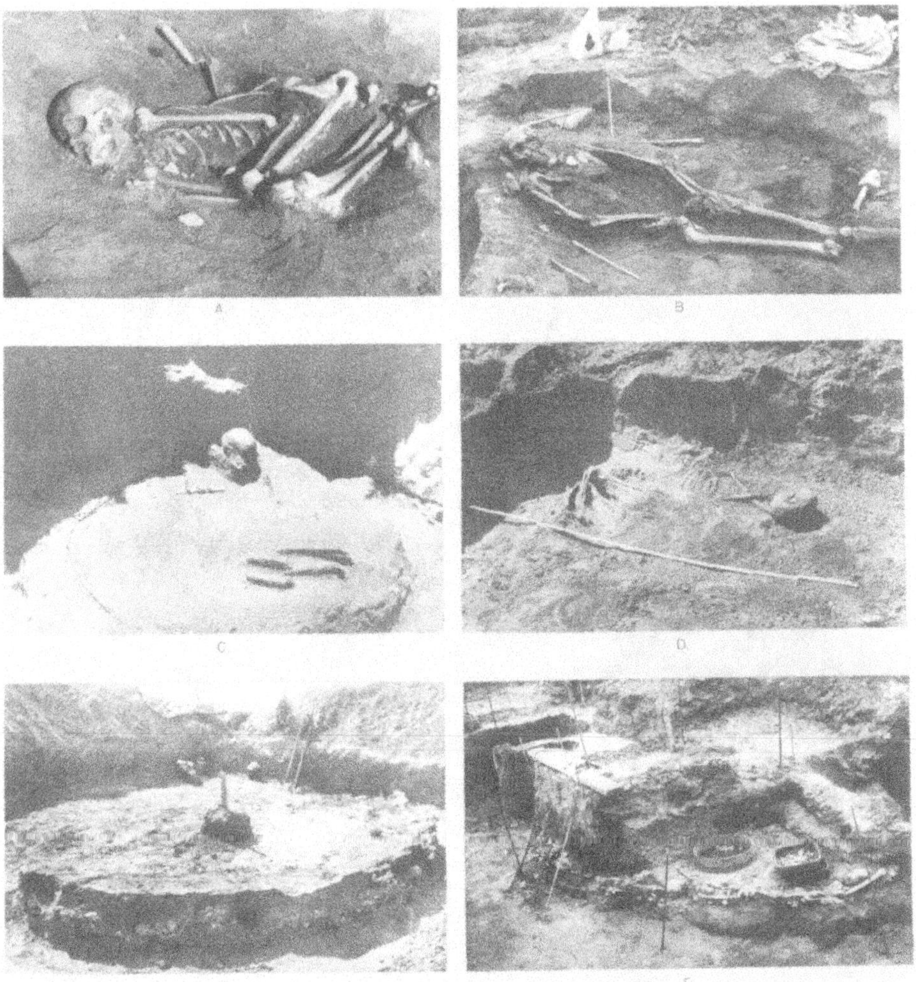

Burials and ossuaries excavated from within the Moyaone area.

A. Flexed burial No. 33.
B. Extended burial No. 38.
C. Fragmentary, semiflexed burial No. 23 showing relation of burial remains to burial pit.
D. Burial No. 29.
E. Ossuary No. 1.
F. Ossuary No. 3.

PLATE IV

Sherds of steatite (soapstone) vessels.

A. Smooth-surfaced rim sherd.
B. Rim sherd with lug.
C. Three joined rim sherds.
D-F. Body sherds showing tool marks.
G. Rim sherd with perforation.
H. Interior view of basal section of a vessel.

PLATE V

Sherds of the pottery type Marcey Creek Plain.

A-E. Sherds showing the basal protrusion or "heal."
F. Rim sherd showing coil marks.
G. Interior of a basal sherd showing the flat base.
H. Rim sherds, with fragment of a lug.
I. Rim sherd with perforation.

PLATE VI

Sherds and vessel sections of the pottery type Pope's Creek Net Impressed.

A-C,F. Exterior views of rimsherds showing different types of net impressions.

D,G. Interior views of rimsherds showing scoring.

E,H. Exterior and interior views respectively of reconstructed vessel section.

I. Large, conical, basal sherd.

PLATE VII

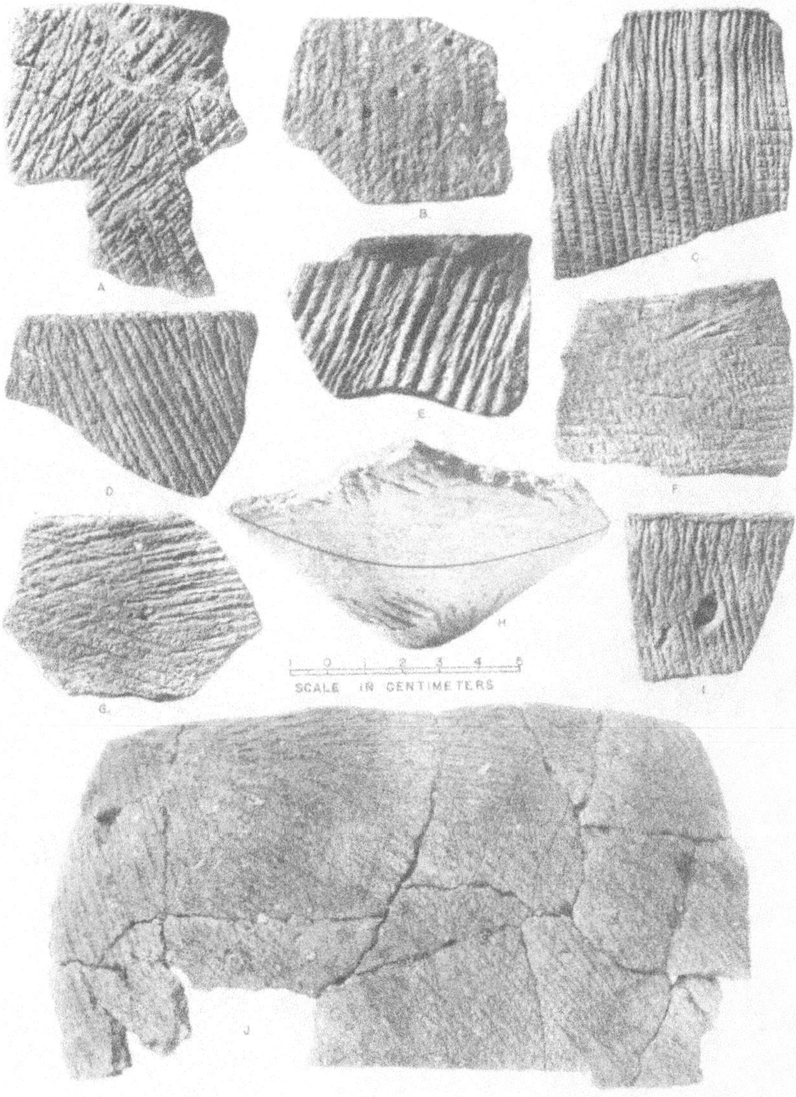

Sherds and vessel sections of the pottery type Accokeek Cord Marked.

A–G,I.	Rim sherds showing various patternings of cord marks.
B.	Has punctate decoration.
H.	Basal sherd.
J.	Reconstructed vessel section from rim to about midpoint of the vessel body. Note the incised decoration around the rim.

PLATE VIII

Sherds of the pottery type Mockley Cord Marked.

A. Body sherd showing coil break at top.
B-C. Body sherds showing various cord markings.
D. Body sherd showing uneven thickness.
G-H. Exterior and Interior views of the same sherd showing holes resulting from leached shell temper.

PLATE IX

Sherds of the pottery type Mockley Net Impressed.

A,G. Rim sherds showing "pimpled" appearance of fine net impressions.

C-F. Rim and body sherds with medium net impressions.

B. Rim sherd with coarse net impressions. Note coil break at top of C.

PLATE X

Sherds of the pottery type Mockley Plain

A-C,E.	Body sherds.
D.	Rim sherd
F-G.	Exterior and interior views of basal section of a vessel. Note the coil breaks and the smoothed basal area.

PLATE XI

Vessel sections of the pottery type Rappahannock Fabric Impressed.

A. Large rim section showing fabric impressions, leached shell temper holes, and decoration of impressions of a cord-wrapped paddle edge.

B. Basal section of a large vessel.

PLATE XII

Vessel section and sherds of the pottery type Rappahannock Incised.

A. Section of a large vessel with fabric-impressed surface and incised decoration on rim. Orifice of this vessel is pentagonal.
B. Rim sherd with rare, punctate decoration.
C-I. Rim sherds with incised decoration.
J. Combined punctate and incised decoration on a rim sherd.
K-L. Rim sherds with incised decoration.

PLATE XIII

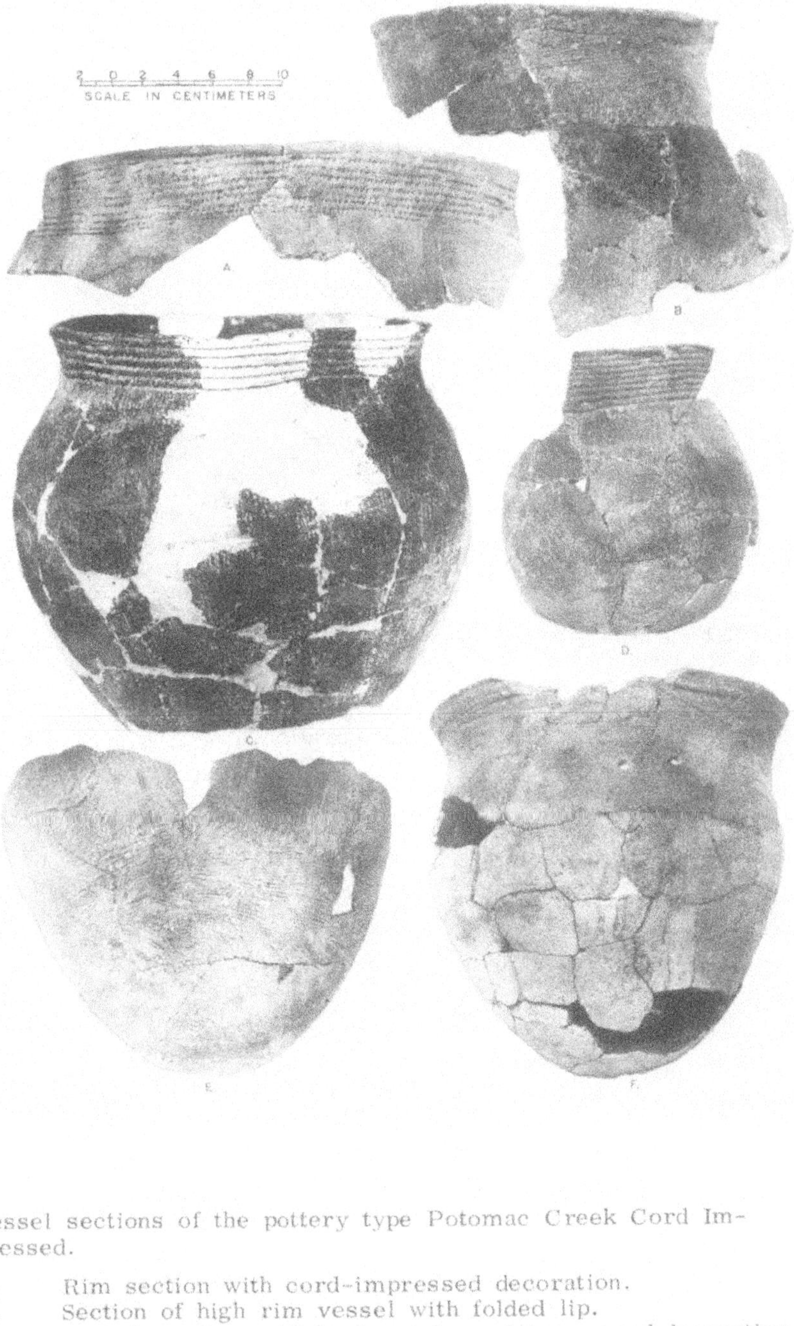

Vessel sections of the pottery type Potomac Creek Cord Impressed.

A. Rim section with cord-impressed decoration.
B. Section of high rim vessel with folded lip.
C-D. Vessel sections with horizontal, cord-impressed decoration.
E. Basal and body section of vessel showing the cord-marked surface.
F. Reconstructed vessel with mending perforations and folded rim.

Vessel sections of the pottery type Potomac Creek Cord Impressed.

A. Unusual vessel shape. Note mending perforations.
B-C. Cord-wrapped dowel impressed, horizontal and vertical decoration on typical vessel form.
D. Single cord-impressed, horizontal decoration.
E. Cord-wrapped dowel impressed decoration.
F. Zoned decoration.

PLATE XIV

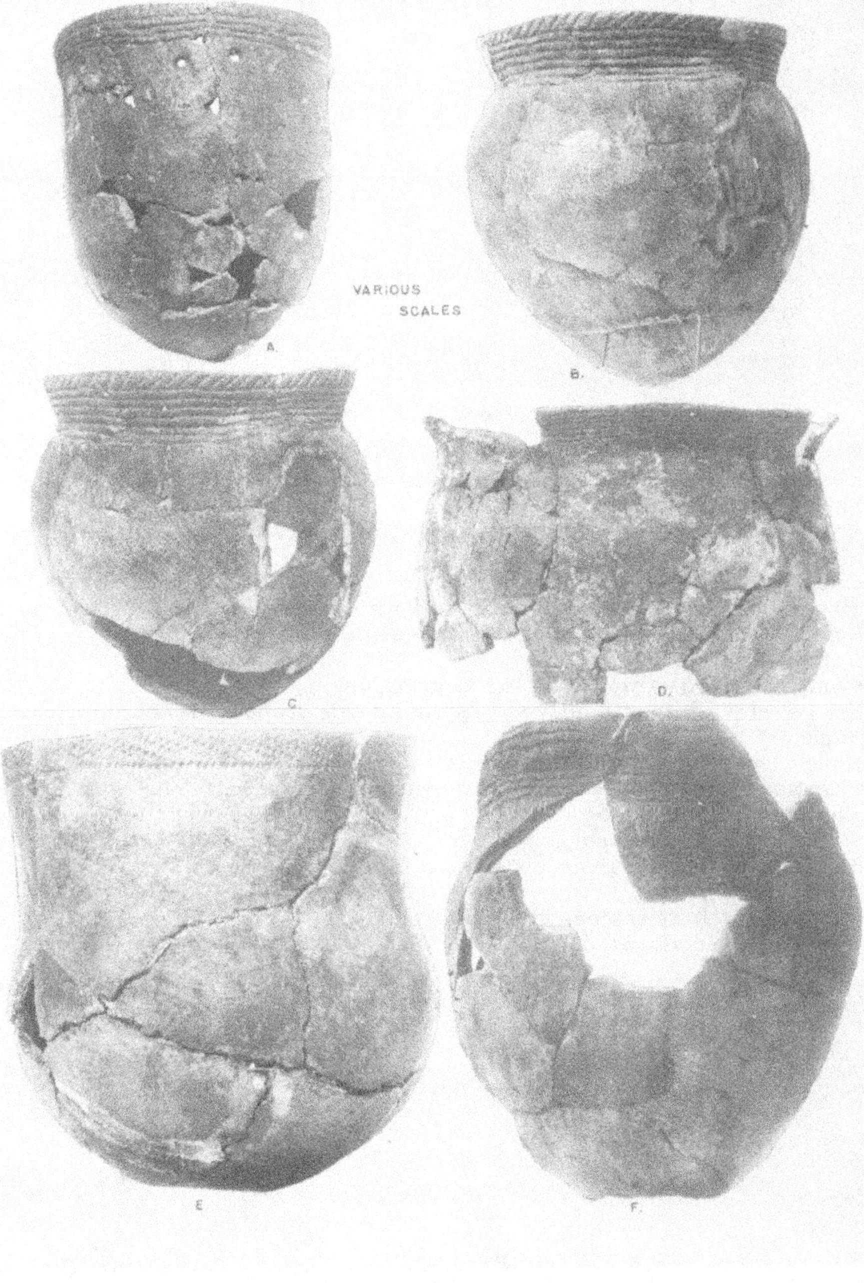

Rim sherds of the pottery type Potomac Creek Cord Impressed.

A. Cord-wrapped dowel impressed decoration on a thickened rim.
B. Single cord decoration.
C. Vertical, cord-wrapped paddle decoration on a smoothed rim.
D. Single cord-impressed decoration.
E. Cord-wrapped dowel impressed decoration with appliqued rim strip.
F. Single cord-impressed vertical decoration.
G. Single cord-impressed diagonal decoration.
H. Folded rim strip.
I. Complex, cord-wrapped dowel decoration.
J. Folded rim strip with heavy, diagonal, cord-wrapped dowel impressions.
K. Rough, cord-wrapped dowel impressions.
L. Complex cord-wrapped dowel impressions on a high rim with appliqued rim strip.
M. Single cord-impressed decoration.
N. Single cord-impressions on interior of rim (scale is twice that of the other sherds).
O. Single cord impressions with thickened lip.
P. Cord-wrapped dowel decoration.

PLATE XV

Rim sherds of the pottery type Potomac Creek Cord Impressed.

A-B. Single cord decoration, (B) with an appliqued rim strip.
C. Complex decoration of single cord impressions.
D. Complex decoration of cord-wrapped dowel impressions on a smoothed body.
E-F. Appliqued and folded rim strips.
G. Cord-wrapped dowel impressions on interior of lip.
H. Broken band of decoration.
I. Folded rim strip.
J. Appliqued rim strip partly separated from vessel body.
K. Jointing of decoration ends.
L. Single cord impressions.
M. Complex, cord-wrapped dowel impressions.
N. Complex, single cord impressions.
O. Banded, single cord decorations.
P. Horizontal and diagonal, cord-wrapped dowel impressions.
Q. Rough, cord-wrapped dowel impressions on smoothed body.
R. Complex, cord-wrapped dowel impressions.

PLATE XVI

Rim sherds of the pottery type Potomac Creek Cord Impressed.

A-E. Various decorations on thickened lips.
F-I. Single cord impressions on thickened lips, (G) with a smoothed body.
J. Rolled lip with cord-wrapped dowel impressions on top of lip.
K. Complex, cord-wrapped dowel decoration.
L. Decoration on a smoothed body.

PLATE XVII

Unusual rim sherds of the pottery type Potomac Creek Cord Impressed, (A-J), and sherds of the pottery type Potomac Creek Plain (K-M).

A. Single cord-impressed decoration combined with punctations.
B. Single cord-impressed decoration combined with finger-nail punctations.
C. Punctate decoration.
D. Vertical, cord-wrapped paddle impressions combined with large punctations.
E. Zoned decoration combined with punctations.
F. Zoned decoration on high rim with pendant punctations.
G. Cord-wrapped dowel impressions with pendant, incised chevrons.
H. Deeply notched lip with complex, cord-wrapped dowel decoration.
I. Incised decoration on thickened rim.
J. Cord-wrapped paddle impressions on thickened rim with incised, pendant chevrons below.
K-M. Rim sherds with plain, smoothed surfaces and no decoration.

PLATE XVIII

Rim sherds of the pottery types Moyaone Incised (A-K), Moyaone Cord Impressed (L-Q), and Moyaone Plain (R).

A. Cord-wrapped dowel-impressed, horizontal decoration with horizontal incising.
B. Incised, filled triangles.
C. Zoned incising with thickened lip.
D-E. Horizontal incising.
F. Horizontal, cord-wrapped dowel impressions with zoned incising below.
G-I. Cross hatched incising.
J. Vertical incising.
E. Cross hatched incising with a thickened lip.
L. Single cord-impressed horizontal decoration.
M-N. Complex, single cord-impressed decoration.
O. Cord-wrapped dowel-impressed decoration.
P-Q. Single cord-impressed decoration.
R. Smoothed surface without decoration.

PLATE XIX

PLATE XX

Rim sherds of miscellaneous pottery groups C, D, F, and G.

A. Rim sherd of Group C showing unwelded, exterior coils
B,C. Rim sherds of Group D.
D-F. Rim sherds of Group F.
G-K. Rim sherds of Group G. Note punctate decoration on (G) and (K); cord marked surface of (I); and thickened or "swollen" rim on (J).

PLATE XXI

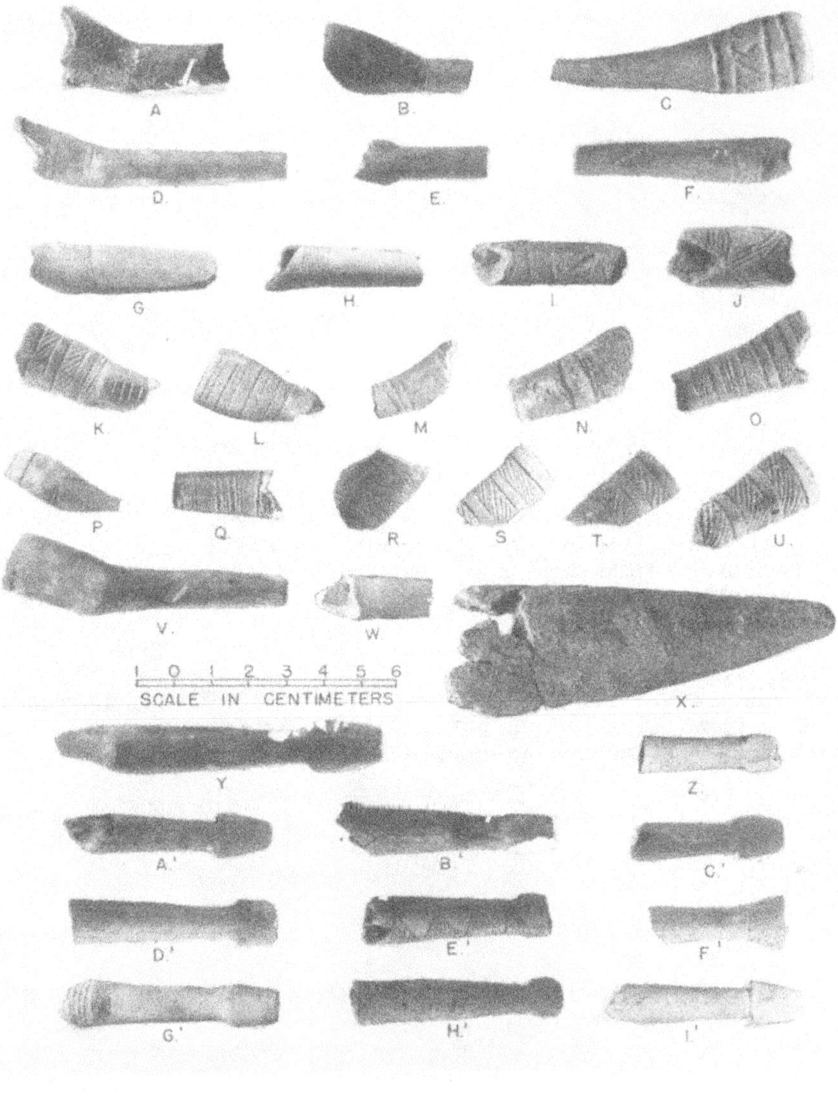

Whole and fragmentary pottery tobacco pipes.

A-U. Sections of bowls, elbows, and stems of the type Potomac Cord Impressed. (C) is a complete specimen.

V-W. Complete and fragmentary specimens of pipes of the type Potomac Plain.

X. Nearly complete example of the type Accokeek Plain.

Y-I'. Stem sections of the type Moyaone Cord Impressed.

Examples of unusual tobacco pipes.

A. Complete specimen of the type Susquehannock Plain (scale is half that of the other specimens in this plate).

B,C. Bowl sections of the type Susquehannock Plain.

D-G. Examples of the tubular variety A of the type Accokeek Plain.

I,K.L. Examples of the tubular variety A of the type Accokeek Cord Impressed.

M. Bird effigy pipe, Variant D of the type Potomac Creek Cord Impressed.

N. Punctated Variant C of the type Potomac Creek Cord Impressed.

O,P. Two views of the stone, platform pipe. Note the opening in the top of the stem making it unsmokable.

PLATE XXII

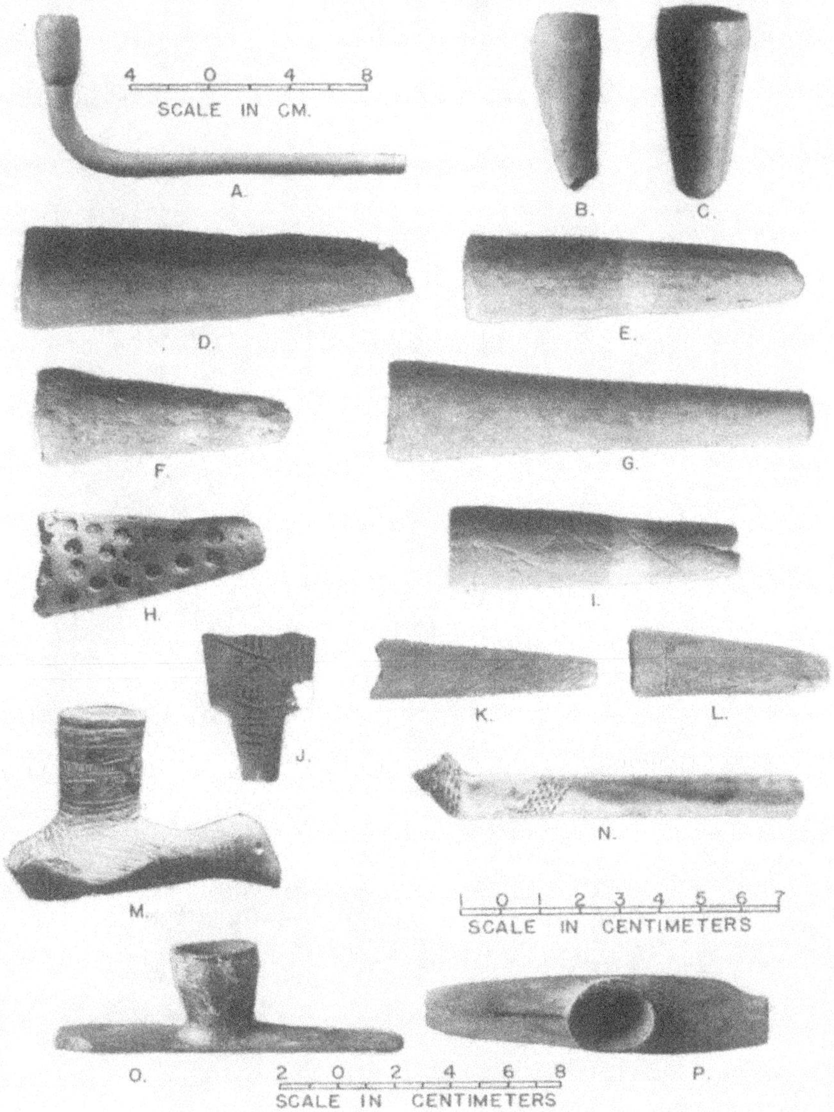
4 0 4 8
SCALE IN CM.
A.
B.
C.
D.
E.
F.
G.
H.
I.
J.
K.
L.
M.
N.
0 1 2 3 4 5 6 7
SCALE IN CENTIMETERS
O.
P.
2 0 2 4 6 8
SCALE IN CENTIMETERS

PLATE XXIII

Projectile points

A-F. Rossville type. G-O. Bare Island type. P-V. Steubenville Stemmed. W-Z. Steubenville Lanceolate.

PLATE XXIV

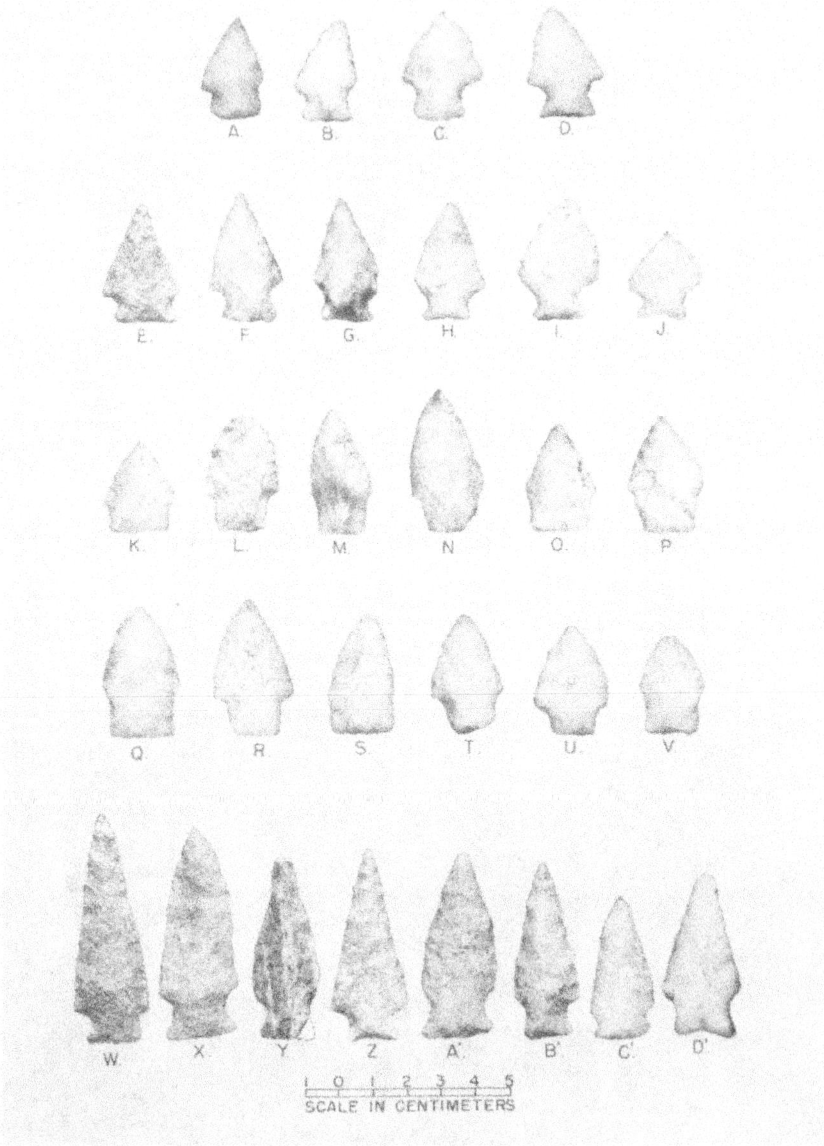

Projectile points

A-J. Vernon type. K-V. Calvert type. W-D'. Clagett type.

PLATE XXV

Projectile points.

A-B. Group A. C-G. Group B. H-J. Group C. K. Group D. L. Group E. M-O. Group F.

PLATE XXVI

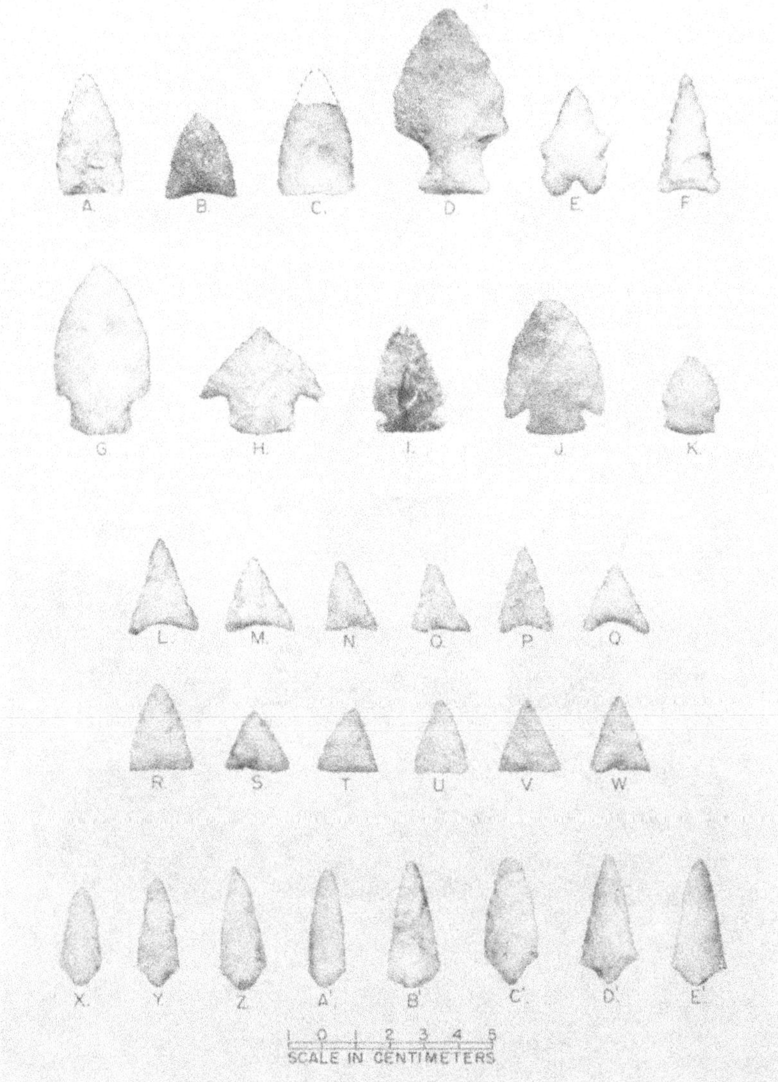

Projectile points.

A-C. Group G. D. Group H. E. Group I. F. Group J. G. Group K. H. Group L. I. Group M. J. Group N. K. Group O.
L-W. Projectile points of the Potomac type. X-E'. Projectile points of the Piscataway type.

PLATE XXVII

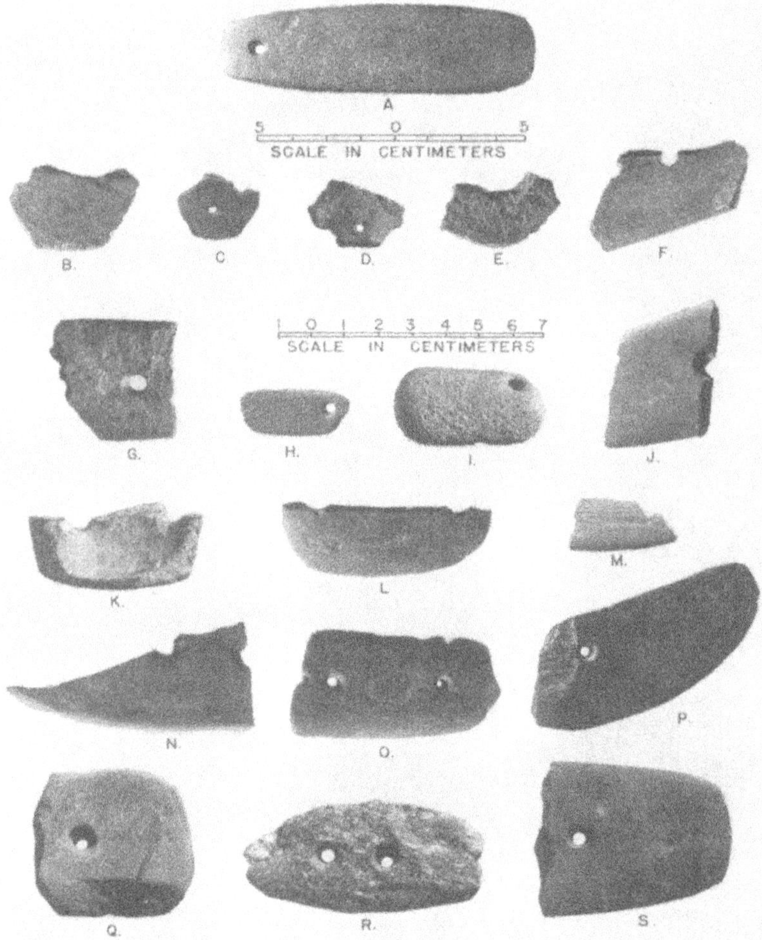

Miscellaneous ground-stone objects.

A. Large pendant or gorget of green granite.
B,E. Ornamental discs of slate.
C,D,F-J. Fragments of drilled pendants or gorgets.
K,L. Fragments of drilled boatstones or atlatl weights.
M. Small sandstone abrader.
N,O,Q-S. Fragments of drilled pendants or gorgets.
P. Half of a large, butterfly bannerstone.

PLATE XXVIII

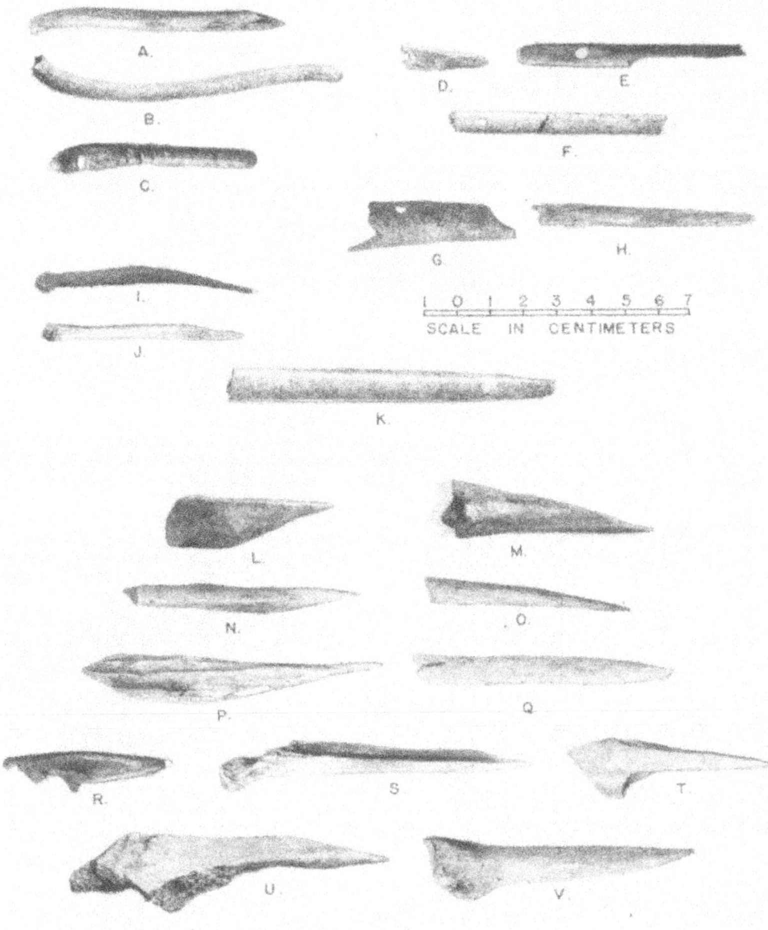

Bone tools and implements.

A-C. Otter penis bone tools.
D-H. Perforated bone bodkins.
I-J. Awls made from bone fragments.
K. Bone flaking tool.
L-Q. Splinter awls made from deer long bones.
R. Ulna awl.
S-T. Splinter awls made from deer long bones.
U,V. Ulna awls.

www.ingramcontent.com/pod-product-compliance
Lightning Source LLC
LaVergne TN
LVHW010859300826
846801LV00012B/140
9781949098259